# Praise for *Outgro*

"Countless people have found solutions to their substance use problems in Stanton Peele's books after many years of painful struggle in treatment, and thought 'I wish I'd read this before I went to my first rehab.' Your child needn't have this bittersweet experience. *Outgrowing Addiction* is a meditation for parents on how to avoid the trap of medicalizing their children's normal life struggles. You instinctively seek to cultivate your child's full potential. Yet you face mounting pressure from institutions to label and limit your child, going directly against your better instincts. With Stanton and Zach Rhoads on your side as voices of reason, you'll be able to resist the pressure from institutions to label and limit your children—and instead rely on your common sense and unique bond to help them grow beyond and benefit from any struggles they may encounter."

—Steven Slate, co-author of *The Freedom Model for Addictions: Escape The Treatment and Recovery Trap*

"The idea that addiction develops isn't new. What is unique and remarkable about this book is the authors' attention to the complexity of that process. Their nuanced model, backed up by rich biographical vignettes as well as clear, reliable data, is especially sensitive to the interplay of developmental timing (stages of development) and the massive impacts of the social environment— both spawning addiction and ultimately helping to overcome it. Peele and Rhoads skillfully refute the faulty (but fashionable) conclusion that addiction is a brain disease. Instead, their view of addiction as a turbulent but natural stage of need fulfillment allows us to replace the bogey man of chronic illness with an emphasis on empowerment, determination, and personal growth. A truly comprehensive and masterful piece of work."

—Marc Lewis, Ph.D., Professor Emeritus, University of Toronto; author of *Memoirs of an Addicted Brain* and *The Biology of Desire: Why Addiction is Not a Disease*

"The evidence keeps pouring in that, over four decades ago when he published *Love and Addiction*, Stanton Peele was fundamentally correct about addiction and how to outgrow it. In this latest work Peele and Rhoads incorporate recent scientific and cultural evidence showing that viewing addiction as a disease is actually harmful, that addiction involves the whole person (not just the brain), that most people will outgrow addiction (and there are ways to accelerate that process), and that pursuing a valued and constructive new life path can move one entirely beyond addiction."

—From the Foreword by Tom Horvath, Ph.D., ABPP, founding president, SMART Recovery

"For decades, Stanton Peele has been one of the leading voices in revising our views of addiction, drug education and drug policy. His new book with Zach Rhoads, *Outgrowing Addiction*, continues and extends this pioneering work to children and stakeholders in child well-being. It is a godsend for anyone seeking a solution to the opioids crisis."

— Carl Hart, Ph.D., Professor of Neuroscience and Psychology, Chair of Department of Psychology, Columbia University; author, *High Price*

"Stanton Peele is a true pioneer of attempts to reveal the inadequacies of the disease view of addiction. His latest book with Zach Rhoads articulates, in clear and accessible language, a rational and evidence-based alternative to the disease view—the developmental model of addiction. Of particular importance here is the understanding the authors provide about the growing minds of adolescents and their chances of becoming and staying addicted. Though aimed at an American readership, the book's topical relevance and its accumulated wisdom apply far beyond the boundaries of the USA."

—Nick Heather, Ph.D., Emeritus Professor of Alcohol & Other Drug Studies, Northumbria University, UK; former director, Australian National Drug and Alcohol Research Centre

"Stanton Peele and Zach Rhoads help us think more deeply about the nature of addiction and the canned rhetoric that we hear every day. Their book explores the vulnerabilities to addiction, the dynamics of self-destructive drug use, and the pathways out. Most critically for users and their families, the book shows how to accelerate the processes that lead users to relinquish drugs. *Outgrowing Addiction* is smart, compassionate, and, most important, optimistic."

—Sally Satel, M.D., coauthor, *Brainwashed: The Seductive Appeal of Mindless Neuroscience*; lecturer, Yale University School of Medicine

"In my clinical work, I often encounter teens and parents who have been mis-led to believe addiction is a life-long condition they can never hope to escape. Stanton Peele and Zach Rhoads combat that mistaken and dangerous mes-sage with research evidence, clear explanations, and above all, the compelling stories of success families need. *Outgrowing Addiction* will have a prominent place on my lending bookshelf for families in my practice."

—Pippa Abston, M.D., Ph.D., FAAP, Assistant Professor of Pediatrics, University of Alabama School of Medicine, Huntsville

"The research behind this book is fascinating. Peele and Rhoads' analysis, in-terpretation, and out of the box thinking about it offers a unique and hopeful perspective of a better future for people struggling with addiction. This book is upbeat, honest and offers realistic and practical strategies for those in addic-tion. In this work addiction is examined through a lens of care and respect. One of the most powerful aspects of this book is the coaching model used to support children. Having these tools enables adults to have difficult and im-portant conversations with children of any and all ages—conversations that could help prevent them from becoming addicted in the first place."

—Robin Ploof, Ph.D., Professor and Program Director, Early Childhood Division of Education and Human Studies, Champlain College, Burlington, Vt.

"Things work until they don't, whether it's an educational system so obsessed with how children perform and what each must become that it has lost sight of who they are and what each is experiencing each day. Could it be what has been highlighted in *Outgrowing Addiction*—a mindset anchored in disease, disorder, and labels that treats symptoms, rather than doing the hard work of adjusting the conditions of children's environments? Whatever the cause, when things don't work, it is time to adjust. Throughout the pages of this book, Zach Rhoads and Stanton Peele present what adjustment requires—ordinary people willing to see differently, think differently, and act differently to achieve extraordinary results."

—Jeanine K. Fitzgerald, creator of The Fitzgerald Institute of Lifelong Learning, author of *The Dance of Interaction: A Guide to Managing Children's Challenging Behaviors*

"Based on compassion, science and good old-fashioned family values, this book empowers us by tapping into our resilience and reinforcing our innate strengths and resources. It embraces person-centered harm reduction approaches that have been the foundation of successful public health policies and programs for decades, thereby offering optimism and hope for people using substances problematically and their loved ones to move forward with their lives in healthy and constructive ways."

—Barry Lessin, CAADC, family therapist, co-founder of
Families for Sensible Drug Policy

"*Outgrowing Addiction* is not afraid to challenge long-held beliefs about drug use, no matter how widespread and entrenched they might be. In the midst of America's opioid epidemic, it has never been more important to raise the questions that Stanton Peele and Zach Rhoads have here."

—Travis Lupick, author of *Fighting for Space: How a Group of Drug Users Transformed One City's Struggle of Addiction*

"Congratulations to Stanton Peele and Zach Rhoads on an eye-opening book, a state-of-the-art guide to scientifically sound information that can help the addiction field move into the twenty-first century. Stanton Peele and Zach Rhoads have written a book that challenges the dominant disease concept of addiction and its treatment. Evidence based treatments are moving past old concepts and should be viewed as new technology for addiction misuse therapy and help. *Outgrowing Addiction* goes step by step to show how the concept of the disease of addiction is not helping recovery programs become successful, and to offer alternative ways of helping people, starting with children."

—Robert J. Meyers, Ph.D., Emeritus Professor,
University of New Mexico, architect of
Community Reinforcement and Family Therapy (CRAFT)

"Stanton Peele is a bold and original thinker with a wide-angle view of the human psyche and spot-on vision. He is a champion of the power people have to change, and has long been a pioneer in rejecting the deterministic belief that addiction is a disease that one has forever and that addicts are powerless in the face of their cravings. He has shown instead that cognitive and life skills are keys to kicking addictions."

—Hara Estroff Marano, Editor,
*Psychology Today*; author of *A Nation of Wimps*

"*Outgrowing Addiction* is a book of hope, and of the liberation that awaits those willing to abandon powerful but bankrupt ideologies in favor of reason, science and clear-eyed self-reflection."

—Ethan Nadelmann, Ph.D., J.D., founding
Executive Director of the Drug Policy Alliance

"Dr. Peele and Zach Rhoads offer a smart, readable, common-sense guide for parents concerned about their children's drug and alcohol use. Persuasively rebutting the alarmist view advanced by the 'experts,' they show the importance of reinforcing children's independence, promoting constructive values, and fostering the ability to learn from mistakes. They also show how to teach youth to recognize the risks in overusing substances and suggest safeguards for the small minority who are at greatest risk for addiction."

—Aaron T. Beck, M.D., Professor of Psychiatry,
University of Pennsylvania, originator of
Cognitive Behavioral Therapy and winner of 2006 Lasker Award

"Stanton Peele has been a groundbreaking pioneer in the addiction field since the days of *Love and Addiction*. In this newest book, Peele and Zach Rhoads continue this breakthrough in our view of addiction, and how it is created and solved, both challenging the status quo and delivering actionable steps in an evidence-based and practical way. Their developmental model of addiction, which traces struggles to early experiences and correctly recognizes addiction as a solvable issue, will be a must-read for anyone struggling with the outdated and insufficient models used in our failing treatment system."

—Adi Jaffe, Ph.D., author, *The Abstinence Myth*; TEDx speaker

## Also By Stanton Peele

*Recover! An Empowering Program to Help You
Stop Thinking Like an Addict and Reclaim Your Life*
(with Ilse Thompson)

*7 Tools to Beat Addiction*

*Love and Addiction*
(with Archie Brodsky)

*How Much Is Too Much*

*Addiction-Proof Your Child*

*The Science of Experience*

*The Meaning of Addiction*

*Visions of Addiction*
(edited volume)

*Diseasing of America*

*The Truth About Addiction and Recovery*
(with Archie Brodsky and Mary Arnold)

*Alcohol and Pleasure*
(edited volume)

*Resisting 12-Step Coercion*
(with Charles Bufe and Archie Brodsky)

# Outgrowing
# Addiction

*"We can't solve problems by using the same kind of thinking we used when we created them."*
—Albert Einstein

*"When we focus less on fixing what we consider to be inadequacies and more on reinforcing our strengths, we can realize potential we didn't even know we had."*
— Lindsay Crouse, in the *New York Times,* about Allie Kieffer, a heavier-than-usual elite marathon runner

Upper Access titles are available at special discounts for bulk purchases. If you are interested in bulk purchases, please contact the publisher, Steve Carlson, at *Steve@UpperAccess.com.*

# Outgrowing Addiction

**With Common Sense
Instead of "Disease" Therapy**

Stanton Peele, Ph.D., J.D.
and
Zach Rhoads

Upper Access Books
Hinesburg, Vermont
https://upperaccess.com

Upper Access Books
87 Upper Access Road
Hinesburg, Vermont 05461
https://upperaccess.com

Library of Congress Cataloging-in-Publication Data

(The CIP data were not available in time for the first printing. You
may obtain this information by emailing the publisher at steve@
upperaccess.com. Please put "CIP Request" in the subject line.)

Trade paper edition, ISBN 978-0-942679-46-5
Also published in e-book formats, ISBN 978-0-942679-47-2

Printed on acid-free paper in the United States of America
19/ 10 9 8 7 6 5 4 3 2 1

For Hadley,

who was born alongside this book

# Contents

# Foreword

For anyone who loves reading Stanton Peele, *Outgrowing Addiction* will be a new treat. The evidence keeps pouring in that, over four decades ago when he published *Love and Addiction,* Peele was fundamentally correct about addiction and how to outgrow it.

In this latest work Peele and Rhoads incorporate recent scientific and cultural developments into the primary themes of Peele's work, including that viewing addiction as a disease is actually harmful, that addiction involves the whole person (not just the brain), that most people will outgrow addiction (and there are ways to accelerate that process), and that pursuing a valued and constructive new life path can move one entirely beyond addiction.

The text is filled with actual stories of change. More than just being inspiring (although they are), the stories are clear. The reader witnesses the processes of change, and discovers they are not mysterious. Outgrowing addiction is very much like other changes people already know how to make.

Peele and Rhoads will help you bring your existing strengths to address any addictive problems you have. The authors also pay attention to parents and children, providing impressively comprehensive and powerful guidance for childrearing by working with children, their strengths, and normal developmental processes, rather than against them.

As with Peele's previous work, this book is written in a clear and easily accessible style. This compelling critique of how the U.S. typically understands and responds to addiction, when more effective (indeed, life-saving) methods are within easy reach, ought to be read by everyone who is an addiction stakeholder.

—Tom Horvath, Ph.D., ABPP
President, Practical Recovery Psychology Group (San Diego)
Past President, SMART Recovery
Past President, Society of Addiction Psychology (APA, Division 50)

# Acknowledgments

We are indebted to the support and help of a number of people, beginning with Will Godfrey, for an early reading and refining of this manuscript, and including Archie Brodsky for his infinite patience and skillful final review before putting this book to bed. We are of course thankful for the support and faith in this book shown by Upper Access editor-in-chief Steve Carlson and his wonderful designer, particularly Kitty Werner.

Finally, Stanton Peele thanks Alta Ann Morris for her graciousness, caring, and perseverance; Zach Rhoads thanks his partner in life, work, and family, Samantha Rhoads and his sister, Molly Rhoads, whose inspiring journey along the Appalachian Trail embodies the spirit of this book.

# Introduction: Why we are writing this book

We Americans fear addiction. The fears are well-founded, as millions of lives are destroyed or damaged, yet what we hear is increasingly confusing. As a society, we respond by tightening the restrictions on painkiller prescriptions and increasing the availability of treatment; yet drug deaths continue to rise unabated. At the same time, many of us struggle when we try to solve the problems that addiction presents for ourselves, our friends, and our families.

How can we prevent and deal with addiction more effectively, both for ourselves and our children?

Many Americans have a fantasy that we can sidestep cultural, community, and personal problems and find medical solutions for addiction and every aspect of all mental disorders. This fantasy grows from a faith in medical technology, from traditions of faith-healing and unscrupulous snake-oil salespeople and some modern equivalents in rehabs, and from a medical theocracy that rules not only our health care, but our personal visions of ourselves and of our collective future as a society.

The authors believe that this is impossible and, in particular, that our society misunderstands addiction. In this book, we will demonstrate how. More importantly, we will set out an alternative model for addressing addiction, one strongly supported by all evidence. Happily, our model—which we name "The Developmental Model of Addiction"—offers a far more optimistic prognosis than the dominant concept in America today: that of addiction as a disease.

This isn't a treatment manual per se. Stanton Peele has created a series of such self-help and treatment books. However, we include in Appendices A and B a readers' guide and a parents' and helpers' manual to assist readers in applying the concepts in this book to their own, their children's, and their help-seeking clients' lives.

Throughout this book we have developed a series of principles around natural recovery and child development that lead us on clear paths to overcoming addiction. These include recovery either in the long run—

that is, growing up—or in here-and-now efforts to change on one's own, through a group or with a treatment provider.

## It's Not a Disease

How does our Developmental Model differ from the standard addiction-as-disease model? We do not see addiction as a permanent personal trait. Instead, we see it as something that ebbs and flows in individuals over time, and that most of us are bound to outgrow. We all encounter addictions in our lives—although for some of us they are far more severe and long-lasting than for others.

No matter how severe an addiction is, we believe that regarding it as an inescapable disease in itself limits our ability to improve. The disease model makes us unduly pessimistic about ourselves and our possibilities, and thus makes challenging addiction more difficult. The damaging nature of this perspective is most obviously true for the young.

People become locked into addictions, rather than pursuing normal life channels, for varying lengths of time. Lifelong addictions are relatively rare. The best way to discourage addiction is not by insisting that people stop, but by allowing, encouraging, and helping people to pursue more constructive life paths—ones that lead to greater satisfaction and self-respect.

People—children and adults—succeed when they learn how it feels to finally become oriented toward greater goals; to treat themselves like people who are worthy of having goals; and to become confident that they can engineer their own positive outcomes.

As we mature, most of us become more emotionally stable. At the same time we develop more connections to life and our actions come to mean more to others, as well as to ourselves. Such improvements enhance our resilience in combating life problems, including emotional ones like anxiety and depression, and practical ones like those at work and with families.

It is this typical pattern of growth and improvement that forms the basis for our Developmental Model.

Addiction and recovery both have strong social tie-ins. Those segments of society with fewer resources and less-positive options are more prone to addiction problems and less likely to recover. In large parts of American society, economic problems and a sense of hopelessness have contributed to a societal demoralization that works against the natural recovery model, increasing addiction and related problems.

Because young people are particularly vulnerable to an addiction model that negates hope, this book is especially concerned with addiction and related problems in childhood. However, many adults also struggle to attain the sense of purpose in life that is their best defense against addiction, so the general principles apply to all ages.

## Overcoming the Effects of Trauma

The widespread idea that specific childhood traumas permanently change people's brains and perpetually predispose them to addiction is really just a variant on the standard disease model. We oppose all disease-theory approaches. Explaining addictions and mental disorders in adults as being caused by trauma leads to circular, negative self-reflection. We oppose the application of such disease theories to children because of how they lead children—and their parents and teachers—to label themselves with permanent childhood conditions such as ADHD, Oppositional-Defiant Disorder, Depression, and Bipolar Disorder.

*All of these labels are becoming increasingly common throughout our society. Somehow, they feed off themselves.*

Underlying our thinking and our approach is a model of ordinary child and adult development. Seemingly neglected in favor of a modish trend toward diagnosing every misstep or slowness to develop that a child shows—or problems that adults display—as a permanent characterological disorder, a developmental model instead says that you or your child can change, grow, and overcome problems that have held you or your child back.

In other words, as you or your child develop personally, you develop out of addiction and a host of other problems. Of course, at times you and your child might benefit from help—but never help that labels you with a disease. Ours is a pragmatic, empowering, and—most of all—an optimistic, non-fatalistic approach. We want and expect our developmental model to be helpful to you in your own life and to all parents, as well as teachers, counselors, and other professionals.

## The Developmental Model of Addiction

Let's step back and define what we mean by addiction. An addiction is a harmful attachment to a habit or behavior that provides rewarding experiences—experiences we continue to pursue, despite their harmful effects, sometimes to the very depths of despair and self-destruction.

There is nothing magical or inherently biological about this definition. What distinguishes addictions from healthful or constructively rewarding behaviors is their negative consequences—for physical health, relationships, careers, or other core aspects of life. Cycles of behavior that are both rewarding and yet have a negative impact can happen with drugs, of course—whether tobacco, alcohol, painkillers, or other legal or illegal substances. But they also occur with Internet use, shopping, gambling, and even with personal attachments—including what some label "love."

The widespread idea that addiction is all about drugs is therefore untrue—as bodies like the World Health Organization and the American Psychiatric Association have only recently come to recognize. But our society still accepts many inaccurate ideas about addiction and drugs as received wisdom.

One misconception is that we are all equally susceptible to drug addictions. We aren't. People experiencing despair and who feel they can't control their lives—whether due to war, poverty, other social deprivation, or serious psychological problems—are more susceptible to addiction.

Equally inaccurate is the idea that research has traced addiction to the brain or a gene. These accepted—but incorrect—ideas lead us to see addiction as a permanent biological trait. This implies that people with addiction can never reconnect in a positive way with the behavior to which they were addicted. In fact, revamping our addictive relationship with a substance or activity is commonplace. In the cases of sex, love, and food addictions, this is the only alternative.

We point out these cultural misconceptions because people who suffer with addictions deserve better. They deserve effective assistance, of course. They also deserve to recognize their own power to improve their lives and to point their children in positive directions. Finally, we need to change our thinking about addiction for the benefit of society as a whole, which is adrift in its drug and other addictive problems. Table 1 summarizes the differences between the disease and the developmental models of addiction.

As the authors of this book, we bring a unique blend of theoretical and practical experience to our subject. Our backgrounds and experiences are very different,* a fact that broadens the perspectives we can offer. We hope that you find the results of our work helpful.

---

* Stanton Peele, Ph.D., J.D., is a widely recognized, award-winning addiction expert who has investigated, written about, and treated addiction over five decades. He has created the Life Process Program, developed for a successful residential rehab center, the online version of which is now used around the world. Zach Rhoads, 40 years younger, is an educational and behavioral consultant for teachers, families, and children, who has put behind him a severe heroin addiction and is a Life Process Program coach. More detailed author biographies are at the end of this book.

Table 1

## Ways of Conceiving Addiction,
### The disease models (AA and brain disease) versus the developmental model

| | Disease | Developmental |
|---|---|---|
| **Nature** | All-or-nothing disease state | Extreme end of continuum of normal human behavior |
| **Cause** | Chemical, biological, trauma | Coping problems, environment |
| **Objects** | Some drugs and alcohol | Range of engulfing experiences |
| **Course** | Irreversible, life-long; held off by meds (brain disease) | Usually reduces or disappears over life course w/o treatment |
| **Human agency** | Individual is powerless, can't control on their own | People exercise choice, display agency, are empowered |
| **Treatment** | Drug Tx (brain disease) or spiritual, group support (AA) | Life developments; skills, purpose, motivational Tx |
| **Community** | Restricted to fellow addicts | Communion with all humans |
| **Self-identity** | "I'm an addict or alcoholic" | "I'm a person with the same needs, capacities as all humans" |
| **Outcomes** | Either abstinence or medication, or else self-destruction and death | Range of goals, from abstinence to normal, reduced, or less harmful use (harm reduction) |
| **Parenting** | Convey disease inheritance | Employ sound, common-sense parenting skills |
| **Value outlook** | Value-free (brain disease) or moralistic (AA) | Harness pro-social, community, purpose and other values |

# Addiction as a Developmental Process

Addiction is a natural response that all people encounter in lesser or greater forms—one that varies with people's personal dispositions and beliefs, life situations and experiences, and opportunities and outlooks.

What tells us that addiction and recovery are typical life processes, ones we have all observed, participated in and experienced? We know this by simply looking around us and at our own lives—as well as making sensible observations about historical and cultural events, from the Vietnam War to the current opioid crisis. As an added benefit, this commonsense exploration of life in the here-and-now will naturally show us the relationship between childhood developmental experiences and addiction.

Addictions have three components:

- The person experiencing the addiction.
- That person's situation, including their physical, social, and cultural environment.
- That person's temporal or developmental circumstances—where that person is in their life.

Each of these components can increase the likelihood of someone becoming addicted, just as each can enable people to avoid, limit, or overcome addiction.

Let's start at the far end of the spectrum of suffering—which is the end that media invariably focus on every time they discuss drugs and addiction*. These obviously addicted individuals tend to reflect extreme formative experiences and current circumstances, including mental illness, terribly deprived environments, and traumas.

---

* It is almost certain that you will never observe a contented cocaine or heroin user on television (although perhaps now we may see some marijuana users), as numerous as these are, or even see a program focused on the overwhelming masses of people who use painkillers in a targeted and successful way, just as you probably have in real life.

A few people have lost most of their ordinary connections to life. For example, we will later describe men and women in "wet housing" (people taken off the streets who are given a residence where they are allowed to drink). Their personal plights are generally severe and long-standing. People in these circumstances are not, by and large, likely to quit heavy drinking. But although they face limits, even for these human beings life improvement is still a strong possibility.

For most people, however, addiction is situational and of limited duration. In some cases, such as people in war zones, like Americans who were sent to Vietnam, the situational nature of addiction is so obvious that everyone has noted it.

## Vietnam Veterans' Natural Recovery from Heroin Addiction

When Stanton and Archie Brodsky wrote about the returning Vietnam War veterans in *Love and Addiction* in 1975, they quoted Richard Wilbur, undersecretary of the army, a physician: "Everything I learned in medical school about addiction—that someone addicted to narcotics remained hooked forever—was proved wrong." In fact, over 90 percent of the returned vets who had been addicted to heroin in Asia ceased being addicted in the States virtually at once.

The Vietnam addiction experience was catalogued by Lee Robins and her colleagues in the classic, *Vietnam Veterans Three Years After Vietnam: How our study changed our view of heroin*, the most careful and detailed study of a group of heroin-addicted people ever conducted. Everything Robins and her colleagues took on faith about heroin was disproved. Most soldiers (85 percent) said they found narcotics readily available to them at home—so we can discount the idea of lack of supply accounting for their mass recovery. Half did try the drugs again in the States. But even among the most vulnerable group, the previously addicted soldiers who used heroin again stateside, *fewer than a third ever became re-addicted.* In other words, non-addicted use of narcotics was not only possible for formerly addicted soldiers, but *more likely than not under their radically transformed circumstances.***

---

** Stanton asks recovering addicts who swear they can never use (a) any psychoactive substance, (b) the particular type of drug to which they were addicted, ever again, under any circumstance: (to opioid addicts) "Have you had a major medical procedure since you recovered? Did you receive a painkiller, in the hospital and perhaps after? If you were to have such a procedure, would you insist on not receiving pain medication?" Of course they accepted the painkiller. This situational idea of addiction and drug use is called "harm reduction," as readers shall see.

What should most impress us about this research is not so much its amazing results, but how the medical experts were completely unprepared for the reality of human addictive behavior—how sensitive it is to individual outlooks, experiences, and settings. Obviously, for most soldiers, addiction was a temporary response to an acutely threatening and disconnected environment. Narcotics no longer held that addictive power over them once they returned to a more comfortable setting. Yet, unlike the medical "experts," most human beings who learn that people leaving a war zone and returning home lose their susceptibility to addiction find this to be simple common sense!

Even this highly publicized result doesn't tell the full story of recovery by Vietnam vets. Robins and her colleagues also discovered that heroin was no more likely to be used regularly or compulsively than other street drugs available to returned vets, such as amphetamines, barbiturates, and marijuana. (In other words, as defined by regular, compulsive use, *heroin, the chief illicit opioid drug, was not wholly more likely to be addictive than other drugs and experiences*, a reality that addiction experts are still struggling to grasp.) Furthermore, Robins *et al.* found that those who entered treatment *actually fared worse* than those who avoided it.

In fact, they found that the small number of men who continued with their addictions had shown these tendencies and life problems before entering the service.

More than a decade after the Vietnam experience, in 1993 Robins wrote a paper entitled "Vietnam Veterans' Rapid Recovery from Heroin Addiction: A fluke or normal expectation?" The clear answer, based on numerous studies: Natural recovery from heroin addiction is the general rule, and not an exception that cropped up in Vietnam.

The significance of this finding is overwhelming. Unlike the widespread assumptions shared by media and the American medical establishment, natural recovery is, by far, the norm. Given a reasonable environment, time, and the expectation that we can and will recover, *almost all of us will.*

Compare and contrast the scientific-sounding fatalism of the following message from the medical body charged with treating addiction in the U.S., the American Board of Addiction Medicine:

"Armed with that understanding [that addiction is a disease], the management of folks with addiction becomes very much like the management of other chronic diseases, such as asthma, hypertension or diabetes," said Dr. Daniel Alford, who oversees the program at Boston University Medical Center. "It's hard necessarily to cure people, but you can certainly manage the problem to the point where they are able to function through a combination of pharmaceuticals and therapy."

William White, widely considered the most balanced and thoughtful among traditional addiction experts***, analyzed 415 scientific reports of recovery in 2012. White (who is "in recovery" himself) confronted the disease philosophy's claims that addiction is a chronic disease that can get worse but never better. He found, "Recovery is not an aberration achieved by a small and morally enlightened minority of addicted people. If there is a natural developmental momentum within the course of these problems, it is toward remission and recovery."

A decisive demonstration of this truth was provided by a 2012-13 national study called NESARC (National Epidemiologic Survey on Alcohol and Related Conditions). The study involved over 43,000 people in face-to-face interviews about their lifetime substance use. This research found that people overwhelmingly overcome drug dependencies (their term for addiction) over the course of their lives: 84 percent in the case of nicotine (smoking), 91 percent for alcohol, 97 percent for cannabis (marijuana), and 99 percent for cocaine. In a separate analysis conducted by the NESARC of subjects who had ever abused or been dependent on a prescription drug—including sedatives, tranquilizers, stimulants (such as amphetamines), and opioids, over their lifetime, 96 percent remitted for all the substances combined, with half the cases remitting between four and five years of the onset of the drug problem. People simply rarely spend their entire lives addicted.****

---

*** *The Atlantic* published a list, "10 People Revolutionizing How We Study Addiction and Recovery." Bill White was listed first on the list and Stanton—called a revolutionary whose work was to be welcomed—was also included, while being labeled "controversial" for "his thesis that AA is not the only way to treat addiction, and that alcoholism is not a disease."

**** Some readers confront the issue of detoxification, or overcoming the effects of withdrawal. We can say that withdrawal varies all over the map, that settings and expectations affect withdrawal as they do addiction, and that some people require, or simply desire, medical or other supervision. Others have quit without such help (think of smoking). We can't tell you what to do. Zach withdrew from heroin gradually, on his own.

Unfortunately, these data are ignored and we allow our societal view of addiction to be shaped primarily by those who have the least success in dealing with it. As addiction journalist and expert Maia Szalavitz asked, "Most people with addiction simply grow out of it. Why is this widely denied?" She wrote: "The idea that addiction is typically a chronic disease that requires treatment is false, the evidence shows. Yet the 'aging out' experience of the majority is ignored by treatment providers and journalists." Nonetheless, Szalavitz herself emphasizes the treatment solution: "many of those who recover do it through professional treatment with medications."

## Changing the Addict Narrative

How is it possible that we hardly ever hear about natural recovery? Propaganda from vested interests in the American recovery industry is one factor. But another is that recovery is so normal, we *don't think anything about it*. Many more 20-somethings misuse and become dependent on drugs and alcohol than 50-year-olds (data we will document), who have usually grown up, gotten jobs, and are supporting families. Everyone knows and accepts this, yet we rarely wonder what those 50-year-olds' lives looked like when they were susceptible young people in their 20s (or sometimes 30s and older).

For most people who formerly had a major drug or alcohol habit, their current absence of addiction has just become part who they are, and they don't see anything special about it. People grow up, become normalized, and settle down emotionally, concentrating on jobs and careers, responsibilities toward their families, raising of their children, or whatever other positive paths their lives take. This is the natural process of recovery, and we rarely give it a second thought.

It is only thanks to the U.S.-rooted recovery movement that people who previously had addictive habits refer to themselves as being "in recovery," and are encouraged—indeed, admonished—to make that the focus of their identity forever.

Similarly, most people who have had a drug or alcohol problem have never thought of themselves as "addicts." And they were right not to do so, since this label is an anchor on their identities. The authors therefore avoid using that word or equivalent labels. Assigning people to that negative, self-fulfilling and self-defeating identity can never be justified. We know this from our work. We also see it in Zach's own life, after he quit a considerable heroin addiction in his 20s.

Zach's story of quick recovery from heroin addiction while still in his early 20s is fairly typical, as NESARC demonstrated. Of course, some of those who quit an addictive drug habit take decades to do so. Here, according to the government's NESARC research, are the turning points by which half of the people who were addicted to each substance quit:

- cigarettes = 26 years
- alcohol =14 years
- marijuana = 6 years
- cocaine= 5 years

Isn't it interesting that addictions to illicit drugs were resolved more quickly: six years on average for marijuana, and five for cocaine? NESARC did not analyze separately the Americans addicted to heroin, but Lee Robins found exactly the same pattern to hold for those addicted to heroin in Vietnam and elsewhere. It seems that major illicit drug habits are so life-disruptive that people are quicker to leave them behind, as so many baseball players did. Keith Hernandez—who himself quit a "massive" cocaine habit—famously said that 40 percent of his fellow players used cocaine.

Some of the people in the NESARC study underwent considerable life changes in the time it took them to remit their dependencies. By the time they recovered, they had developed into very different people from when their addictions began. This is an ordinary developmental process, and the opposite of the disease theory.

### Case Study: Am I Really an Alcoholic?

Margaret contacted Stanton to decide whether she was actually an alcoholic. She joined Alcoholics Anonymous at 17. She had been homeless and drank from an open bottle with a group of other street kids. However, she never enjoyed alcohol, and only mouthed the bottle when one was passed around. Social services placed her in AA after she moved in with a foster family.

Fifteen years later, Margaret was married and had a child. She joined a new-mothers' group in a well-off neighborhood. Drinking wine was a regular part of their weekly get-togethers, and Margaret felt how she stuck out by abstaining. But she hadn't drunk alcohol at all in 15 years, and had never consumed wine casually, which she now wanted to do.

This case might seem like a no-brainer. If you never liked drinking alcohol, then how could you possibly be an alcoholic?

But there is a more fundamental argument within this case: If someone like Margaret had actually been drinking alcoholically as a teen, why should the risk of drinking for the Margaret of her early 30s, settled in marriage and motherhood, bear any relation to that for the adolescent Margaret, who had been enduring homelessness and turmoil?

Life is more complex than simply asserting that Margaret never really drank, ergo she can't be an alcoholic. Margaret had grown into adulthood *thinking of herself* as an alcoholic. Changing a person's self-image and perceived place in the world can involve considerable effort. Moreover, Margaret was married to an AA member who wanted to continue in AA, adding another wrinkle that she and Stanton worked on as she "recovered" from a disease she never had.

While Margaret presents a stark example of self-labeling, the people questioned in the NESARC study objectively qualified, according to clinical standards, as alcohol- or drug-dependent due to their past drug use or drinking. Some were lectured that their addictions are lifelong. Yet even in those cases, most didn't think of themselves as addicts or alcoholics based on a bad patch—even an extended one—in their lives. Proving their point, NESARC found that the majority of formerly alcohol-dependent Americans now drank alcohol without problems.

The possibility of former addicts resuming moderate use has been a cultural and therapeutic flashpoint for decades, if not centuries. We can't say that moderation is the recommended path for everyone, but the data show that it is possible for most. We see this all around us. Zach drinks alcohol socially, now that he no longer uses heroin. Maia Szalavitz, author of the bestseller *Unbroken Brain*, was once addicted to heroin and cocaine, but now drinks alcohol moderately. A few media stars, such as Drew Barrymore (whose story we tell below), are emboldened to reveal that they have recovered from addiction but are not "in recovery."

Maia Szalavitz was piqued when describing how this typical situation is denied: "For some, recovery is a members-only club for people who are totally abstinent. This leaves most of us out in the cold."

Think of people you know who have been addicted. Would they really ever go back to their former addicted lives if they used again? What if they had an operation and left the hospital with a prescription for pain relievers? What if they drank the holiday punch, not realizing it contained alcohol?

People do occasionally become re-addicted. But most formerly addicted people would simply have to sacrifice too much to do so. People don't like to sacrifice good and meaningful things in their lives.

### Case Study: Joseph Couldn't Dream of Using Again

Joseph grew up on the streets of New York City where he was addicted to heroin. Everyone knew it: he was registered as an addict with the police. He never finished high school, and he could barely read. He had been in and out of prison. But when, in his mid-twenties, Joseph married a college-educated woman—a social worker—he changed. He got an equivalency diploma and then graduated community college. He and his wife moved to a suburban community, where Joseph became a counselor himself. He developed a following of people for whom his life story was compelling.

One day Joseph burned himself in a small kitchen fire. The treating physician, having no idea of Joseph's life story, prescribed a refillable course of Percocet. Joseph smiled as he contemplated the script. He thought how, in time gone by, he would have relished this open door to drugs. Now, he imagined what he would give up to use drugs again: his marriage, his home, his work, the respect of his community. After the burn had healed, he smiled again as he threw out the remainder of the prescription.

Of course, the point is, he *did* use opioids again—for a short time—because he was in pain. The evidence about prescribed painkiller use and addiction tells us that Joseph joined legions of people in using his Percocet without further problems. At the same time, his story illustrates how purpose and human connection are far more powerful than drugs' effects. So, too, are other kinds of values.

## Case Study: Uncle Ozzie Forgets He Was Addicted

At his grandfather's funeral in the early 1960s, Stanton noticed that his Uncle Ozzie, then aged 42, no longer smoked. Ozzie explained that he had quit smoking after 25 years. This was a couple of years before the 1964 Surgeon General's Report indicating that smoking caused cancer.

Stanton asked his uncle what made him quit. Ozzie described how he had made his decision because of a co-worker's comment. (They repaired TVs together.) Ozzie was placing an extra nickel in the cigarette machine after the price of cigarettes had been raised when his co-worker remarked that Ozzie was a "sucker for the tobacco companies."

"You're right," Ozzie responded. "I'm quitting." After finishing the pack he had just purchased he never smoked again.

Talking with Stanton, Ozzie didn't cut himself a break about his former habit. "It was filthy," Ozzie told Stanton. "I had smoked four packs of cigarettes a day since I was 18. I kept one lit on my work-bench all day long." And yet, Ozzie said, "I had never considered quitting before that moment."

Decades later, Stanton quizzed Ozzie at his 90th birthday party about his famous decision to quit smoking almost 50 years earlier. After a half century without cigarettes, Ozzie was puzzled by Stanton's question.

"I smoked?"

But you don't have to wait a half-century to change your narrative.

There are some key facts about Ozzie's personal background that we should be aware of in considering his story. Ozzie was a shop steward for his union, a staunch anti-capitalist, and an anti-big-business crusader. Indeed, in the 1950s, he was in real danger of being labeled a "commie."

So why did Ozzie quit a four-pack-a-day, quarter-century addiction, never to smoke again for the remainder of his long life, based on an off-hand remark from a co-worker? We'll return to this question, because it has broad relevance for both quitting and preventing addictions. In the meantime, think purpose and values.

As unique a personality as Ozzie was, his story is another example of a normal developmental process. While people's life parabolas (and, of course, chance encounters) vary all over the map, most people outgrow addiction. They do so because of values, goals, and ideas about themselves that they hold concurrently with being addicted, as Stanton and Ilse Thompson describe and work with in their book, *Recover! An Empowering Program to Help You Stop Thinking Like an Addict and Reclaim Your Life.*

We feel that this is remarkably good news—and we marvel (like Maia Szalavitz) at the perversity of its being withheld from the public.

As an experiment, try looking for examples of this phenomenon among your own friends. Simply quiz them to discover how typical it is to quit smoking—which is by far the longest-lasting addiction recorded in NESARC—without any formal assistance. You'll find this feat is commonplace among people you know. How amazing is *that*?

## Developing Resilience

Even if people can and do regularly quit addictions, it's still preferable not to become addicted in the first place. So what can we do to help children who are not yet addicted, but may be at high risk due to their difficult life situations?

First, let's consider the label "high risk." In a school setting, everyone knows who the high-risk children are. The authors are against labeling. But being aware of children in circumstances requiring special help is simply sensible educational policy. Yet we are at a loss for dealing with such kids. The best approach is to have a task force for the school and the community to offer such children helping resources. Here is one such system, as described by conservative *New York Times* columnist David Brooks in a column titled, "A Really Good Thing Happening in America":

> Around the table was just about anybody in town who might touch a child's life. There were school superintendents and principals, but there were also the heads of the Chamber of Commerce and the local United Way, the police chief, a former mayor and the newspaper editor . . . everybody who might have any influence (on the child)—parents, religious leaders, doctors, nutrition experts, etc. And then together, as a community-wide system, they ask questions: Where are children falling off track? Why? What assets do we have in our system that can be applied to this problem? How can we work together to apply those assets?

At a more basic level, we all understand the concept of resilience, which has particular relevance for children raised under adverse conditions. In practice, even among children facing such challenges, the substantial majority (according to the very research used to establish childhood adversity measures) don't become addicted, and instead establish positive outlooks and relationships. How does that happen, and how can we expand that resilience for the children we know?

Psychologist Angela Duckworth, in her book *Grit*—a popular term for the resilience that all of us want for our children—relates child developmental issues to mental health. *Grit* describes the perseverance people need to succeed in life endeavors. Such perseverance, in turn, requires a positive, optimistic outlook.

Duckworth's work focuses teachers and parents on fostering optimism in children. This optimism is especially important for children who face challenges, like those who are diagnosed with the conditions we discuss in this book. But hopefulness and perseverance are important qualities for *all* children.

We are failing to foster this optimism and resilience in sizable numbers of children in our contemporary world, even beyond traditionally high-risk children, with many kids who feel insufficiently equipped to meet the demands placed on them. This is increasingly the case for even the privileged children who go to leading colleges and who are reporting alarmingly high levels of anxiety and depression. Nonetheless, bad outcomes more often occur for children in inner cities and pockets of rural poverty such as Appalachia. As Maia Szalavitz has pointed out, "Addictions are harder to kick when you're poor."

The task of instilling in challenged children the confidence to proceed in life is a tough one, made tougher without the additional resources available to well-off people. No matter who the person is, creating a path of hopefulness and belief in oneself is the best guarantee against addiction. If children in some groups are more ensnared by trauma, mental disorders, and addiction than ever, that is because we are failing them. We must as a society devote ourselves to reversing this process.

But we aren't doing that well in inspiring grit even in the best-off of children.

# Addictive Experiences

## 2

For the proper perspective, we need to examine the general nature of addiction, not just dependence on drugs and alcohol. People seek and find addictive relief in different experiences at different times in their lives under certain circumstances, and these experiences may satisfy their needs, while simultaneously harming them, in ways ranging from small to large, until they find superior ways of gaining life sustenance.

Drug use is *not* a special, separate category of behavior, one that usually leads to addiction. In fact, addictions based on many non-drug behaviors and experiences are common, as now recognized by the American psychiatric establishment. At the same time, most drug use does not lead to addiction. Yet our drug-addiction caricature is firmly embedded in the American mind, centered around the demonization of opiates.

Opiates have been known and used since antiquity, sometimes in massive quantities. Historians and popular authors differ on the impact of the widespread use of opiates in the nineteenth century in America and England, which we view through our modern biases. David Courtwright contended in his 1982 book, *Dark Paradise*, that the U.S. was awash in drug addicts during that period of history, but Virginia Berridge's 1998 book, *Opium and the People*, instead showed that there was no evidence to support the idea of widespread opioid addiction in England. In practice, it was only at the turn of the twentieth century that organized medicine defined opiates (including morphine and heroin) as special agents of addiction, alone among the world's substances and activities.

The belief that addiction is a disease has become "normal" science, while dissenting views are ignored. Disease advocates assert that the disease model is humane, since it regards drug users as victims. That belief is well-intentioned, but ignores the disease theory's effects in the real world. The supposedly diseased opiate habituées were turned into despised social outcasts early in the 20th century. With the passage of the 1914 Harrison Tax Act, they became criminals. Both the medical-disease view of addiction and the criminal one dehumanize drug users based on the come-lately (in the history of humankind) judgment that drug use is inherently bad and uncontrollable—*that drugs possess us.*

## American Painkiller Hysteria

Politicians, public health officials, and media reinforce this caricature of drug use by publicizing accounts of the worst examples of drug use they can find. This approach has carried over to our current opioid crisis. But, as always, every premise of the new drug hysteria is incorrect. For example, the *National Survey on Drug Use and Health* calculated that 98 million of us used opioid painkillers, legally or illegally, in 2015. Between one and two percent of users encountered any sort of a problem, let alone something as severe as dependence or an overdose.

### Exercise: What We All (Should) Know About Painkillers

If many tens of millions of people take painkillers without becoming addicted, why then do we believe opiates (and, as Sam Quinones points out in *Dreamland*, the same molecule is involved from heroin to Percocet and Demerol) are inherently addictive?

Stanton has an exercise for this. He asks those present in a group if they have ever taken a painkiller. Everyone raises their hands. "How many of you became addicted to the drug?" No one raises their hand. Stanton then asks several people, "How come you didn't become addicted to this 'highly addictive' drug?"

Stanton is on the board of the Above and Beyond Family Recovery Center in inner-city Chicago, the brainchild of Bryan Cressey, a healthcare investment pioneer who realized that comprehensive help had to be provided to those facing addiction in the most deprived parts of the country, rather than our preferred approach of devoting costly (if ineffective) care to the most privileged.

When Stanton did his exercise with the board, comprising a dozen people with successful places in society, and no one had become addicted, Cressey spoke up: "I was given painkillers after I had a knee replacement operation. I found taking them disoriented me and interfered with the work I had going on in my life. I was so anxious to get back to my life that I stopped using the pills as soon as I could, after a couple of days."

The CEO of the organization then spoke. He termed this answer, and the approach Stanton was identifying for Above and Beyond, "The purpose and meaning approach to addiction."

Cressey's answer is the one given by millions of ordinary people. People don't become addicted to opiates as a rule because they have other purposes in their lives with which using the drugs interferes. This common-sense point, one that is present in nearly everyone's mind, is the key to the solution for addiction.

It's always important, of course, to be mindful of the risks of prescription drug use. But overwhelming data like these prove that painkillers are not particularly dangerous or lethal. How, then, can our primary approach to the opioid crisis be to make it harder for those with opioid prescriptions to obtain needed painkillers? This has, demonstrably, had the effect of increasing opioid problems, since people have been forced to turn to illicit street supplies of painkillers, including heroin.

### Case Study: The Prince Story

Prince died in 2016, aged 57. As Stanton noted at the time, he couldn't have died from drugs he was prescribed. Rather, his death was caused by some mix of unregulated opioids. Two years later, in 2018, the county attorney reported that Prince was using counterfeit Vicodin containing fentanyl along with Percocet provided by his bodyguard, who had a prescription for the drug.

This story is typical of painkiller deaths, in that Prince was mixing drugs for which he had no prescriptions. According to a twisted logic, Prince prided himself on not drinking or taking illicit drugs. He died due to consuming opioids whose contents were thrown together by street chemists, combined with other painkillers that he used without medical supervision.

We often hear of drug toxicology results long after a person dies, or not at all. Here are the drugs found in prominent drug fatalities:

- Tom Petty—fentanyl, oxycodone, temazepam, alprazolam, citalopram, acetyl fentanyl and despropionyl fentanyl (the last two drugs are street formulations);
- Carrie Fisher—cocaine, methadone, ecstasy, alcohol,

antidepressants, and opiates (Fisher was a recovery spokesperson);

- Philip Seymour Hoffman—heroin, cocaine, benzodiazepines, amphetamines;

- Amy Winehouse—alcohol, benzodiazepines (people are often prescribed benzodiazepines in treatment, as they are at the Priory Clinic, where Winehouse was treated).

People don't die from taking pure heroin or from using prescribed painkillers. We will see that giving people access to these drugs in a controlled environment never results in death. If Prince had been given a single opioid source, no matter how powerful the opioid was, he would still be alive. His legal drug providers might have discussed with him whether he was relying on the drugs too much, the reasons for this dependence, and whether he could have benefited from alternative forms of pain relief. But he would be alive.

## The Campaign against Painkillers

The fundamental mistaken idea about addiction underlying the painkiller scare is the belief that addiction is the biological result of regular use of narcotics. Opioid hysteria websites broadcast alarming claims: "Dependence on prescription opioids can happen after just five days." But that idea is no truer than that regularly eating, having sex, shopping or drinking alcohol inevitably causes addiction to those things, to which some people become addicted. The truth is, addictions are created only when an involvement develops a special place in or meaning for a person's life.

The CDC issued stringent painkiller prescription guidelines in 2016. These guidelines embody the dominant misunderstanding of addiction and the extreme dangers of this erroneous thinking. They are based on the idea that taking painkillers for a long time equals addiction. A group of analgesic (painkiller) experts published a critique that challenged the CDC recommendations "that opioid prescriptions for acute pain last no longer than seven days" and that prescribers should avoid extended-release or long-acting opioids (ER/LA) because they keep painkillers in people's systems too long.

The group of seven experts noted that these recommendations attributed the addictions that some people (generally those with long addictive histories) form with opioids to everyone who uses them, converting a personal susceptibility into a characteristic of drugs. They wrote: "If prescribers must forego the use of ER/LA opioids in patients who could possibly benefit from them, it essentially punishes the chronic pain patient for offenses committed by drug abusers."

Constant messaging like that issued by the most visible public health officials (such as the Surgeon General) and politicians helps to ensure that America views addiction as an inescapable, unavoidable, consequence of using drugs. They say these things not only because they are chasing funding and votes, but because, unfortunately, they actually believe them.

## Normal Drug Use

The facts contradict these beliefs. Like many other involvements, drugs can have powerful negative consequences. But they usually don't. An extended study of prescribed opioid users published in 2018 in *The BMJ* (British Medical Journal) found that fewer than 1 percent suffered any negative consequences—including any kind of substance-use disorder or, at the extreme, overdose—following years of use. (This is the same figure as computed by the 2015 National Survey on Drug Use and Health cited above.)

Prescribed opioid users nearly always use their drugs as prescribed. This structure is absent for most illicit drug users. Yet to a remarkable and rarely recognized extent, even illicit users, given a fair chance (reasonable lifestyles and uncontaminated supplies), do regulate their narcotics habits and don't become addicted. The following quote is from Professor Paul Hayes, who was CEO of the British National Treatment Agency for Substance Misuse from 2001 to 2013:

> Most drug users are intelligent, resourceful people with good life skills, supportive networks and loving families. These assets enable them to manage the risks associated with their drug use, avoiding the most dangerous drugs and managing their frequency and scale of use to reduce harm and maximise pleasure. Crucially they will have access to support from family and friends should they begin to devel-

op problems, and a realistic prospect of a job, a house and a stake in society to focus and sustain their motivation to get back on track. . . .

In short what determines whether or not drug use escalates into addiction, and the prognosis once it has, is less to do with the power of the drug and more to do with the social, personal and economic circumstances of the user. . . .

Unfortunately the strong relationship between social distress and addiction is ignored by politicians and media commentators in favour of an assumption that addiction is a random risk driven by the power of the drug.

It does happen. But the atypical experience of the relatively small number of drug users from stable backgrounds who stumble into addiction and can legitimately attribute the chaos of their subsequent lives to this one event drowns out the experience of **the overwhelming majority of addicts for whom social isolation, economic exclusion, criminality and fragile mental health preceded their drug use rather than being caused by it.** (Our emphasis.)

A survey of drug users conducted on behalf of the website Addiction. com—a platform for trumpeting the dangers of drugs and addiction—made the same discovery:

### Drug Users Are Usually Normal People

### Survey depicts a day in a drug user's life, and it's pretty normal

"As we started collecting the data (from over a thousand regular drug users), we found out that most drug addicts are pretty similar to everyday people" (according to lead researcher, Logan Freedman).

Despite a few outliers, Freedman's findings seemed painfully mundane.

"These habits (sleep patterns, eggs for breakfast, home lives, etc.) don't seem to fit the stereotypes we typically associate with these drugs," Freedman said.

"Most of these people have jobs, wake up at a normal time and eat breakfast. . ."

The 2016 National Survey on Drug Use and Health revealed about 28.6 million people aged 12 or older—slightly over 10 percent of Americans—reported using illicit drugs in the 30 days prior to being asked. When you consider in addition people who drink, or use pharmaceutical drugs or other legal substances, it adds up to virtually all of us using potentially addictive drugs of some kind. How do we all avoid drug addiction and alcoholism?

Of course, given all of those who take drugs, many people do have negative drug outcomes. We certainly read and hear about them all the time. Consider, however, that a large number of people meet horrible deaths in car crashes. We could focus on this facet of the driving experience. But the overwhelming majority of people don't die driving cars over their whole lives, and we choose to drive, out of convenience and necessity.

Taking drugs recreationally is less necessary than driving, and so, while many do use drugs, their number is far smaller than those who drive. That's fine. You don't have to take drugs if you don't want to. Nonetheless, imagine what the media/public health debate on driving would be like if the air waves were constantly filled with dire warnings and graphic pictures of horrible auto accidents. You could be made to fear stepping out in the street, let alone getting behind the wheel!

## Fear Itself

The brilliant British researcher John Davies found, in his native Scotland in the 1970s, that adolescents with the most negative—and fearful—attitudes toward drugs *before* ever using them were the most likely to misuse them. They generally came from less well-off families, and were warned incessantly about the dangers of drugs, which they then vowed, in their early teens, to avoid at all costs. When many did, instead, start using drugs, they were much more likely than average users to encounter problems.

The fear-inspiration approach is used by DARE (Drug Abuse Resistance Education) and most American drug programs that claim to prevent drug use. These programs have been shown not to work, and in fact often are counterproductive, as Stanton described in his book, *Addiction-Proof Your Child*.

## A Note about Psychedelics

We are—if not in the midst of—on the cusp of a society in which drugs are used as tools for every aspect of our existences. One of the key examples is the use of psychedelics in therapy, for conditions like depression or for dealing with crises including life-threatening or life-ending medical conditions, but also as simply a window into the unknown—our own and the universe's. Psychedelic experiences are now being touted by mainstream authors like Michael Pollan in his book, *How to Change Your Mind*.

Pollan was a generally successful and mentally stable man who had not experimented with drugs prior to his research for the book. Indeed, that's what concerned him:

> Like many people in late middle age, I had developed a set of fairly dependable mental algorithms for navigating whatever life threw at me, and while these are undeniably useful tools for coping with everyday life and getting things done, they leave little space for surprise or wonder or change. After interviewing several dozen people who had undergone psychedelic therapy, I envied the radical new perspectives they had achieved. I also wasn't sure I'd ever had a spiritual experience, and time was growing short. The idea of "shaking the snow globe" of my mental life, as one psychedelic researcher put it, had come to seem appealing.

We can all benefit from shaking up our assumptions and looking at life anew, as Pollan came to do himself. There is widespread agreement on that issue among experts: for example, the trauma addiction specialist with whom we often disagree, Gabor Maté, administers the psychedelic ayahausca in international settings for people to liberate themselves from past experiences.

And, then, there is the need to reintegrate that experience into our ongoing lives. According to the *New York Times* reviewer of Pollan's book:

> Unlike people drunk or high who feel compelled the next day to shake their heads at what they did or thought under the influence, psychedelic users often feel the opposite, as if it's important to keep a foot in the place they were while gone. They might not credit the man in their shoulder, but their philosophical revelations about self and relationships and need and perspective last longer than you might expect. Pollan writes: "The traces these experiences inscribed remain indelible and accessible."

That solid-life basis for assimilating the drug experience, having a sense of purpose in pursuing and having control over it, and finding benefits from the time spent under the influence, are parts of the roadmap for using all drugs.

## Vulnerability to Addiction

Resisting efforts to exaggerate the dangers of drugs does not mean we should ignore them. People suffer, and sometimes lose their lives, around excessive, compulsive, and chaotic drug and alcohol use. But people's likelihood of harmful and fatal substance use is linked, like so much else, to their place in society. Addressing social concerns remains the key element to improving our alarming addiction profile and the proliferation of drug deaths in America. It is also the key, as we will show, to dealing with individual addictions.

Although drug and alcohol harms are far more typical on the margins of society, they do sometimes appear in privileged America, frightening all of us. Terry McGovern, the daughter of former presidential candidate George McGovern, was a 45-year-old mother of two who died of exposure on the street due to extreme intoxication. In explaining his daughter's long-standing alcohol problem, McGovern said: "She knew what it meant to love other people. But she fell short of loving herself."

Any theory of addiction—and any form of treatment or prevention— has to deal with people who "fall short of loving" themselves or who have other mental disorders. But that task is always easier when people have support and resources and communities. And those things, which are more available to the well-off, need to be found, or created, in order to help the marginalized.

The state with by far the highest rate of drug deaths (the CDC refers to these as "drug poisonings," rather than overdoses, for reasons we will explain) is West Virginia, which had 52 such deaths per 100,000 in 2016—no other state had as many as 40 per 100,000 that year. West Virginia's health commissioner set his department on the task of identifying every one of these opioid deaths.

> "We wanted to know who each person was and what we could have done to help them," Dr. Rahul Gupta said. . . . The findings ultimately would show a depressing pattern: **If you're a male between the ages of 35 to 54, with less than a high school education, you're single and you've worked in a blue-collar industry, you pretty much are at a very, very high risk of overdosing.**" (Our emphasis.)

The identical process takes place in many American inner-cities, where, as in rural Appalachia, opioid and other drug addictions are most typical among middle-aged male users: "According to the Office of the Medical Examiner in Washington, D.C., **overall opioid overdose deaths (read poisonings) among black men between the ages of 40 and 69 increased 245 percent from 2014–2017.**" (Our emphasis.)

This awareness of the link between social context and drug deaths is absent in American public health and drug policies. Addiction experts and political leaders ignore the reality of addicted people's lives by describing addiction as an "equal opportunity destroyer." Do they really believe that the Obama daughters, for instance, with their solid two-parent family, private schools, year abroad, and Harvard attendance have the same chance of becoming addicted as unemployed blue-collar workers in West Virginia, or as African-American children who grow up amidst Baltimore's chaos of violence and drug sales?

One of America's foremost and insightful medical critics, the former Editor-in-Chief of the *New England Journal of Medicine*, Marcia Angell, reviewing many books on the opioid crisis, rejects the idea that our drug-death epidemic is due to overproduction and over-prescription of narcotics. (It should be noted that Angell is a long-time critic of pharmaceutical companies.) In her piece in *New York Review of Books*, "Opioid Nation," Angell notes, "We also need to remember an essential and crucial fact: opioids do have a legitimate purpose, and it's an enormously important one. They treat severe pain." Rather, for Angell, "As long as this country tolerates the chasm between the rich and the poor, and fails even to pretend to provide for the most basic needs of our citizens, such as health care, education, and child care, some people will want to use drugs to escape."

## The "Non-Addictive Analgesic"

One of the books that Angell reviewed, *American Overdose: The Opioid Tragedy in Three Acts*, by British journalist Chris McGreal, is less hysterical than the other works. McGreal first notes how American-centric the opioid crisis is: the U.S. consumes 85 percent of the world's prescription painkillers. Therefore, McGreal devotes some space to exploring Americans' aversion to pain. But he ends up laying the major blame at the feet of American pharmaceutical companies. In doing so, he emphasizes their marketing of prescription medications, such as OxyContin and Vicodin, with claims that they were "nonaddictive painkillers."

The search for non-addictive analgesic is as old as pharmaceuticals; it began in the nineteenth century with the marketing of morphine and heroin (which was first made from the opium poppy/morphine in 1874). It is our central point that people do not become addicted to the chemical side effects of drugs, but rather to the direct experiences that they engender, which is the basis of addiction. *The search for the non-addictive painkiller is thus a contradiction in terms, since it is the search for pain relief* in itself *that is the object of the addiction process.*

## The Definition and Natural History of Addiction

Although addiction is an identifiable negative pattern of behavior, no person is by definition an "addict" whose fate is sealed by some accident of birth or traumatic event—or even by a persistently traumatic upbringing.

Most of us seek out powerful experiences at some point in our lives, especially when younger, often with some greater or lesser negative consequences. We may persist for a longer or shorter time before reducing the behavior or ceasing it entirely. These experiences are capable of dominating our consciousness and emotions, with the potential for creating an addictive process for varying lengths of time. Although drugs produce direct, intense experiences, they are not alone in their ability to do this. And there is nothing chemical about drugs that makes them inevitably— or singularly among all that we experience—the sources of addiction.

### The Addictive Process

Addictive involvements do the following:

1. Diminish awareness of surroundings and feelings.

2. Provide immediate, predictable, and encompassing sensations.

3. Offer a false sense of control and personal value.

4. Reduce healthful options (impairing the person).

5. Worsen negative feelings about self (causing distress).

Addictions occur along a continuum of severity and reverse as people engage in positive life experiences ("recovery").

Despite their negative consequences, addictions do not entail losing all control of our behavior. People with addictions recognize boundaries and are capable of changing with their circumstances. When smoking was banned from workplaces, daily smokers learned to wait for a break to smoke; people who drink problematically are usually not inclined to get drunk in front of their parents; frequent users of illegal drugs have places where they prefer to take drugs and can defer their use in exchange for small rewards—as Carl Hart showed in the case of regular crack users in his book, *High Price*.

### Seattle's Wet Housing Residents

Hart's experiment speaks to all of us: We respond positively and delay and eliminate addictions when we see better options open for us. Seattle, like other cities, has a famous skid row populated by long-term street drinkers. These men and women often ended up in hospitals and prisons, at great public expense. In order to get these homeless drinkers off the street, Seattle offered them "wet housing"—safe residences where they could drink as they wished. Here is the result, as described in *Time* by Maia Szalavitz:

> The homeless residents in the study cut the number of drinks they consumed daily by 40% over the course of two years in a home that did not require abstinence. Moreover, for every three months of their stay, participants consumed 8% fewer drinks on average on their heaviest drinking days. The occurrence of delirium tremens, or DTs—potentially life-threatening withdrawal symptoms—also declined by more than half, with 65% of residents reporting suffering DTs in the month before being housed, compared with just 23% in the month afterward.

Curtailing people's worst addictive excesses (e.g., how much they drank at their highest-consumption moments), as we shall see, is harm reduction. We might all pray that people would cure their addictions and cease drinking altogether. But for a large, and possibly growing, number of people, ones often at the bottom's of society's ladder, that doesn't happen. And these are human beings who are capable of living better and feeling better about themselves, as described in interviews with the residents and staff.

From a staff member, many of whom originally opposed the program:

> "I would like to see our residents never drink again. I would like to see abstinence. But . . . that's an unrealistic hope for our population . . . that's an option that will only do more harm than good . . . so you want them to have the liberty to drink, but not hurt themselves or anyone else."

One resident said:

> "You've got to maintain a certain amount of intelligence to be able to stay here and get drunk at the same time. You don't have to get drunk, just enough to go down, lay down, take a good, nice sleep . . . . Maintain. That's it."

One of the few women in the housing said:

> "I'm not a bad person. You know, I feel like I'm not a bad person. I wanna help, you know? I wanna be. . . I don't feel like a bad person . . . . I'll get out of hand, but I stop myself, you know. . . . I'm trying to turn from . . . this person [to] that person. This person was a bad person, and that person is a good person. So I'm tryin' to. . . [tails off]."

Evidence like this provided by people who are among the clearest examples of addiction makes us aware that addicted people are human beings operating under value systems that they struggle to realize. Their failures can kill them or doom them to society's permanent underside. But they are seeking satisfaction, comfort, and self-respect—like all of us.

With addiction seemingly all around us, including areas of life where we never previously considered it, like gaming and electronic devices, eating, sex, and love, finding a balance between being exposed to powerful experiences and maintaining a stable life is a task we may all face. A negative bias against drugs does nothing to help achieve this balance—quite the opposite.

# Expanding Life Experience

3

People become locked into addictions, rather than pursuing normal life channels, for varying lengths of time. Yet lifelong addictions are relatively rare. The best way to discourage addiction is not by insisting that people stop, but by allowing, encouraging, and helping people to pursue more constructive life paths—ones that lead to greater satisfaction and self-respect.

We have already referred to the data showing that over 90 percent of Vietnam veterans quit their addictions when they returned home. These vets didn't ultimately quit heroin because they couldn't get the drug—or didn't use it or another drug in the U.S. The explanation for their recovery is that they found compelling involvements that were incompatible with drug addiction. They returned to or started families, got involved in school or careers, found sports or other entertainments—and people to share them with—that had nothing to do with drugs.

Think also of Margaret, who switched from AA to a mothers' group; Ozzie, who needed to see himself as an anti-capitalist activist; and Joseph, whose life no longer had room for an opioid habit. Margaret freed herself at around the 16-year point, and Ozzie at the 24-year point, just where half of those dependent on their substances (alcohol and cigarettes) matured out according to NESARC.

We saw also that those addicted to illicit drugs quit, on average, more quickly, as was true for Joseph. It's hard for people in normal circumstances to maintain an illicit-drug addiction. In fact, as Lee Robins's paper pointed out, Vietnam vets were simply accelerated, but typical, examples of young men who outgrew heroin addiction. They are a template for the standard developmental process, one that one author of this book underwent.

## Case Study: Zach Rhoads's Youthful Maze

Zach struggled in school and got a lot of negative feedback from teachers, even though he had many positive interests. As an uninhibited child who had little academic success, he ended up in the crowd who used drugs. After graduation, Zach became a musician. In that career, he became deeply involved with heroin. After nearly dying from a fentanyl-heroin mix and realizing he was violating his values, Zach decided to change. He began working with children, where he discovered that he had a gift for understanding and helping kids with a variety of problems and labels, labels that had been applied to Zach himself as a kid.

The skills he demonstrated by working with such children made Zach highly employable. He worked in several school systems, and was hired by one even though he hadn't applied for a job there! He was also sought after outside of school as a helper for families with children facing problems. Zach found helping such kids very rewarding. In his personal life, Zach formed a stable relationship with a woman. They created a sharing but independent union, married, and had a child while this book was being written!

Although still only in his early 30s, it has been a decade since Zach quit heroin. Like Joseph, he is separated from his former world of drug addiction by an existential gap that would take a tectonic life shift to reverse, one that Zach can't even imagine. This was true before Zach became a parent; but parenthood was always something Zach intended.

Zach, Joseph, Margaret, and Ozzie recovered at different times in their lives. Joseph and Zach, like the Vietnam vets, quit after accepting adulthood, which is the most common path to recovery. Margaret was somewhat older, and a new parent, also a turning point for many addicted people. Ozzie's recovery was later, in middle age (his children were nine and 13). Although recovery follows clear patterns, all individuals need to find their unique paths. These paths reflect who they are, where they are in life, their values and skills, and their human involvements.

Gene Heyman, a Boston College researcher, made a remarkable discovery: A certain proportion of addicted people recover at every point in the addiction cycle, and there *is no end to recovery*. Heyman summarized his research findings:

The half-life for cocaine dependence was four years (NESARC researchers said five), but for alcohol dependence it was 16 years, and although most dependent cocaine users remitted before age 30, about 5 percent remained heavy cocaine users well into their 40s. Although varied, the remission results were orderly—each year **a constant proportion of those still addicted remitted, independent of the number of years since the onset of dependence**. (Our emphasis.)

Translation: Although some people don't recover from their addiction at the typical period for recovery, as Zach did, the percentage of this remaining group of addicted people who recover remains the same throughout the life span.

### Case Study: The Delayed Recovery of Keith Richards

Keith Richards, who was born in 1943, published his memoir, *Life*, in 2010, soon after becoming a senior citizen.

Lord, he's taken a lot of drugs! His heavy use of and addiction to drugs extended throughout his early, most productive years, when (with Mick Jagger) he wrote and produced *Beggars Banquet*, *Let It Bleed*, *Sticky Fingers*, and *Exile on Main Street*. According to Liz Phair, "Pulled by the poppy and pushed by cocaine, Keith acquired a taste for working unholy hours that damn nearly kill his colleagues."

Keith carried on taking drugs longer than his bandmates. He, alone, was arrested in his mid-thirties on tour in Toronto in 1977 when police found heroin in his hotel room.

Richards took his first child, Marlon, on a European band tour after his arrest. (Marlon was born in 1969. Keith had three children with Anita Pallenberg, one of whom died of SIDS at 2 months while Richards was on an earlier tour.) Richards had no time for Marlon and barricaded himself in his room when not working. This left Mick Jagger to look after Marlon, introducing him to hamburgers, for instance, when they stayed in Hamburg.

Richards is not a carefree individual. He was plagued with guilt over the death of his baby. And he expressed guilt over his treatment of Marlon, whose description of the tour is included in Richards's memoir. For his part, Marlon said Keith needn't have worried. He was okay and had fun. (Marlon now has three children of his own.)

Richards married Patti Hansen in 1983. He had two daughters with Hansen, both now in their thirties. Richards still drinks quite a bit and smokes marijuana, having given up heroin and pharmaceuticals more than 30 years earlier. (As you may surmise, Richards didn't join AA.) The family lives in suburban Connecticut, where Keith drove his daughters and wife around to school and shopping malls.

Richards persevered in good part through his early life due to his love of music. The Rolling Stones recorded their first album, *Out of Our Heads*, in 1965. Speaking in 2018, in the midst of a world tour, Richards, age 74, was asked about how he can still play old standards he has performed for decades. He described with evident glee both resonating to the old chords and improvising on top of them for new audiences: "Even though they're old songs, they're still growing. . . . I'm still learning how to play them properly."

The Stones announced that they would be doing a world tour in 2019, Long live Keith!

### Case Study: Even Later Recovery of Richard Harris

Richard Harris achieved early stage and screen success—starring, for instance, in *Camelot* in 1967. But, as noted in his Wikipedia biography:

> At the height of his stardom in the 1960s and early 1970s, Harris was almost as well known for his hell-raiser lifestyle and heavy drinking as he was for his acting career. He gave up drugs after almost dying from a cocaine overdose in 1978. He was a longtime alcoholic until he became a teetotaler in 1981, although he did resume drinking Guinness a decade later.

Harris regularly confessed his alcoholism and recovery to national television audiences, including the *Tonight Show*, until, in his 60s, as a grandfather who reunited with his children and grandchildren, he reflected on how his dead Irish relations would "turn over in their graves" if they knew he was still living and not imbibing the national drink. So he took to turning up at local pub and having a pint or two.

Moral: a senior citizen may no longer be the alcoholic he was, even as late as middle age.

## The Path to Recovery—embrace life and the opportunities and joy it presents

*You*, anyone, can strive to create connections with people, events, and experience. This process is called "living in the here-and-now." In the classic American novel *A Tree Grows in Brooklyn*, the teenage heroine, Francie, grows up in threadbare poverty, albeit in an extremely nurturing family. Her beloved father dies from alcoholism when she's an early teen. Although she went to work instead of high school, Francie resolves to live life fully:

> Let me be something every minute of every hour of my life. Let me be gay; let me be sad. Let me be cold; let me be warm. Let me be hungry… have too much to eat. Let me be ragged or well dressed. Let me be sincere—be deceitful. Let me be truthful; let me be a liar. Let me be honorable and let me sin. Only let me be something every blessed minute.

You don't *have* to sin or be deceitful! And you certainly deserve some downtime. But you get the idea. Live life as fully as you can. Savor the good with the bad. Life is a field open for exploration, not a prison.

Yet some of us can struggle for years, even decades, with this process. Obviously people with addictive problems may benefit from help—just not the kind that involves being taught that they have an incurable disease.

## The Life Process Program

In 2008, based on his books *The Truth About Addiction and Recovery* (1991, written with Archie Brodsky and Mary Arnold) and *7 Tools To Beat Addiction* (2004), Stanton developed the Life Process Program (the LPP) for a residential rehab center. LPP is now administered online around the world with the use of coaches.

LPP is a nonjudgmental, harm reduction program, meaning that—through motivational interviewing—clients determine their own goals with their coaches, and review progress towards these. (See Appendix C for a more detailed description of LPP.)

LPP is based on the concept that the best antidotes to addiction are to put it in a realistic perspective (it is not a lifelong disease), address emotional and other problems clients may have without letting them determine the person's life, and expand people's skills and involvements with other people and the world.

The LPP is built around people's self-beliefs, their values, their resources and strengths, and their hopefulness. Above all, it focuses on purpose. In its online version, clients send responses and queries to their coaches around modules they read and questions they answer dealing with different aspects of their addictions, themselves, and their lives; they may talk via videoconferencing with coaches.

Here's one simple, sample query from a woman drinking alcoholically: "I'm thinking of getting a dog. But I wonder if this is a foolish distraction from my real problems, and that I would do better directing my attention towards them."

The coach responded: "Taking care of and relating to another living thing can always be a worthwhile endeavor. But try to think of it as another window to the world—getting out more and walking in the open air, meeting other dog owners, learning about animals. Don't stop with having found one furry living thing that responds to you and that you love—there's a lot more out there."

Although dog ownership may be one of the easier life-moves a person can make when fighting addiction, getting a pet illustrates the larger point of this section: Enhancing your life experience reduces the addictive side of your life.

The good news is, this is a natural progression that we are all able— even inclined—to make. Dealing with emotional problems along the way may not be as simple. It's not something we take on ourselves with clients in the LPP; instead we recommend that people find reasonable, practical aid from professionals and other helpers. At the same time we encourage people to pick up on career and educational opportunities. We encourage intimacy and community. And we ask people to review and surface their values—to find purpose in their lives.

Here is an LPP coach's description of a client who progressed through LPP. "Roy" exemplifies a larger version of embracing life than getting a dog. Parenthood was in his positive life parabola, coming later than it did for Zach and earlier than for Keith Richards.

## Case Study: Embracing Life Fully Through LPP

Roy gave up regular heavy drinking very early on in LPP and has not looked back. He got into fitness —improving his health and diet—took up swimming and skateboarding (something he can do with his son) and has embarked on a whole new career.

A scientist and an atheist, Roy would never have gone to AA. He feels that the LPP outlook and values approach have made all the difference in his life. One critical value of his is to live a long healthy life to be with his young son. He has also reached out to others, volunteering to help immigrants in his community.

Roy is a poster boy for the LPP outlook of embracing life and its opportunities.

Recovery is not a result of magically leaving something behind. It is about embracing life and expanding your horizons. There is no better way to fight addiction.

# The Life Process of Children

4

The authors don't think that children become addicted due to genetic inheritance, to trauma, or to any fixed combination of factors. But we certainly recognize that children may face difficult circumstances and develop problems. Zach works with such children daily. How shall we, as a society, conceive of these problems?

In many cases, current thinking classifies such problems exactly as the disease theory conceives of addiction: as permanent biological and brain malfunctions. We, the authors, don't believe that. We simply see young human beings coping as best they can with their circumstances. Sometimes their coping mechanisms, while understandable, lead them in problematic directions.

## Doing the Best They Can

We all know that children often behave in ways that gain negative adult attention. Have you ever watched a child do something deliberately that will inevitably result in punishment? This behavior sometimes persists despite adults' cajoling, coercing, bribing, yelling at, or even hitting them. If such children know that they will be punished, why do they repeat the behavior?

Zach fields this question regularly, sometimes during fraught emotional outbursts, through his job working with children of all ages. He is asked it by parents, teachers, and even kids themselves: "Why do I keep doing this?"

The answer: If a child lacks the skills to meet the expectations or demands she or he faces, then any kind of predictability is rewarding. Children will naturally seek these rewards and that predictability, even if it lowers their self-esteem and causes problems for others. Child development specialist Dr. Ross Greene addresses children who "act out" in his book *The Explosive Child*. Greene explains:

There's a spectrum of things kids do when life's demands exceed their capacity to respond adaptively. Some cry, or sulk, or pout, or whine, or withdraw—that would be the milder end of the spectrum. As we move toward the more difficult end of the spectrum, we find screaming, swearing, spitting, hitting, kicking, destroying property, lying, and truancy. And as we move even further toward the extreme end of the spectrum, we find self-induced vomiting, self-injurious behavior, drinking or using drugs to excess, stabbing, and shooting.

This default behavior causes adults and other children to react negatively, so that the child internalizes a negative self-image. Children ordinarily outgrow this stage. But they may be slow to leave it behind if they lack the tools to create positive experiences for themselves. According to Greene:

> These behaviors occur when the demands being placed on a kid exceed that kid's capacity to respond adaptively. Why do some kids respond at the milder end of the spectrum while others are at the more severe end? Some kids have the skills to "hold it together" when pushed to their limits and some don't.

Just as people labeled addicts and alcoholics are seeking the best rewards they can get, so too are children. Jeanine Fitzgerald provides another description of this process in *The Dance of Interaction*:

> There is a concept known as the "soggy potato chip theory." This theory is based on the idea that if a child is offered a choice between a nice crisp potato chip and a soggy potato chip, he will choose the better potato chip. However, when a child is offered the choice between getting something, even a soggy potato chip, or getting nothing (no potato chip at all), the child will choose the soggy potato chip.
> The analogy of the potato chip directly connects to the use of positive attention, negative attention, and being ignored. When there is a choice between positive attention (crisp potato chip) and negative attention (soggy potato chip), a child prefers and chooses the positive. But when given a choice between negative attention and being ignored (no potato chip at all) the child chooses negative attention.

## Counterwill

And so why not command children to behave—just as some people tell others to stop their addictive behaviors?

The most popular form of addiction therapy (even among chronic brain disease specialists) is called motivational interviewing (MI). Developed by psychologist William Miller and his colleagues, MI is based on the phenomenon of resistance—that telling people to do something instantly produces an opposite reaction to resist or contradict the input. For example: "You should quit smoking" elicits the response "I need to smoke to keep my weight down." Children are (to say the least) equally susceptible to this reaction, one that developmental psychologist Gordon Neufeld calls "counterwill":

> Counterwill is a name for the instinctive reaction of a child to resist being controlled. This resistance can take many forms: opposition, negativism, laziness, noncompliance, disrespect, lack of motivation, belligerence, incorrigibility and even antisocial attitudes and actions. It can also express itself in resistance to learning.
>
> Despite the multitude of manifestations, the underlying dynamic is deceptively simple—a defensive reaction to perceived control or coercion.

## The Consequences of Commanding Children

Why, then—given its lack of success—do adults command children to behave? Imagine the following scenarios:

- A mother and her child are finished grocery shopping. The mother, with her arms full of groceries, tells the child it's time to leave; the child refuses.

- A child spitting and swearing at his parents in response to their direction, "Clean your room."

- A student who refuses to stop throwing pencils across a classroom despite a teacher telling the student to stop.

Perhaps the most natural reaction for an adult in each of these scenarios is to command the child to behave—possibly to physically remove the child from the situation. That natural reaction is perfectly understandable. This may or may not stop the child's unwanted behavior, but it is not likely to prevent it from being repeated in the future. (If, in the off-chance, it does work to prevent the behavior from happening in the future, it will almost surely only be true for you and your child, not in other contexts, and with potential of resentment or fear on the child's side.)

Acting swiftly to enforce rules is sometimes necessary but it is not in the child's best interest developmentally. There is a response that will work better than giving an order, which has spotty results even in the short term.

This isn't a new idea. Rudolph Dreikurs presented it early in the 20th century in his book, *The New Approach to Discipline*. Dreikurs's theories have been rediscovered by PBIS (Positive Behavioral Interventions and Supports)—a program encouraging teachers to exercise positive discipline in schools.

Shari Carr, PBIS Universal Coordinator, described positive discipline in an interview with Zach when he asked her, "What are the most effective ways to discipline children? Can we do better than punishment?" She answered:

> I do agree with consequences, but those should be small consequences, they should be related to what happened, and they should be meaningful. A consequence shouldn't be something used to hurt the child. The learning experience for the child doesn't come from withholding a privilege, it comes from fixing the problem, making it right with the other people involved, and figuring out how to behave positively in the future.
>
> When kids make a bad choice, it's an opportunity to learn. They haven't been bad; they made a bad choice.
>
> The onus is on adults to help students accept responsibility for what they choose to do. When kids act out, they are giving us a message and we can help them discover new tools to get what they need or want in the same situation next time so that they don't keep making the same mistake. This way they can be productive and successful rather than thinking things like, "I don't want to go to school today" or "This negative thing is going to happen again" or "Oh no, that teacher doesn't like me." Under the auspices of positive discipline, everybody is liked and respected, so that's not a problem—now

we can figure out some basic fine tuning of social and cognitive skills.

There are non-negotiables: safety is non-negotiable along with breaking the law and being kind to other people—everybody has the right to be treated with respect. But everything else is probably small stuff. So we have to have a general understanding of "What are the rules?" and "What are the consequences if you don't follow the rules?" but solving these problems shouldn't be viewed as a punishment. When kids see this process as inherently punitive, they also see it as negative—something to be avoided; so they will favor their original choices over engagement with adults.

## The Childhood Acting-Out Cycle— understanding the rewards of contrariness

The process of seeking predictable rewards despite their negative kickback is thus at the heart of child development problems—just as it is in the addiction process. In both addiction and instances where children act out despite negative consequences, we see human beings accepting temporary, illusory rewards at the cost of longer-term misery. Drawing this parallel between children's misbehavior and adult addiction helps us to see the normalcy of both behaviors, even when these get out of hand, and to understand the commonsense nature and routes out of both self-defeating syndromes.

In the case of children, we have seen that even punishments may serve as stop-gap replacements for healthy rewards and positive acknowledgment.

Most of Zach's young charges experience this confusing social paradox. Here's what the cycle looks like for them—a sequence that strongly resembles the addictive process:

1. They experience demands being made of them socially or academically that they are unable to meet.

2. They act in negative and inappropriate ways instead of meeting these demands.

3. Acting out makes them feel powerless, even while they are trying to exert control and seek reliable rewards in their lives.

4. The most consistent form of social interaction for them becomes: (a) they are expected to behave in a particular way, (b) they behave some other way, (c) they get a negative response.

5. They don't enjoy the lack of control they feel or the negative reactions they receive but they continue to behave in the same negative ways.

6. The more often they behave this way, the more distress they experience, and the more embedded their image (and self-image) of "problem child" becomes.

7. This pattern perpetuates itself until they find constructive ways to meet their needs for recognition and emerge from their childhood "disorder."

### Case Study: Why Can't This Child Do Something Positive?

Zach was asked to work with a 17-year-old with diagnoses of "oppositional defiant disorder"—a clinical term meaning that the boy didn't do what he was supposed to—and, secondarily, ADHD. The child, DJ, was not completing writing assignments, despite his apparent intelligence. His teacher felt DJ was intentionally disrupting the class.

Zach was shown this note from DJ's teacher by his parents:

> DJ is clearly intelligent and quite well versed in current events. But he refuses to complete short writing assignments that he's capable of doing. I told him this is affecting his grade, but nothing I say makes an impression on him. He simply will not complete the assignments. And when I remind him of his missed assignments, he has a tantrum.

This teacher concluded that DJ's failures to complete assignments showed that DJ was antisocial, which led to his oppositional disorder diagnosis.

DJ's guidance counselor observed the friction between DJ and his teacher and referred the parents to Zach. For her part, the counselor suggested accommodating to DJ's "disabilities" in this way:

DJ has a diagnosis of oppositional defiant disorder along with a reading and writing disability. We will need to discuss accommodations to those conditions, including assignments without reading or writing components.

DJ was caught between the teacher's perspective ("he's doing this to disturb the class and to make me angry") and his counselor's sympathy ("he shouldn't have to do writing assignments that he isn't able to do").

Nowhere in the school's file that was presented to Zach was there any record of DJ's own view of what was happening. So Zach asked him. DJ said: "I know how to read and I know how to write, and I know a lot about current events. But asking me to sit there and write journal entries out of thin air? You may as well be asking me to fly an airplane."

DJ's resistance to writing had sparked a power struggle between him and his teacher, which created his antisocial reaction. Worse, he bought into this image of himself as a troublemaker who couldn't make a positive contribution in class.

Putting aside DJ's oppositional diagnosis, Zach helped DJ map a blueprint for a successful future in this class. The first step was for DJ to understand the destructive cycle in which he'd become entangled, which he analyzed with Zach's help:

- He was asked to expend mental energy on writing assignments that he wasn't sure how to do.

- He then refused to write and became defensive and resorted to yelling and name-calling to hide his embarrassment.

- His feeling of powerlessness left him seeking negative reactions instead of positive ones he wasn't receiving.

- DJ knew how to create one predictable routine: (a) he was asked to write (b) he refused to write (c) he got a negative response.

- DJ did not enjoy his lack of self-control or the negative responses to his behavior, but he continued on this path anyway.

Zach saw that no one was working with DJ on escaping this cycle. The options that had been tried—cajoling, coercing, demanding, punishing—hadn't worked. Then there was the counselor's suggested approach of eliminating all written assignments.

In place of giving up on participating in class in a positive way, DJ and Zach came up with a third option: reprogramming his destructive behavior cycle in order to achieve goals he was capable of meeting. DJ, working with Zach, identified what he was missing:

- Motivation

- Self-control

- Finding options

- Gaining the rewards of positive experiences for DJ and positive reactions from others

- Connection with others

With Zach's help, DJ set about gaining the pieces he was missing by using his genuine skills and passions.

Zach asked DJ, "You said you know how to read and write. What kinds of things are you writing about?" DJ pulled out a spiral notebook with page after page of cartoons he had drawn, complete with witty storylines and captions!

"DJ, I had no idea you were writing these things. I'm so impressed," Zach exclaimed. Zach sought a way to harness DJ's skills and interests in the classroom setting. He worked to craft a doable lesson plan with DJ and his teacher. In every class period DJ followed the material along with everyone else. But instead of writing the journal assignment, DJ would draw a political cartoon that demonstrated his understanding of the subject-matter along with a couple of sentences describing the drawing. DJ signed on to the plan.

On day one, DJ worked enthusiastically on his first cartoon, something he was confident of his ability to do and that he enjoyed. It was a picture of two well-known political figures with balloons capturing each of their most prominent talking points.

DJ's skill as an illustrator and his understanding of the political landscape impressed Zach along with everyone else. Political cartoons became a regular part of DJ's assignments. He began displaying them to his classmates, and his teacher even used DJ's drawings as tools for explaining the material.

Achieving positive results using his existing gifts, DJ began writing a whole page to describe each cartoon so that he ended up writing much more than he had originally agreed to do.

Zach decided to expand the scope of DJ's creativity: "You are holding up your end of the deal, so I'll make you another offer. If you write a few sentences describing each of your drawings, I will have your pictures color-printed and published in a book."

DJ, filled with pride, jumped at the chance. And, as promised, he is now the author of a published comic book.

DJ hadn't misbehaved out of spite or because of some brain disorder. Nor was he incapable of doing school work, someone to be relegated permanently into a handicapped category. Avoiding these unnecessarily drastic options, DJ and Zach had re-imagined DJ's reward structure in school. They did so by addressing these issues:

- **Motivation** = He utilized authentic skills and passions to find meaning in life.

- **Self-control** = He developed a positive routine that he controlled.

- **Options** = He found a way to express himself positively.

- **Rewards** = He generated positive responses that boosted his self-esteem.

- **Connection** = He formed healthy connections with Zach, his teacher, and his classmates.

## Learning Zones vs Mental Disorders

Lev Vygotsky, an early 20th-century developmental theorist, described this style of childhood learning with the help of an adult as the "zone of proximal development." When tasks are too challenging for children, their frustration means that no learning will occur. On the other hand, tasks that don't challenge children leave them tediously stuck at their current skill level. Per Vygotsky, tasks that are just beyond a child's present ability exist in the zone of proximal development—what we might call the learning zone.

Tasks in this learning zone are things children can imagine doing—in fact, they're enticed by the prospect—but that they need help from others to accomplish. With this help, kids move beyond where they are currently at by mastering the skills and being able to do them on their own. Their reaction is, "What's next?"

Focusing on this learning zone shifts the teacher, parent, or other helper away from seeing the child as having a disability or disorder. Instead, a learning problem is viewed as a task to work through with the child, so that the child will move along a learning curve. Simply reconceiving the process as normal development allows children to escape destructive cycles that they and others have come to see as inevitable, like those DJ had repeatedly found himself in.

Such cycles also characterize addiction. DJ was pursuing the rewards that were available to him, leading to negative results that made him unhappy, hampered his life, and locked him into a pattern that he couldn't break. Of course, we wouldn't use the term "addiction" (as we describe in the next section) when the actor is a child and the harm is temporary and remediable.

As a culture, we concentrate on labeling people with mental disorders rather than on helping them to escape destructive cycles by expanding their life experiences and self-conceptions. Change is about learning, or relearning, and diagnoses like "learning disability" and "addiction" are useful only to the extent that they assist in this task.

Zach helps children to broaden their horizons—this is how he overcame his own developmental problems, including addiction. Thankfully, most people track into this normal developmental process, as Zach did, on their own. Doing so, they display the incredible potential we all have to address our mental health and addictive problems.

(More detailed steps for helping children are described in Appendix B, "Parents' Addiction and Development Manual.")

# Children and Addiction

5

We have seen that most people outgrow addiction. This is most notable for young people, as we would expect. There is a large bump in drug use and, above all, alcohol disorders and dependence among people in their late teens and early 20s.

According to the 2016 National Survey on Drug Use and Health, 15 percent of Americans age 18-25 had a substance use disorder* (drugs or alcohol)—an SUD. Here is a pocket definition of an SUD: "A pattern of repeated drug or alcohol use that often interferes with health, work, or social relationships." Substance use disorder thus exists along a continuum, as described in Chapter 2, from serious problems to all-consuming addiction. *And between 1 in 6 and 1 in 7 young people display this condition.*

The good news: From the age of 26 and older, the SUD figure was 6.6 percent—1 in 15—a precipitous drop of 56 percent. Youth is certainly a high-risk time for drinking and other substance use problems. But older teens and young adults often sober up in a few short years, so that the percentage of people with an SUD after age 26 drops to fewer than half the number of the younger group. The many people discussed in this book of whom this was true, such as Maia Szalavitz and author Zach Rhoads, are the mainstream. And people steadily drop off the group with a disorder as time progresses all along their life spans (from Joseph and Ozzie to Keith Richards and Richard Harris).

These results nonetheless raise several critical questions:

1. How can we convince more teens and young people to eschew problematic drinking and drug use by maturing at an earlier age?

2. What is the consequence of telling young people with an

---

\* Substance use disorder includes both dependence, or addiction, and the milder category of "abuse." This distinction prevailed in the earlier edition of DSM (DSM-IV) but was abandoned in DSM-5 for ranking SUDs on a continuum from "mild" to "moderate" to "severe."

alcohol or drug problem that they are lifelong alcoholics or addicts?

3.   How can we build on the natural ameliorative tendencies of age to get even more people to recover from their drinking and drug problems?

## The Teenage "Addict"

We previously noted how Ross Greene described one end of the spectrum of kids with behavioral issues like DJ's as involving excessive drinking and drug use. Zach was one such case.

DJ didn't have a substance problem, so no one was labeling him an alcoholic or drug addict, although they were applying other labels to him. Such labeling is harmful if it replaces dealing with the real child, including his own thinking and perspective and his goals, skills, and motivation—all keynotes for Zach's work. As for teens who do use alcohol and drugs excessively and problematically, a label denoting a permanent disease can be especially damaging.

### Case Study: Drew Barrymore, "America's Youngest Addict"

Drew Barrymore appeared on the cover of *People* in 1989 under the banner "America's Youngest Addict." She had been consuming marijuana, alcohol and cocaine on her own since she was 12. She confessed, "I'm Drew, and I'm an addict and alcoholic"—i.e., she was "in recovery," meaning, presumably, that she now abstained from all psychoactive substances.

She entered rehab at 14, attempted suicide, and spent 18 months in a mental health institution. She then went to live with David Crosby because she "needed to be around some people that were committed to sobriety." In 1990, age 15, she published a memoir, *Little Girl Lost*.

Addiction experts had a field day with Barrymore—a name associated with alcoholism and addiction. They explained how Drew had inherited her disease from her famous paternal alcoholic grandfather, John, and from a father who was addicted to heroin (her parents divorced when she was nine). The solution: a lifetime of abstinence.

That didn't happen. Barrymore outgrew her addiction to become a film power player as an actress and a producer while, early on, she combined this success with being a wild child. She posed nude in

*Playboy* in 1995, at age 19. The same year she formed her own production company, often making films in which she starred. In 2009 she won a Screen Actors Guild Award and a Golden Globe for her role in *Grey Gardens*. She also directed her first film in 2009.

In 2013, at age 38, Barrymore re-appeared in *People* with the new byline, "Drew Barrymore: She's a Vintner," "unveiling her eponymous pinot grigio at the Nantucket Wine Festival. . . . [Drew has] lots of knowledge and is passionate about her wine."

Barrymore had come a long way from being institutionalized in her early teens for mental illness and addiction. But she doesn't make a big thing about it. In 2009, then in her early 30s, she confessed, "I'm not sober" (meaning she, like Maia Szalavitz, drinks). Rather, she said, she had found "balance" in her life.

In 2017, now in her 40s with two daughters, she starred in the popular Netflix series *Santa Clarita Diet*. In 2018, she did a deep interview with Willie Geist around the show's new season. Barrymore had retreated from acting prior to Santa Clarita in order to raise her two young daughters, and because she thought she was overexposed. In that time, her marriage broke up and she was in a "dark and fearful place" when she signed on for the TV series.

We should first note that neither Barrymore, nor anyone who knows her, considers Drew's relapsing to addiction as the remotest of possibilities. Barrymore embraces her entire life, accepting the adversity she faced as a child. Rather than seeing this as a lifelong disease, she announces that it made her the person she is.

Indeed, she worries about how her daughters might never face adversity, which she feels people must in order to fully develop—she only cautions her children about maintaining two primary guide lights: *kindness* and *safety.*

We will return to Drew's wisdom (although she makes no pretense of being a guru) with children in embracing life, facing adversity, and maintaining safety when we discuss harm reduction.

A life like Drew Barrymore's—a large life, but, in outgrowing drug addiction, not an unusual one—undercuts the American recovery meme that not only adults, but increasingly children, must be permanently diagnosed as addicts. Here is how the Orchid Recovery Center addressed "Childhood Drug Addiction, Drew Barrymore":

Though Drew certainly went through some very rough years, she seems to have kept her sobriety for a long time. Though she has done some quirky and questionable things as a celebrity, there have been no reports of her relapsing into drug use. She seems to have found good work that matches her talents, service and charity efforts she believes in, and good people around her.

This version of Drew views her as being on the precipice of being re-addicted at all moments, which she is somehow barely avoiding. But even this perspective grants Barrymore too much, according to one commenter on Stanton's blog about Barrymore in *Psychology Today*: "She's just in denial and I hope SOMEONE around her will sit her ass down and tell her the TRUTH that she is bound to die addicted and alcoholic."

As extreme as that thinking is, it is actually the fundamental view that our society applies to addiction. Yet the millions of undisclosed people who have been addicted usually resemble Barrymore in that regard. Recall the NESARC odds that a person, over their lifetimes, will leave a drug dependence (i.e., addiction) behind are 84 percent for nicotine, 91 percent for alcohol, 97 percent for cannabis, and 99 percent for cocaine. And the majority of those who escape alcohol dependence, especially in their youth, like Drew, continue drinking.

Barrymore doesn't lecture on the topic of how she outgrew addiction. She would rather focus on her accomplishments. But there are essential, helpful lessons to glean from this process in Drew's and so many others' lives.

In the U.S., a long list of U.S. Surgeons General and Drug Czars have claimed that addiction is a brain disease that can never be escaped. *And yet government research itself, as well as the experiences of people all around us, shows that the opposite is true.*

### The Reality of Childhood/Youthful Drug Misuse

- No one is destined to be addicted.

- Early childhood recreational substance use may (or may not) have downsides, perhaps severely negative ones, but such experiences are not lifetime sentences.

- The route out of early substance problems is to embrace as full—and as fully rewarding—a life as possible.

- This goal is not enhanced by calling a child (or anyone else) an addict, and we shouldn't do so.

## A Case of Childhood Addiction

It is clear that young people often enter self-defeating involvements with alcohol and other substances that may cause serious, possibly permanent, damage. But these involvements do not exhaust the kinds of problems that children encounter. Not all addictions involve substances.

In 2018 gaming addiction was classified as a disorder by the World Health Organization. This condition occurs, according to WHO, when *gaming has priority over other life activities and there is continuation or escalation of gaming despite negative consequences.*

### Case Study: Mark's Gaming Involvement

Mark was an 11-year-old 5th grader. He complained that nobody liked him and that even the few people who were nice to him had no interest in being his friend.

Mark had many academic skills: visual/spatial, linguistic, and logical/mathematical. After school, Mark played video games, often speaking remotely with strangers as they played, because "it's super fun, and the people on the other end actually understand me and like me because they're gamers too." That is, video games gave Mark a feeling of excitement and connection that compensated for the lack of such experiences at school and in the rest of his life.

Mark became so involved with video games—and so out of touch with other aspects of life—that he began staying home from school, even pretending to be sick, in order to play games all day. He fell behind on his assignments and lost touch with his school life. When he returned to school, he had to do his missed schoolwork during recess. Perversely, Mark's missing recess deprived him of the opportunity to do what he needed most—to bond with people.

Mark was trapped in a negative, self-perpetuating loop like others we have seen in this book. His difficulty making connections was a problem that led him to isolate himself, a consequence of which was his falling further outside of a rewarding engagement in school, which made it harder for him to make friends. On top of this, he also faced the stress of overdue homework and additional burdens being placed on him at school, to which his response was to play more video games—the one thing he knew to do to relieve stress and gain self-esteem and form connections, however short-lived and artificial.

We can see that Mark was embarked on a deepening negative path. And *he was only 11 years old*, with so much life before him, a life to be lived fully.

Mark could clearly articulate what a good life was and what that looked and felt like: "being a good person, which means being honest, polite, taking care of yourself like eating good food and exercise, and doing well in school."

Instead, Mark felt bad about his own life. Rather than acting according to his expressed values, he did the opposite: He secluded himself; he missed school; he fell behind on class work; he was alienated from his schoolmates; he lied to his parents about what he was up to—for fear that by admitting the truth (that he was going downstairs to play video games instead of doing homework) he would cause his parents to punish him and forbid the one thing that made him feel good.

Mark's developing problem with excessive, detrimental gaming needed to be addressed by finding avenues into real experience, with real people—which is precisely how Mark's teacher helped him.

### Mark's Retracking

Mark's parents brought up their concerns about their son to his teacher, Mr. Stevens, who took their concerns seriously but didn't panic. The next school day, Mr. Stevens began a technology unit— one he had already planned for Mark's class.

Mr. Stevens gathered his students into small groups in which they would study different video games. The aim of the project was to create their own games using computer software. Mr. Stevens knew that being in groups made Mark anxious. But he knew that Mark had strong computer skills, that he wanted to be helpful, and that he knew a lot about video games. On that basis, Mr. Stevens made Mark his technical point person with all the groups.

It didn't take long for Mark to become the most sought-after person in the class, answering questions from "How do I do this?" to "What is your favorite console?" This *was* Mark's area of expertise.

In short order, Mr. Stevens asked Mark to set up an online discussion board for students in the class. Mark happily created this clearing service at home, which added another way for him to interact with classmates.

Mark was now going to school, engaging in class, and playing with friends during recess. His parents reported that he was much politer and more present at home. He wasn't actually playing fewer games; he was playing a wider variety of video games with the purpose of building his knowledge base. But, at the same time, he was balancing his gaming with personal, social, and academic involvements.

Although he certainly didn't consider himself an addiction expert, Mr. Stevens was a sensitive and flexible teacher. By drawing on Mark's strengths and the available opportunities in the classroom, he created a new pathway for Mark, one that integrated Mark's skill set within the class environment. With this support, Mark was able to find a positive balance in his life without having to give up his gaming passion—an example of harm reduction.

Mark's case illustrates how gaming, in and of itself, isn't a disorder, but becomes one when it curbs a young person's cognitive and social development. Rather than simply labeling gaming "addictive," a better way to describe this process is to say that young people who are not well adjusted may seek out gaming as one kind of unhealthy outlet.

We should question whether it would have helped in this situation to diagnose Mark with "gaming disorder."** And, no matter how much his behavioral cycle resembled an addiction, under no circumstances, no matter what categories WHO creates, should we define Mark a "gaming addict," as though this were an embedded part of his being.

---

** In a You-Tube video at https://www.youtube.com/watch?v=q61v9K578OA, Stanton discusses with a group of teens their own ability to come to grips with what it means for gaming to tilt over into the unhealthy, even the addictive, realm, what causes this imbalance, and how to help friends with that potential addiction—all using resources and insights these young people had and recognized themselves.

# Diseases, Disorders and Self-Fulfilling Prophecies

6

People develop addictions to a range of things, including drugs. But drugs themselves contain no irresistible chemical draw that makes them addictive. No biological mechanism exists that turns addiction on or off. As Maia Szalavitz shows in *Unbroken Brain* and Marc Lewis in *The Biology of Desire*, addiction operates through human beings' normal reward and brain systems. Addiction happens when a person becomes involved in a substance or an activity that provides needed rewards— perhaps pleasure, but more often psychological relief or compensation— in the absence of adequate rewards in other areas of the person's life.

When people with addictions find attractive alternatives to destructive behavior, they can develop positive new patterns (which both Maia and Marc, like so many others, did themselves). This is a normal life process, one that children are particularly likely to undergo, but which is possible for all of us.

Mainstream U.S. responses to addiction, following the disease blueprint, represent the intrusion of a historical American anomaly, our tradition of temperance, into the present. Recent examples include the Obama Administration Surgeon General's 2016 Report on the opioid crisis, and the Trump Administration's Christie Commission—even as Marc Lewis, Stanton, and others increasingly show that the disease approach is inaccurate and ineffective.

Meanwhile, featured televised addiction series after series—from Bill Moyers' 5-part 1998 PBS series *Close to Home* (the first episode was titled "The Hijacked Brain"); to the 2007 Nora Volkow/National Institute on Drug Abuse-inspired HBO addiction series widely used in American schools; to PBS's latest, 2018 addiction series—all claim to prove (as *NOVA* once again states in 2018) "how opioid addiction affects the brain and how evidence-based treatments are saving lives." *NOVA* nonetheless points out, after decades of such programs, that the U.S. is undergoing "an epidemic of addiction—the deadliest in U.S. history." PBS had just completed showing another special, "Dealing with Addiction," in December, 2017, teaching people how to understand addiction.

Two things are notable about all of these series:

- Undeterred by the failure of the brain disease model of addiction to stem the addiction tide thus far, each series reinitiates the approach as though they have made a scientific breakthrough while upping the estimates of the prevalence of addiction and the damage it causes.

- No treatments based on the brain disease model are ever presented, instead going from Moyers' love of AA and the 12 steps, to the HBO series' highlighting of motivational interviewing as the best addiction treatment, to *NOVA's* emphasis on harm reduction, meaning mainly providing narcotic antagonists (like Narcon/naloxone) to reverse overdoses and substitutes (like buprenorphine and methadone) as arguably safer versions of narcotic addiction.

No notice is ever given in such shows to the anti-disease movement that has accelerated in recent years. It's as though science—and certainly all those disease true believers—can't tolerate such a challenge.

In any case, despite all such advances, in 2017, opioid deaths—both painkillers and heroin—topped record levels yet again. At the same time cocaine and methamphetamine deaths surged. So too did benzodiazepine deaths peak. All this, after the seemingly unmatchable 350 percent rise in opioid deaths from 1999 through 2015, and further sharp increases in deaths due to synthetic opioids, heroin, cocaine, and methamphetamine in 2016. This record growth has occurred even though painkiller prescriptions had been declining since 2013, creating headlines such as "Number of prescriptions for opioid painkillers drops dramatically in U.S.," alongside "West Virginia dispensed 31 million fewer pills, while opioid OD deaths still rose" in this, the highest drug-mortality state in the country.

This rise took place even in states that assiduously practiced the latest techniques in medicine-assisted treatment (MAT). Claims are finally being made that, due to the application of modern treatment approaches, drug deaths are leveling off. While this remains to be seen, and how across-the-board this plateauing is, there are still deep pockets of drug deaths throughout the United States. We have entered a period in which management of drug use and its consequences have us looking everywhere for a magical, medical cure to an ever-encroaching social problem.

In several of his writings, including a *Psychology Today* article titled "Why our Drug Death Epidemic is Worse than Ever," Stanton has predicted that America's perverse efforts at addressing these problems would lead to negative outcomes. The chronic, irreversible brain disease theory—and its close relation, the school of thought that traces all addiction and mental health issues back to childhood traumas—fail to address the actual causes of drug addiction and death. These approaches mire people in addictive situations and mindsets, instead of allowing them to escape these pasts—as Drew Barrymore did, as Zach, Maia Szalavitz, Marc Lewis, and as most of us do given the space, time, and opportunity.

## Positive Psychology

Martin Seligman, director of the Positive Psychology Center at the University of Pennsylvania, is a strong advocate for encouraging positive options to deal with conditions that are labeled as mental disorders. Seligman and his colleagues don't specifically address addiction, but their perspective is highly relevant to addiction and other clinical syndromes, along with child development.

As Seligman and John Tierney wrote in the *New York Times*:

> While most people tend to be optimistic, those suffering from depression and anxiety have a bleak view of the future—and that in fact seems to be the chief cause of their problems, not their past traumas nor their view of the present. While traumas do have a lasting impact, most people actually emerge stronger afterward. Others continue struggling because they over-predict failure and rejection. Studies have shown depressed people are distinguished from the norm by their tendency to imagine fewer positive scenarios while overestimating future risks.

This piece—titled "Why the Future is Always on Your Mind" (in reference to the ways we as a species inexorably approach the world in a forward-looking way)—shows that it is self-defeating to anchor yourself in the past. Rather, people dissipate depression, and feel better, planning forward. "When making plans, they reported higher levels of happiness and lower levels of stress." Yet this preoccupation with the past is now the primary method of treating depression, through trauma therapy.

### Case Study: Anthony Bourdain

#### The Best Way to Help Depressed and Lost People

Stanton was interviewed by a highly insightful journalist exploring, among other things, the role of love in the death of Anthony Bourdain, who had recently committed suicide while he was in a possibly problematic love relationship.

Stanton, in order to involve the journalist, asked her, "I know you're not a therapist, but how would you have tried to help Bourdain if you had the opportunity to interact with him before his death?"

Tentatively, she suggested, "Explore his earlier traumas?"

Stanton had been so taken with his interrogator's good sense that he couldn't help but be shocked by how the trauma meme had so conquered America that it dictated her wrong-headed suggestion here. He said quizzically, "Focus a depressed person on the worst moments of his life?"

Stanton recovered and offered his own vision of helpfulness: "I would review with him his purposes in life: his 11-year-old daughter, his popular work and especially how he had been increasingly able to learn about cultural and political realities wherever he went, his ability to relate to all people, and the *joie de vivre* he showed, his plans for his television show for the coming year, especially the current episode." These weren't cover-ups for his trauma—they were real, if possibly overlooked for the moment, parts of him.

The genetic labels children are given are part of the danger of anchoring in the past. A prominent example is ADHD (attention deficit and hyperactivity disorder). Between 2003 and 2011, the number of children ages 4 to 17 who were diagnosed with ADHD and medicated increased by over 40 percent, and now account for over 10 percent of American youths. The diagnosis is so popular that ADHD parents have their own magazines and websites. The parents are told—even though this is never measured—that ADHD results from dopamine deficiencies in the brain that cause youngsters to seek extra stimulation "through nicotine, caffeine, alcohol, opiates, risky sex, pornography, gambling, physical risk-taking, reckless driving, and compulsive buying."

Why are these diagnoses growing so rapidly in the young? This growth, which nearly always leads to prescriptions for powerful amphetamines or amphetamine-like drugs, has raised a culture-wide concern. We have more such diagnoses than other countries, and the consequences of them can be severe. Among other things are the consequences of taking powerful drugs like Adderall. One young man, introduced to an ADHD diagnosis in 2005, described his decade-long dependence on Adderall, including stealing drugs from medicine cabinets, in the *New York Times* in a piece titled "Generation Adderall."

These diagnoses may seem to help many children, and people usually accept them for their kids. It takes a heroic assertiveness to resist—even for the many parents who are uneasy about the ADHD label and who worry what it means to tell children, as soon as they start thinking about themselves, that they have a mental disorder. Such labels are potentially harmful for people of all ages, but especially for children, who can so easily become defined by them. ("I'm not surprised he threw a fit, he has ADHD.")

This is not to deny that, of course, children and adults have different temperaments, and that some people struggle in some areas, and that some may require treatment for a time. We should, however, use mental health diagnoses with great caution, constantly checking in to assess their effects for fear of their inherently self-defeating features, and looking for other avenues to pursue.

The argument today is that we fail our children when we don't diagnose them for one disorder or another. In fact, most children dislike labeling themselves negatively, in what might be called "denial."Research on the effects of self-labeling at the University of Wisconsin investigated children who do or do not label themselves as disabled. The investigators found that "only a minority of adolescents" with some kind of problem self-labeled. More critically, the research found, "adolescents who self-labeled reported higher ratings on self-stigma and depression, and a trend toward a lower sense of mastery." In other words, they viewed themselves more negatively and were less able to improve. Additional research has found that along with "lower expectations for themselves...teachers and parents are more likely to perceive disabilities in, and hold lower educational expectations for, labeled adolescents than for similarly achieving and behaving adolescents not labeled with disabilities."

So, there is a cost that accompanies any proposed benefits for the diagnoses of children. Young people are particularly difficult to diagnose definitively. Children live predominantly in the immediate present. As one exasperated parent expressed when his children were diagnosed and their behaviors projected into the future, "They're kids!" A child's psychiatric track record is so sparse, a future course so impossible to predict, and developmental factors so unknown that any clinical picture of a kid is limited and time-bound. Yet, as Stanton showed in his book, *Diseasing of America*, we Americans are especially—and ever-increasingly—prone to using psychiatric diagnostic labels.

Zach has a close-knit family. His parents were and are nurturing and he is in a loving and supportive marriage. He has taken opportunities to use his skills in creative ways to find a fulfilling career, including music and working with children. But his future was once not so bright. As a child, he was a poor, alienated student. It seemed to make perfect sense to the adults in his life to label him with ADHD. He didn't form positive relationships as an adolescent, and he began using alcohol and other drugs problematically in his early teens. The negative prospects for Zach's life encased in his diagnosis might have characterized him for a long time—perhaps forever.

In his early 20s, working as a musician, he became entangled in a cycle of heroin use and addiction that lasted several years. He was eventually hospitalized, near death, after accidentally using a combination of fentanyl and heroin. Reviewing his options, and with his family's support, he decided to change the course of his life. The process wasn't instantaneous. But he got a job through his mother, who is a teacher, working with kids.

This proved to be work at which he thrived, and it led to other good jobs based on his skill set. He gained pride in his accomplishments, and recognition and appreciation from others.

Zach's personality is marked by quick shifts in attention and outbursts of energy. He expressed this style as an obstreperous child and then as an on-the-edge rock musician. But he developed a personal and professional life that harnessed these traits in positive ways. He was now seen by his wife, coworkers, and the families he worked with as a constructive and helpful person. As he accumulated and reflected on his successes and the esteem of others, Zach gained a new sense of himself. He decided to stop referring to himself as being ADHD, a label he once accepted. He also rejected calling himself an addict. Doing these things took some independence of will and thought.

Zach's personal experience alerted him to the potential of the children he worked with, many of whom had been sidetracked by cycles of self-defeating behavior like the one in which DJ engaged. He looked to find paths to expand the lives of these children, just as his own life had expanded. Instead of seeing and labeling their conditions, Zach set his radar to perceive their strengths and gifts, even while recognizing the traps they sometimes got caught up in. When Zach had been caught in such a trap, enough people had faith in him, and he had enough of an idea of who he could become, that he found a fruitful life path. This only happened for Zach after he left school. Nonetheless, he was able to remain optimistic about his possibilities, to retain what Angela Duckworth described as grit. For young people today, this can be a difficult feat to pull off.

In encouraging choices like Zach made, the advice in this book is the opposite of the advice you are likely to hear from most specialists in childhood behavior and addiction. These professionals tell people that the best way forward is to decide on the appropriate defining label for their—or their children's—behavior. We instead build on Seligman's positive psychology and the developmental work of Gordon Neufeld and the grit and perseverance work of Angela Duckworth. This work tells us that everyone is ultimately capable of designing and following their own positive route through life.

Anything that reduces the fatalism of childhood diagnoses is to be welcomed. Both Zach and Stanton worked with Gerard, a 10-year-old boy with attention-deficit and other related diagnoses. Gerard had, however, been given a relatively hopeful prognosis—an improvement on those we normally see applied to children like him. He was told that his disorders would not be permanent. A restless soul who tended to scoot from one thing to the next, Gerard explained: "I can't concentrate now because I have this condition. But I will grow out of it. So I shouldn't get down on myself until that happens." This helpful insight may give Gerard more patience with himself and perseverance in his tasks. Still, we should be wary. Why do we need this label to accomplish these purposes?

The question, ultimately, is whether—in our efforts to engage children, accommodate their learning styles, and support them in realizing their potential—diagnoses of disorders help or hinder. We believe the latter is more often true than the former.

# 7

# Beyond Labeling

## Children and Mental Disorders

The standard figure given for mental disorders among children—proffered by the CDC in 2013—is one in five, and "estimates appear to be increasing."

Our questions are these:

- Does one in five children in the world have a disabling mental illness?

- Is there anything going on in children's lives to cause this epidemic, or have one-fifth of American (and all) children always been mentally ill?

- Have we improved the health of children since discovering this alarming rate of mental disorders, as we did previously in regard to smallpox, malaria, and AIDS?

In answer to the last question, here's a recent review in MedicineNet claiming "about one-fourth of children and teens experience some type of mental disorder in any given year, one-third at some time in their lives."

> ADHD affects 8%–10% of school-aged children. Depression occurs at a rate [annually] of about 2% during childhood and from 4%–7% during adolescence, *affecting up to about 20% of adolescents by the time they reach adulthood* [our italics]. In teens more frequently than in younger children, addictions, bipolar disorder, and less often, early onset schizophrenia may manifest.
>
> Although not as commonly occurring, developmental disabilities like autism spectrum disorders can have a significant lifelong impact on the life of the child and his or her family. . . . . Statistics about autism conclude that it afflicts one out of every 88 children, *a 78% increase in the past 10 years.* [Our italics]

This summary omits anxiety, even though the section lists anxiety as one of the most common childhood conditions, along with ADHD and depression. In 2017, the *New York Times* asked, "Why Are More American Teenagers Than Ever Suffering From Severe Anxiety?": "In 1985, the Higher Education Research Institute at U.C.L.A. began asking incoming college freshmen if they 'felt overwhelmed by all I had to do' during the previous year. In 1985, 18 percent said they did. By 2010, that number had increased to 29 percent. Last year (2016), it surged to 41 percent." This growth is stunning.

It may be impossible to separate all of this out. But we can safely conclude:

- Young people have startlingly high rates of diagnosis for mental illness and related conditions (for ADHD, 10 percent; for depression during childhood, 20 percent; for SUDs among 18-25 year-olds, 15 percent, or one in 6 or 7 young people); for anxiety among college-bound 18-year-olds, 40 percent).

- These rates are increasing substantially and rapidly for some conditions (ADHD, bipolar disorder, anxiety).

- Regardless of whether these rates are due to too-eager diagnoses or to changing situations children face, they are highly alarming.

- What we're doing to help isn't working.

And we should therefore ask ourselves the following questions:

- If more children really are anxious and depressed and have alcohol use disorders, what can we do about that as parents, as helpers, and as a society?

- Even with maturity, a certain percentage will continue to have these problems through adulthood (after all, 16 percent of 30-44 year-olds have alcohol-use disorders). What can we do to prevent this extension of adolescent problems?

- And if children are diagnosed with, treated for, and even helped by thinking they have a disorder, how do we handle that as the child progresses?

We will later return directly to these central questions. First, let's continue to trace Zach's story as one template for this passage beyond ADHD and addiction.

## Zach's Alternative Story

Zach was impulsive, distractible and seemingly incorrigible throughout his school career. His inattentiveness and hyperactivity were disruptive to his life, both academically and socially, as a teen and young adult. So it was reassuring at one time for him to see these characteristics as symptoms of ADHD. But at some point seeing himself as disabled stopped being helpful.

Zach came to find that emphasizing these negative traits in his identity ignored the positive qualities that were also true about him, and on which he was to build a more successful identity. Zach recalls:

- I was labeled *impulsive*—a trait that got me into trouble in school. But I got little credit for being spontaneous, which helped me think creatively in the moment and led me to some of my successful exploits.

- I was called *incorrigible* and *out-of-control*—a self-fulfilling prophecy when it came to drug-taking. From another perspective, I am a sensation-seeker, which is how I created a vocational path as a traveling musician, a consultant for children and families, and a writer and podcaster. These involvements all excite and engage me. I'd be a far less satisfied person without them.

- I was *distractible* and *disorganized* in school, which led to my feeling lost and falling behind in class, both of which caused me to doubt my intelligence. But the same traits allowed me to hyper-focus at other times, and I'd spend endless hours researching and writing about and doing things that appealed to me. I've always had a strong interest in abstract concepts in science, literature, and the arts, which have led me to several career tracks and, ultimately, real happiness.

Zach's natural attributes presented challenges in some contexts while fueling him in others. That's true for all of us. As Zach realized this, he came to reject the ADHD label as insulting and self-limiting. Later, this same self-awareness and independence allowed him to reject his heroin addiction. Instead, he focused his life around the things that gave him purpose and joy.

Zach is now a trained professional in his 30s who is equipped to reach his own conclusions about himself. But how many children in situations Zach once faced have the resources that he now has? Through his work, Zach has found, distressingly, that many well-meaning professionals at American schools are eager to categorize children in ways that highlight their deficits while minimizing their potential. When we tell young people that they have ADHD or addiction, we don't simultaneously convey that they also have abilities that they can build their lives around—a truth that Zach was fortunate to have the space to discover for himself.

Let's return to Gerard, the 10-year-old who was diagnosed with ADHD, with accompanying claims about how his brain made him feel and act the way he did. Zach wrote an assessment of Gerard after interacting with him in a variety of contexts.

### Zach's Report on Gerard

First and foremost, it was a pleasure to spend time with Gerard. He is such an alive, fun child! Below are my observations regarding Gerard's skills and areas for growth in (a) flexibility, (b) problem solving, and (c) emotional regulation. To be sure, flexibility, problem solving, and emotional regulation are skills within a developmental process; no kid can master all of them suddenly, or all of the time. Recognizing this gives the teacher or helper a more incremental, day-to-day way to deal with the child. Once the narrative changes from "This child has problems" to "I want to help this child develop these skills," things become easier for everyone involved.

Let me begin with my observations about Gerard and his temperament (notes to the reader are in parentheses). Gerard is:

- creative
- risk-taking
- self-starting
- people-oriented

- interactive
- impatient and impulsive
- spontaneous
- outgoing and talkative
- convincing and persuasive
- fun and fun-loving
- generally optimistic
- sometimes shy
- warm and caring

(In this list we can see both sides of some of Gerard's tendencies—for example, that he is both impulsive and spontaneous, as well as fun-loving. We can also see that he is not fully evolved, and that he can be one thing and then its opposite—for example, that he is outgoing and talkative, and yet sometimes shy.)

Teachers have many obligations competing for their time and attention, and so they may not always respond to Gerard's complex set of natural tendencies. But ignoring them may lead to displays of Gerard's "challenging behavior."

Conversely, this list of temperamental traits provides any number of ways he could contribute to his family, peer group, or classroom:

- He speaks openly.
- He has leadership qualities.
- He can act independently.
- He enjoys people.
- He is entertaining.
- He cares that people are happy.
- He can diffuse tension with funny comments.
- He can make people laugh.
- He's cooperative and helpful.
- He's kind.

Most people in Gerard's life know all of this about him to some degree, and there's a lot to work with there.*

---

\* Zach's list of characteristics, emphasizing their positive nature, is adopted from Jeanine Fitzgerald's work, discussed in Chapter 4.

(What a relief it was to Gerard's parents to see these positive lists about him—even though, or especially because—they recognized these traits as a true picture of their son.)

Of course, he has temperamental blind spots as well, ones that can cause confusion or get him into trouble:

- He tends to speak before thinking things through.
- He would rather chat than work.
- He might skip over important details.
- He can be overly sensitive at times.
- He may overstep authority.
- He gets bored with routine.
- He sometimes asserts control to show his independence.

The issue is, what is the best environment—including physical environment, social environment, parenting styles, and teaching styles—for making use of Gerard's skills and guiding growth needed in other areas?

This in turn requires everyone working with Gerard to ask two key questions: How can I effectively communicate with Gerard (address his concerns and needs and communicate my own)? How can I help him develop stronger flexibility, emotional regulation, and problem-solving skills?**

This is what I would suggest to those working with Gerard:

**1. Guiding Gerard forward:**

- Answer his "Who Else" questions. Let him know who else is involved in what you want him to do. (In a sense, his whole life is like a big social gathering.)

- When appropriate, call on him to make things fun for everyone in order to gain recognition and approval from peers.

- Provide a foundation of love and approval he can rely on when his emotions get "out of control." (His parents already do this, but perhaps being aware of this process will highlight it.)

- Because he starts things enthusiastically but may not have

---

** These concepts are emphasized in the work of Ross Greene, discussed in Chapter 4.

the patience to finish them, provide him with achievable short-term tasks so he can be successful; teach him to pace himself while slowly extending the length or rigor of his required tasks; use this engagement as a way to foster his longer-term focus.

- Because sometimes he likes to be independent, he often debates anything adults suggest to him. So he needs to be certain that you mean what you say. Adults should take time to explain situations, then provide reasonable choices so that he can still be involved in the decision-making process, but then be decisive.

- Gerard is a contributing, loving person by nature. I can imagine a situation where maintaining social harmony is so important that he neglects his own needs.

- Communicate with him in a way that expresses the objective needs and intentions of other people while considering his own needs as well.

**2. Providing appropriate encouragement for Gerard:**

- Let him know how much positive energy he has and how much fun he is.

- Offer him as many opportunities as possible to be helpful and to contribute, and praise him when he does so.

- Let him know you appreciate that he shares his thoughts and feelings so freely.

- Tell him when he's used his sense of humor in a valuable way.

- Tell him when you notice him being confident and responding quickly and well.

- Tell him you understand that when he wants to do something that's important to him, and that telling him to wait doesn't mean you don't think it's important too—it just means that you want to maintain balance and include everybody so he can continue to pursue his passions (like his love of animals).

- Tell him you notice when he's being caring and responding to the needs of others.

### 3. Supporting Gerard's learning style in school

After these issues on Gerard's personal behavior/identifying his authentic values and preferences/communication/encouragement become well-established, the focus can shift to his learning style in school, which will improve as he becomes more flexible, regulated, and able to solve problems.

I haven't tried to teach Gerard anything in an academic sense, but it seems he learns best in the following ways (we can use reading as an example):

**Cooperative/groups:** Gerard likes to work with people. He should be given opportunities, both in class and during free time, to work and play in groups where his leadership qualities can come to the fore.

**Verbal/auditory:** Gerard likes to listen to concepts and talk things out, rather than reading about them. He also likes to listen to music, sing and hum, or hear white noise while he works.

**Kinesthetic:** Gerard likes to use concrete materials to work through a problem. He's most comfortable (like most of us) with subjects he's familiar with and activities he's done in the past.

**Interactive:** As well as interacting with others in play and tasks, use Gerard's reading and writing for interactions—for example, in writing and reading emails and letters.

- Gerard doesn't always stick with reading material for a long time, because he likes *doing* and not just thinking. He likes things broken into short sections. This works for his approaching larger tasks and projects, and also for reading assignments.

- Gerard learns best, and is happiest with, a balance of life experience (he loves nature and animals) and application of those experiences to academic topics. This type of balance will guide him comfortably through school and the larger world, while making it possible to limit nagging from adults to change his style and the tension this produces for him.

Gerard is going to be just fine, especially if you keep taking him on adventures—as meeting me was for him—and demonstrating that life is an adventure! I would *love* to be his teacher.

## A Note on Accessing Special Resources

Note how absent of labels Zach's report is, how steeped in appreciation for what Gerard already does well and which directions he can pursue, to improve his undeveloped areas and, more importantly, to build on his strengths. This is a strength-based—as opposed to disorder-labeling—approach. The critical thing is for Gerard to be confident and motivated enough to proceed in positive directions in school and out.

Zach operates independently, in cooperation with schools and families, due to his local placement and reputation. He himself represents a special program for the children he works with. The fact is that kids who are not labeled often can't access the kinds of help he provides. It is through diagnostic labels that kids gain such extra help and services—including medications as these are occasionally useful.

This often leaves a concerned parent striving to find an appropriate disease label, as a person and their doctor might search for a diagnostic label in order to provide a medical test the doctor wants to perform that is prohibitively expensive. Indeed, parents, doctors, and helpers do this consciously, often joking together: "We need to call you this in order to get that." There are two conclusions to be drawn from this rigmarole that parents must go through:

- As much as it is possible, don't allow yourself to follow the label down the rabbit hole and to accept it as the "real" child, the human being with whom you are dealing.

- As was the case with Mark, sensitive and skilled teachers often take the kinds of steps Zach outlined for these cases. Counselors vary all over the lot in how well they use the kind of strengths-based, non-labeling process that Zach practices. We hope to encourage more parents, teachers, and counselors to follow their instincts in this direction (and both authors know that many parents and professionals follow disease prescriptions with deep reservations and worries). This means being mindful when people enter into negotiations with school authorities to procure extra services, and to know what it is that they are seeking for their child. And, of course, the authors look forward to a visionary system when people can avoid labeling, but simply discuss in here-and-now terms what a non-diseased, unlabeled child can benefit from, and that the school or other system is able to provide it sans labeling.

## Children's Strengths, Grit, and Perseverance

Angela Duckworth found that when people fulfilled their positive potential, they did so not because they have more skill or ability, but because of grit:

> There are no shortcuts to excellence. Developing real expertise, figuring out really hard problems, it all takes time—longer than most people imagine. You've got to apply those skills and produce goods or services that are valuable to people. Grit is about working on something you care about so much that you're willing to stay loyal to it. . . It's doing what you love, but not just falling in love—staying in love.

Duckworth extends Seligman's positive psychology emphasis on optimism into the behavioral realm of perseverance and the spiritual one of purpose—that is, seeing life in positive terms and having life goals. Children succeed—both in individual tasks, and overall—when they believe that their efforts are worthwhile and that they should continue to pursue their goals.

Seligman's and Duckworth's theories of positive psychology are the antithesis of diagnostic labels of addiction and mental illness. Notice how these concepts apply to Zach's life story, and to how he approaches children like Gerard. Zach saw his own life turn from one of problems being diagnosed to a life of optimism, perseverance, and positive work and relationships. This is a roadmap for developmental improvements with children.

What Seligman and Duckworth have discovered through research, Zach has discovered in his own life and his work with children, and Stanton and Zach have discovered in their working and research with people facing addictions: We are all correctable, improvable, developable, on our own terms even if we sometimes need help. We all are predisposed to lead a successful life on earth, if only we look for what is available in the here-and-now and acquaint ourselves with our potential and how to surface it.

# Behavioral Addictions and What They Show Us

8

When Stanton introduced the idea of love and sex addiction in his 1975 book with Archie Brodsky, *Love and Addiction*, the idea was ridiculed. A prominent addiction researcher spoke after Stanton at a conference: "I read the newspaper every morning; that doesn't mean that I'm addicted to newspapers."

Dial forward to 2013, when the American Psychiatric Association introduced its new edition of its diagnostic manual, called DSM-5 (*Diagnostic and Statistical Manual of Mental Disorders—5th Edition*). There were several remarkable elements to this psychiatric reference book.

One was that the word "addiction" isn't applied to any of the 11 categories of drugs that DSM lists, including alcohol and caffeine along with such standbys as cannabis (marijuana), opioids, stimulants (cocaine and amphetamines), tobacco (nicotine), and so on. "Addiction" wasn't used by DSM's predecessor III and IV volumes either, but rather "dependence." However, "dependence" was also omitted in DSM-5's substance-use disorder categories.

Yet the term "addiction" does show up in DSM-5, resuscitated after having been omitted completely in previous volumes. In the same section as substance-use disorders, DSM-5 lists one addictive disorder: compulsive gambling. Everybody finds these categorical gymnastics confusing: addiction and dependence are terms, ideas, not employed with drugs in DSM-5, even though they remain common in professional and popular usage. The term, the concept, of addiction, does appear—applied to only a single, non-drug involvement, gambling—and is listed in the same section as substance use disorders.

Whenever something seems so antithetical to common sense, we are looking at a revolution in our thinking, however poorly realized the revolution as yet may be. Rather than defining substance-related disorders with terms like addiction or dependence, DSM-5 categorizes them from "mild" to "moderate" to "severe"—summing various problems the user experiences, using similar criteria across all drug types. These categories reflect that people who have problems with substances simply refuse to display traditional symptoms of addiction in their drug use; yet their lives are nonetheless wedded unhealthily to these drugs.

So, if a person can't be called addicted by the fabled, traditional criteria—like the person's climbing the walls in withdrawal when they can't take a drug, *a la The Man with The Golden Arm*—then why say that they have a problem at all? Thus, critics complained, the mild-use disorder category isn't a real psychiatric disorder. They're wrong. Overarching the entire DSM-5 classification is the principle that a behavior or syndrome must cause impairment and distress. The process definition of addiction described in Chapter 2 of this book is also anchored in these two concepts (which rules out reading the morning newspaper as an addictive disorder).

Here are other startling conclusions from the sensible aspect of DSM-5. Cocaine or heroin use, by itself, doesn't constitute a disorder. In fact, DSM provides a list of symptoms or problems. As to impairment, consider criterion 5, "Recurrent substance use resulting in failure to fulfill major role obligations at work, school, or home," and 7, "Important social, occupational, or recreational activities given up or reduced because of substance use," along with tolerance, withdrawal, and craving. Even scoring one such problem, on its own, does not create a disorder. That doesn't mean that it's advisable to take drugs. But taking drugs—like playing video games—is not *per se* a problem or a psychological condition, let alone comprising an addiction. Indeed, as we have seen, most drug users do not show the impairments DSM identifies.

### How Stanton Studied DSM

Stanton has often been asked by physicians or their lawyers to evaluate their "addiction charts." These are the doctors' hospital records when they have been required to go through a stint at a private rehab (the most famous of which is Hazelden Betty Ford, but which proliferate around the country, most notably in Southern California and Florida) due to having illicitly taken pharmaceuticals, a DUI, or an accusation by a spouse during a divorce proceeding that the doctor had a drinking or a drug problem.

Doctors in this position are generally presented with a choice by their Physician Health Program (the medical equivalent of an employee assistance program, always comprised entirely of AA members in Stanton's experience): Enter a rehab, virtually all of which are 12-step-based, for several months, or lose their license. Faced with that choice, doctors agree to losing the time from their practices and the $100,000-or-so cost as necessary evils, even if they don't believe that they are addicted or out of control.

Many then encounter a number of concerns they hadn't anticipated, such as:

- They must instantly "confess" that they are an addict or alcoholic and that they are powerless over their substance use.

- They are required to embark on a "spiritual" program as part of their rehab.

- They must attend 12-step meetings.

Many are shocked by these elements in a supposedly medical program, so different from how they themselves practice medicine, where the individual patient's beliefs and preferences are respected. But they reluctantly consent because otherwise they'll be kicked out of rehab and won't be allowed to practice medicine.

On completing their purgatory, however, they discover that they must continue with all of these requirements indefinitely *after* they leave the facility. They are also tested to guarantee that they remain absolutely abstinent, including no wine or beer—even if drinking was never an issue for them.

For some, this continuing charade is too much to bear, and they hire a lawyer to contest these requirements. The doctor or the lawyer may then hire Stanton to question their diagnosis as an addict or alcoholic (or, in the terms used by the old DSM-IV, as being "dependent").

Although the programs are invariably 12-step based, they must justify their actions in terms of DSM criteria in the charts Stanton examines. These two approaches to addiction are not the same. Indeed, Stanton was on the DSM-IV advisory group for substance use disorders, and played a role in formulating the DSM criteria:

- As noted, DSM doesn't use the terms "addiction" or "alcoholism," "addict" or "alcoholic."

- Use of any substance, even regular use, is not defined as a disorder without meeting several problem criteria.

- Abstinence isn't required for remission (a.k.a. recovery)—only the absence of substance-use problems. Note: this makes DSM a harm-reduction document (see next chapter).

- After a year of the absence of such problems, the individual is certified as having achieved long-term remission ("recovery"). That is, DSM recognizes addiction or its equivalents as time-limited conditions.

Of course, it is very possible that the individual may have a problem they should address with their preferred mode of treatment—anxiety, marital discord, lack of other life diversions, loss of work motivation. They just don't happen to be drug addicts or alcoholics or have a substance use disorder at all! It seems remarkable that Stanton would even need to be called in to offer his expertise in cases like these. Clearly, even many psychiatrists—and certainly rehabs—don't recognize that these elements are part of their own diagnostic bible, which contradicts 12-step ideology.

## Evolving Definitions

By 2013, American psychiatry, as represented by its latest diagnostic manual, had finally recognized, as Stanton and Archie Brodsky had shown in 1975, that addiction is not limited to, or defined by, drugs. This is good, as far as it went. But the idea that people *can* be addicted to gambling—but *not* to sex, or shopping, or eating, or television and video games and iPhones, or anything else that people become involved in compulsively and destructively—is patently absurd.

The truth is, addiction is not in the *thing*, but in our lives—in the processes and the consequences of our activities and involvements. DSM-5 partly recognizes this, but isn't permitted to declare this recognition openly. Or, perhaps, DSM-5 and its addiction expert authors simply haven't yet caught on to the full implications of their own reasoning. Or both.

Despite DSM-5, anyone who works to help others needs to be able to recognize the addiction process. People can become involved in destructive ways with any all-encompassing experience, as defined in Chapters 1 and 2. The key things to consider are very straightforward: how much an activity or involvement is harming you or others; and how much you want to change it. Stanton's Life Process Program doesn't diagnose people's habits as addiction, alcoholism, etc. Rather, it focuses people on the problems their habits cause them and their motivation to change.

Do people really respond to the idea that they are involved in addictive behavior that doesn't involve drugs or alcohol? Yes, they do.

### LPP Case Study: Eating and Exercise Addictions

A woman from a deep-red state began working with an LPP coach (also a woman) due to compulsive eating and depression and anxiety, which she linked to trying to be a perfect mother, wife, and Christian. Her coach noted:

> "Bea is a Southern Baptist. She was raised with major restrictions in her life: no alcohol, dancing, etc., plus a rigorous focus on perfectionism in keeping God's commandments via church doctrine.
>
> "Her father became an outcast from her church due to drinking; he died at least in part due to alcoholism. She had adored him, but when he became a drinker, she was humiliated and broke off all contact with him.
>
> "She is emotionally distressed and curtails her social relations and daily activities because of her binge eating, which she offsets with compulsive exercise."

LPP deals with addictive eating behavior, like that displayed in anorexia and bulimia, where abstinence and excess often alternate. That these behaviors are addictive is easily apparent to a woman who witnessed the same pattern with her father's drinking. She understands at a gut level—as do our other clients and many other people—that the process of addiction is not a function of drugs or alcohol.

The coach deeply respected Bea's dedication to her values of family and faith. But these weren't proving good lodestars for her personal health and happiness. Along with her eating, Bea exercised in ways that were preoccupying and sometimes damaging. She was also experiencing sharp mood swings. Bea recognized that she had to find more natural, less restrictive, eating and exercise patterns, and a more supportive, calming lifestyle.

Her coach worked with Bea on developing a moderate exercise program, as well as taking pressure off herself as a parent. Bea wanted to be less perfectionistic with her children, so that she could enjoy her time with them more. She also took time from her family for her own interests, hobbies, and passions. Expressing these things provided naturalistic ways of addressing her mood problems. For instance, she enjoyed her garden and found it relaxing to watch the birds fly through its trees.

Bea also needed to find support for her change efforts. First, of course, she had to communicate her needs to her husband and children, who were supportive. As she turned away from intensive, isolated workouts, she began walking a few times a week with several neighbors. This offered Bea her first friendships outside of the church.

The coach was applying the Life Process Program of focusing on overall mental health, values, personal skills and resources, family communication, relationships and community, and purpose as the fundamental building blocks for combating addictions of all sorts.

### Love and Drug Addiction

How can a relationship prove addictive? Are such addictions for real—and really serious? When Stanton speaks with groups at Above and Beyond, an inner-city addiction recovery center, he often brings up the question of love addiction. *People in this hard environment instantly identify with the idea that relationships can be the most destructive of addictions, and that they are often sources for drug and alcohol addictions.*

For women, the story is most often of being led into drugs and addiction by a boyfriend or partner; men most often tell a story of a failed relationship being the driving force in their addiction—of loss and of feeling betrayed. Of course, we don't want to blame other people for our own addictions. And these examples are very present for middle-class people as well. But in a starker environment, where substance addictions are so disruptive, the stories of love addiction stand out in bold relief.

### On Childhood Addictions

The spotlight is now on gaming and other tech devices that children are especially prone to use addictively. The correspondent document to DSM-5, the American psychiatric manual, is the ICD-11—the World

Health Organization's *International Classification of Diseases*, now in its eleventh edition. This latest edition has identified gaming as a primary addiction. Even though DSM-5 hasn't recognized this idea, if a child refuses to play with other kids or to read or to leave the house because they spend all of their time playing video games (as described in Chapter 5), this is an addictive problem. It is an attachment to a destructive, self-feeding process that prevents their being engaged in life, that impairs and distresses them, as discussed in Chapter 2.

The issue of technology in our lives, and in our children's lives, is massive. As Franklin Foer describes in *World Without Mind: The Existential Threat of Big Tech*, we are being re-engineered as human beings so that technology is central to our consciousness. Children and young people now live their lives through technology, so that texting, e-mail, *et al.* have replaced human contact, even phone calls, as children's (and many of our) primary ways of interacting with other people. And, yet, so many people are lonely.

Technology companies have mastered how to engage our consciousness, so that few people today—and always fewer—can spend substantial time in activity uninterrupted by electronic devices. This is not a topic to be resolved easily, for adults or children. Yet Foer isn't completely pessimistic. He likens learning to use ubiquitous cell phones and electronics moderately to a child's learning to eat reasonably amidst a sea of sweet treats. Of course, while many of us learn how to do so, the constant presence of addictively alluring food is also causing our worldwide obesity crisis, starting in America.

As for children and drug use, we can readily accept that an adult uses a drug or drinks alcohol (or uses social media) within healthy boundaries. For young people, however, we may be concerned about the implications of any drug use. But this doesn't mean that kids who use drugs are addicts who must abstain for the rest of their lives. Harm reduction is an approach that focuses on consequences rather than on substances. HR doesn't require zero tolerance. It requires a child to be engaged in life, in ways that may be reflected by their report cards, who they hang out with, their cooperation at home, and how they spend their time.

# Abstinence and Harm Reduction, in Adolescence and Recovery

9

This book takes a harm-reduction approach to addiction—quite unlike an abstinence-only approach, in which the only accepted outcome of treatment is to stop use of a specific substance, or of all psychoactive substances, or an addictive activity. (Abstinence made no sense, of course, for Bea's eating and exercises addictions, or for electronics or love addictions.) Using harm reduction (HR) in treatment means that abstinence isn't the end-all goal; the aim instead is to improve the person's situation—their life overall.

HR also has implications for America's "just-say-no" approach, which insists that young people should never take drugs.

## Harm Reduction and Youthful Drinking

Before turning to HR's most high-profile forms—preserving lives and treating people who use opioids, especially heroin—let's first continue with children and youthful substance use. Does HR really apply to kids?

America has a temperance tradition, and an abstinence fixation that manifested itself in alcohol prohibition throughout the 1920s until it was repealed in 1933. But Nancy Reagan's "just say no" has really never lost its primary status in America, especially when it comes to children and drugs. Most people wish that their children would never consume illicit drugs. But marijuana is now legal recreationally for a third of American adults since California took that route. Canada has become the first Western nation to legalize the drug nationally for adults, and any number of states are considering doing likewise. The cat is out of that bag.

We have reviewed, in Chapter 2, the extent of normal drug use. The National Survey on Drug Use and Health tells us that nearly 100 million Americans consume a prescription painkiller annually; 28 million Americans over the age of 12 use an illicit drug in the course of a year (more than 10%), and 86 percent of Americans have drunk alcohol during their lifetimes (70 percent over the past year, and 56 percent in the past month). So you and your child are unlikely indeed to avoid all contact with these substances. The question rather is, *when and how* will a young person learn to deal with alcohol and drugs?

Put another way, we might ask: Who will teach your child to drink? A high school kid? A college fraternity or sorority member? A fellow military service person? Someone your kid meets on the street? *Or could it, perhaps, be you?*

This question leads to a further one: At what age should your child be allowed to consume a psychoactive substance? The age limit of 21 is the one embedded in the law for legal alcohol use in the United States. This age has been replicated for marijuana use since that drug has been legalized in a growing number of states. Yet the United States' 21-year-old drinking age stands alone among western nations.

Research consistently shows that countries in which the drinking age is lowest—France, Greece, Spain, Italy, Portugal, Cyprus, Hungary—have fewer drinking problems among the young, and fewer alcohol problems overall.* Likewise—in a remarkable finding—countries where the most alcohol is consumed have the fewest drinking problems, up to and including death from alcohol due to causes such as cirrhosis and accidental deaths (see "Temperance and Policy" below**).

How is this seemingly incredible anomaly achieved? Countries in which alcohol is most commonly and casually drunk, like France, Spain, Italy, and Greece, serve wine with meals in sedate age-and-gender-integrated surroundings, where misbehavior not only isn't countenanced, but is almost impossible to imagine. Note that this whole approach to drinking belies the American idea that the substances *per se* and the

---

\* This statement has become remarkably controversial in itself, and it is now popularly claimed that youth drinking in Europe is worse than in the U.S. This is simply not true although drinking is pushed somewhat further back age-wise here. In general, moderate-drinking European cultures persist in encouraging more moderate drinking by their youths.

\*\* Stanton has spent a good deal of his professional life addressing such cultural differences in drinking and drug use and their implications for theory and practice and treatment in addiction and alcoholism. A few of the milestones in this work are: "The limitations of control-of-supply models for explaining and preventing alcoholism and drug addiction," *Journal of Studies on Alcohol*, 1988 (this paper won the Mark Keller award presented by the Rutgers Center of Alcohol Studies); "End Alcoholism—Bomb Spain," *Psychology Today Blogs*, 2008; "Alcohol as evil: Temperance and policy," *Addiction Research and Theory*, 2010; "I'm single-handedly preserving the world's wine cultures—Any help out there?" *Huffington Post*, 2010; In 2018, the Temperance movement still grips America, *Filter Magazine*, 2018.

amount consumed determine outcomes, up to and including addiction.

In one study comparing drinking by Italians and Finns (Finland has one of the highest levels of alcohol problems in the world), nationals of both countries were asked when they had first consumed alcohol. Finns could invariably identify the exact time and place that they first drank: in their early teens (around age 15) where they drank throughout a night with others their age, getting completely drunk.

Italians, on the other hand, couldn't answer the question. They simply had been sipping wine, often mixed with water when they were small, their entire lives, even before they were conscious of alcohol. Italians don't think of wine as a dangerous substance with overwhelming powers to corrupt. Rather, wine is felt as an adjunct to a good time, consumed with people they love in a natural social setting that embodies an entire community's approach to socializing—to life, in fact. Italians typically prize community, family, food, and relaxed socializing. In town squares throughout Italy, taverns and cafes exist directly across from churches and are filled with families following Sunday services. Imagine American families going to a bar right after church!

Whether and how this model can be spread to other cultures, and possibly other substances and activities, has been debated for decades and longer. As we saw in the table beginning Chapter 5, it is an urgent issue, since alcohol and other substance-use disorders are rampant for young Americans. If we tried to recreate the Italian approach at an American university, we might set up a tavern where alcohol is served, along with food, for members of the university community of all ages—rather than having 18–21-year-olds imbibe in isolated groups, like the typical college fraternity party. But, among the other reasons this is rarely attempted, most college students are too young to drink legally in America.

However, how *you* deal with this issue is something you ought to think through as a parent. This is true even (perhaps especially) *if you yourself have had substance use problems.* That's how one of Stanton's colleagues dealt with introducing his daughter to alcohol.

### Abstinent Father Let His Daughter Drink at Age 14

Stanton was presenting at a conference with a colleague who became interested in drug policy after he was arrested and spent time in county jail because of his drug use. As a part of his battle for custody of his daughter, and for other reasons, the colleague gave up all drug use, including alcohol.

Some time later, he took his 14-year-old daughter, now living with him, to Italy. The drinking age in that country (as in Spain, Greece, and France) was 16. It has recently been raised to 18 in Italy due to pressure from the World Health Organization, led by Northern European nations with worse drinking problems than their Southern European counterparts.

But restricting drinking to adults is still not the custom in Italy, despite the recent change in laws, and the server placed a glass of wine each in front of the colleague and his daughter. He sent his own wine back. But he told his daughter that she could drink her wine if she wanted to. "I figured," he said, "that making all of these things forbidden fruit was part of my problem." She drank the wine carefully.

The colleague was expressing, through his permission for his daughter to drink on a special occasion, his belief that she is a much better-balanced person than he was at her age. He has made sure that she is involved in many productive activities that he himself didn't come to until later in life. This is the self-image he wants to encourage for her. All signs are that his encouragement is taking root. We will return to this larger, critical matter of parenting and addiction prevention.

## Harm Reduction in Treating Substance Use Problems

HR conceives that helping a person doesn't necessarily mean that they quit using drugs. It may mean that a person reduces their use to less dangerous levels, or uses or administers the drug in ways that are less harmful. The primary example of harm reduction has been distributing and using clean needles to avoid HIV infections. Needle-exchange programs curtailed the AIDS epidemic in Europe and the United States, but only belatedly here, with resistance and delays that cost of hundreds of thousands of lives.

In the case of clean-needle programs, to some extent, the person's heroin addiction has been accepted. But, as we shall see, the contact provided with health care workers—or simply concerned helpers—is an ameliorative factor that moves many to quit injecting drugs, or heroin use, altogether. We saw this impact in Chapter 2 in regards to "wet housing" in Seattle, where homeless street drinkers were provided secure residences without a demand that they abstain, and they reduced their drinking substantially. Although they still might be classified as "alcoholics," they nonetheless significantly improved their health, along with their living conditions.

The HR concept of drug and addiction treatment has gained traction worldwide. This is true even as HR is a difficult idea for many people to grasp when applied to people who have serious drug-related problems. The United States has, as usual, been especially slow to adopt the HR idea and approaches. Our slowness in this regard—as with so much else that we confront in this book—is due to the trifecta of American temperance, our abstinence fixation, and the 12-step approach to substance use problems.

As expressed by the leading American figure in drug policy reform, Ethan Nadelmann:

> Where the 12-step thing has the most to own up to is its role in impeding harm reduction interventions to stem the spread of HIV/AIDS. Why was it that Australia and England and the Netherlands were able to stop the spread, and keep the number for injecting drug users under 5–10%, and the U.S. was not? It's that notion that abstinence is the only permissible approach, that we are not going to "enable" a junkie by giving him a clean needle. There has to be a kind of owning up to that role in hundreds of thousands of people dying unnecessarily.

This American distaste for addressing substance issues in ways that don't involve abstinence derails our thinking—even as, according to a series of large national research studies (such as NESARC, described in Chapter 2), most of the many people who outgrow alcohol dependence here in the United States cut back without abstaining entirely. This is certainly true for young people, as many of us can testify.

Harm reduction, of course, may make more or less sense depending on the person, their age, their environment and life circumstances, the severity of their addictive problem, and the substance or addictive involvement.

But harm reduction is nonetheless relevant for every sort of drug and every sort of habit. For example, HR at first didn't seem like a realistic option for smokers, since that addiction was extremely hard to cut back without quitting. But HR has now become a major focus in smoking, with people getting nicotine using a less harmful intake method, like "vaping"—smoking e-cigarettes—or through nicotine patches or gum.

It is also true that even regular smokers have cut back their smoking radically—an accomplishment that at one time was considered impossible. According to Gallup surveys, only one percent of U.S. smokers now smoke more than one pack of cigarettes per day, while 68 percent smoke less than a pack a day, each a record in Gallup surveys dating back to 1944. (The percentage who smoke one pack a day has remained fairly constant at about 31 percent.) Smokers have been spurred to cut back by the many restrictions imposed in work places, their homes, restaurants and bars, etc. There are just not enough places a person can smoke and not enough time for them to do so to maintain old-style addictive smoking habits. And people—even smokers we would call addicted—adjust by smoking less.

## Mindfulness Harm Reduction Therapy for Smoking

Pavel Somov and Marla Somova wrote a mindfulness manual for smokers, *The Smoke-Free, Smoke Break*. Its radical goals were described in the foreword by harm-reduction psychotherapist Andrew Tatarsky: "changing your relationship to smoking, whether that means quitting, cutting back, or simply smoking more mindfully."

In other words, Somov and Somova aim to give people greater mind control over their smoking, to make it more a matter of choice, which then opens the possibility of cutting back or quitting entirely. Among the numerous techniques they employ for instilling such mindfulness is to save the ashes from one day's smoking and to finger paint with them, refuse to smoke in the place where you smoke most commonly, switch the hand you smoke with—and other of myriad ways of introducing choice points and reflection into the addiction process.

Unlike with opioids and alcohol, the U.S. has radically decreased the amount of smoking and number of smokers over the past half century (down to 14 percent from well over 40 percent of Americans when the 1964 Surgeon General's Report, *Smoking and Health*, was released). Much of this reduction in addiction is due to the natural mindfulness brought about by smoking regulations, which cause people to think through where and when they will smoke. Could we do something similar for marijuana and heroin, if legalized use were accepted but not encouraged, but where nonetheless moderation, healthfulness, and self-respect were encouraged for users?

## Harm Reduction for Opioids

Narcotic substitution therapies are another prominent HR technique. Pharmaceuticals such as methadone, buprenorphine, and Suboxone (buprenorphine plus naloxone) provide safer ways of consuming narcotics through regulated prescriptions for people who use opioids. These therapeutic drugs have been shown to reduce drug-related deaths. Still, some people prefer to remain on heroin. Or they use the drugs in dangerous ways (as did Anna Nicole Smith and her son, both of whom died from their unregulated methadone use). Or they may simply become unhealthily addicted to the substitute drug itself, as many people report occurs for Suboxone.

The easiest drug to administer in a life-saving way is naloxone (Narcan), a narcotic antagonist that reverses the effects of opioid drug use and revives comatose drug users. It has become widely popular for police and emergency medical and other care workers to be equipped with naloxone kits. (Zach carries Narcan with him in his work with teenagers.)

Of course, people are still addicted to an opioid or narcotic drug with these substitution or one-shot reversal therapies, so just allowing people to take their existing drug of choice safely accomplishes the same goal. Enter drug consumption sites (DCS, also called by other names such as supervised injection facilities), in which people use an opiate or other drug in an antiseptic environment with trained personnel available. No fatality has ever been reported in a drug consumption site in Europe, where most of the 100 DCSs are located (including sites in Switzerland, Germany, Spain, and Denmark). In a smaller number of countries, pharmaceutical-grade heroin is provided to long-term users (called HAT, or heroin-assisted treatment), with similarly beneficial outcomes.

Safe injection sites are now being set up across Canada. *There is currently not a single DCS in the U.S.* Although such sites have been planned for Seattle, New York, Baltimore, Philadelphia, and San Francisco in response to our utter failure to stem drug deaths, the Trump administration opposes them tooth and nail.

While successful at reducing mortality and other problems, these HR therapies are not actually addiction remedies. As is true for vaping and nicotine replacement patches and gums, the person may still be entirely dependent on the target drugs (nicotine or opioids). On the other hand, these therapies greatly reduce present risks, and may also provide a transition route to further reductions or ending use entirely.

Amid the nationwide movement toward legalizing marijuana, marijuana is increasingly being seen as a possible pathway for quitting opioid addictions. In fact, states with dispensaries for medical marijuana have witnessed a decline in opioids deaths relative to other states. Indeed, this has been one of the few strategies that has proved effective in reversing the opioid-death epidemic in America. For some people, at least, marijuana is an effective pain reliever and an acceptable replacement for opioids. And people don't die from marijuana, even if they can be addicted to it.

Yet the U.S. establishment continues to rule out anything but abstinence, despite the many harms this thinking has caused us. In the 1980s, New Jersey Governor Christine Whitman adamantly refused the recommendation of her own AIDS Commission when it proposed clean needle programs—which the committee estimated would save the lives of 700 drug users a year. Her opposition led to a 10-year delay in the implementation of clean needles in New Jersey, which, according to her AIDS commission, caused 7,000 deaths.

Whitman's refusal to allow needle programs was not based on any evidence that the programs encouraged drug use. In practice, research conducted by New Jersey's Robert Wood Johnson Foundation found the programs led to more people quitting drugs. As well, per usual, the Trump administration—through Assistant Attorney General Rod Rosenstein—has indicated that they will quickly shut down any drug administration sites, for example in a Philadelphia neighborhood inundated with drug deaths, because, they claim, such sites encourage drug use.

It's hard not to note at this point that American attitudes toward drugs and treatment resist change regardless of all the evidence.

Harm-reduction policies display an essential feature of our developmental approach. When people are encouraged to use drugs in healthier (or less harmful) ways, they more often quit altogether. This is because through the ability to take control of their behaviors, to take drugs more safely, they empower themselves. The same is true when people smoke in only selected spots at permitted times. Drug users in clean needle and drug administration programs are also working with supportive people, including others who have quit using injectable drugs. In this way those who are addicted to drugs show greater regard for themselves, which leads to greater self-acceptance and a better chance of embarking on a non-drug-using lifestyle, rather than encouraging them to continue using drugs, as Whitman and Rosenstein falsely claimed.

## Harm Reduction and Childhood-Youthful Drug Problems

We have covered two bold issues so far around applying harm reduction to children—that we should avoid making alcohol forbidden fruit for children, but rather gradually introduce them to drinking, and that we should focus on children's overall lifestyles rather than on whether they use a substance or not. But nothing scares us more than the idea of young people taking drugs, becoming addicted, and dying.

### Case Study: David Sheff's *Beautiful Boy*

David Sheff's *Beautiful Boy,* a #1 *New York Times* best-selling book and a major film starring Timothee Chalamet and Steve Carell, describes the youthful drug addiction of Sheff's son, Nic. The younger Sheff, despite also using heroin, preferred meth. Nic recovered and wrote a best seller, *Tweak: Growing Up On Methamphetamines,* meant for younger readers, on which the film is also based.

David Sheff has continued to write about addiction in a follow-up book, *Clean: Overcoming Addiction and Ending America's Greatest Tragedy.* Nic also wrote a follow-up book, *We All Fall Down: Living with Addiction.* In his later work, the elder Sheff proposes a view of addiction very much like that in this book—other than being transfixed by his son's brain disease and demonizing drugs, in his son's case meth (meth's chemical structure, as Carl Hart points out, is virtually identical to Adderall).

Sheff tries to thread the needle by favoring harm reduction, while still regarding and treating addiction as a disease caused by drug use. He thus stigmatizes drugs, drug users, and addiction in a way that he deplores, while *defeating* the impulses toward social and family change that motivate him.

The film shows David Sheff himself snorting *something* after a character in the movie tells him that a meth high is akin to cocaine times a thousand. It isn't, and the two drugs are categorized together as stimulants in the psychiatric diagnostic manual DSM-5. But, in any case, why doesn't Sheff become addicted to whatever he's taking?

Sheff and the film never address this question, which is in essence unknowable. Nic is an example of a socially advantaged boy with good (if divorced) parents, a solid home in upscale Marin County, California, and no observable traumas. So what went wrong for Nic? And, more important, what could have helped him avoid addiction or rerouted him instead of experiencing repeated failed resolutions to quit while undergoing contemporary treatments, accompanied by his self-recriminations and the demoralization of his father?

The father, hamstrung in finding ways to cope, responded with fear and intolerance of drugs. (From *Beautiful Boy*): "Through Nic's drug addiction. . . .I shock myself with my ability to rationalize and tolerate things once unthinkable. The rationalizations escalate. . . . It's only marijuana. He gets high only on weekends. At least he's not using hard drug. . . ."

And so the solution would be: Forbidding his son to ever take drugs? Punishing him when he did? Deciding that taking marijuana is the same as shooting up meth or heroin? Sheff has his finger on a true worry, that his desire to see the best version of Nic led to wishful thinking. But does that rule out safe use of drugs for everyone, including, seemingly, himself?

As for Nic, he didn't always feel he was addicted to meth and other drugs he took, but that he was more acting out of rebellion. Eventually he agreed that he was irreparably addicted to drugs and required emergency treatment. This transformation, a complex one, no more argues for the disease theory of drugs and addiction than does his father's trying drugs without becoming addicted and Nic sometimes controlling his drug use do.

As a parent, Sheff discovered that he had less control over his son's life than he believed, maybe none—a lesson worth a parent's learning. He might have used this recognition constructively. Instead, he depicts himself as another victim of his boy's disease, as though he is hypnotized into self-deceit by Nic's drug use.

But what if Sheff had followed his own parenting instincts rather than reifying his son's challenging behavior? Adolescents seek purpose, a community to connect with, and the skills to meet life's—and parents'—expectations. Nic communicated, through his behavior, that he was struggling to find those things. He was a confused adolescent, desperate for guidance. His father's fear of drugs and lack of connection to his son made him miss what his own good sense told him.

None of us but Sheff understand his options, of course. But under the general rules of harm reduction prevention and therapy, he might have focused his energy on regaining family order. This might have involved acknowledging the truth about his son's drug use, setting clear limits for Nic, keeping his son safe when he failed at those limits, and establishing honest communication with him. These are strategies Sheff now values, but that he surrendered at the time due to his fear of drugs.

Does Sheff expect his son never to have a drink for the rest of his life, or not smoke marijuana, or not take a painkiller? Or, indeed, never use a stimulant? Does he expect that his other children will never do, or never did, any of these things before the age of 26? Because that's not going to happen. And everything else is harm reduction.

In the meantime, we can rejoice through the film that Sheff's son is a lucky person with supportive parents, financial resources, and academic and intellectual skills and that he thus has a strong foundation from which to quit meth and focus on his writing career.

How do we—can we—apply the logic of harm reduction to adolescents who encounter substance problems? Yes, even for children, an HR approach is superior to the DARE one. DARE (Drug Abuse Resistance Education) is the standard, abstinence-only, police-based approach used throughout the United States, despite never having been shown to be effective, and in fact often resulting in more drug use. This is because DARE doesn't address—cannot even conceive—that children are able to expand their experiences and meet their basic responsibilities, and smart enough to know that the answers are more complex than just whether or not they are doing drugs.

Barry Lessin, a psychologist and co-founder, with Carol Katz Beyer, of the nonprofit organization Families For Sensible Drug Policy, explains how harm reduction made him a much better therapist through his work with a teenage boy named Matt. According to Lessin, "Harm reduction teaches us a number of important lessons: (1) Hitting bottom isn't required for lasting change; (2) people use drugs for reasons; (3) helping people change is easier when we start where they're at; (4) change includes taking small positive steps; (5) ultimately change involves engaging the young person in their own larger life solutions." Following is his description of his work with Matt:

### Case Study: Barry Lessin's Harm Reduction with a Teenager

Matt was a month from his 18th birthday, during the summer before his senior year of high school, when his father called me about Matt's marijuana use. Matt's father reported that he and Matt's mother were extremely worried about their son's seemingly depressed mood, insomnia, underachieving in school and lack of motivation about making a decision about his future. They had lost their trust in him since he had been lying about his marijuana use.

My treatment with Matt focused on his developing healthy strategies and tools to reduce anxiety and improve his mood. He used our sessions to explore career options; after speaking with a military recruiter, he decided that the military was a realistic option for him to get training in his mechanical interests, develop motivation and independence, and to help his parents pay for college when he was ready to enroll.

The requirement of the military for Matt to be drug-free at the time of his enrollment evaluation, together with his excitement about his newfound sense of purpose, motivated him to decide to "end his relationship" with marijuana at that point. He was able to fairly easily stop using. In his case, abstinence wasn't imposed by therapy or parents, but by the real demands of a situation he himself wanted and valued; his treatment ended once he was accepted into the military.

In my previous life as an abstinence-based therapist, Matt and his family probably wouldn't have gotten past their initial phone call to me.

Harm reduction therapy allows me now to offer families like Matt's some hope and a compassionate partner to walk with them through an often very difficult period. I didn't have to reinvent myself as a psychologist. A recipe of compassion, collaboration, evidence-based treatments and a menu of options offers me the opportunity to be more effective with more people.

Parents don't have to reinvent themselves, either. Harm reduction uses time-tested parenting principles and values, along with common sense, to offer parents some hope and the skills to cope more effectively with the challenge of their children's risky behaviors. A more hopeful parent means a more effective parent and more opportunities for family healing.

Perhaps Matt's problem seems relatively easy to solve (although that certainly wasn't clear to his parents at the time). But what about cases where a child is embarked on a serious involvement with an opioid?

### HR and Natural Recovery vs. Rehab

The following case is related (with prior approval) by a professional who has worked with Stanton on a family drug concern:

> When talking with my daughter about family issues, I think she's especially helpful due to her own experience. She is now in her mid-20s. When she was 17, she got into snorting Oxycontin. Her friends were doing it, and she had a dare-devil streak. I think now that it was developmental, due a lot to her having no idea what career she wanted despite her obvious natural ability.
>
> Beth asked to go to rehab, and we sent her, three times. We followed all the advice of the counselors, to no avail. After the third rehab, when she was 21, I decided they were wrong and I took her to a halfway house. I relied instead on my own instincts of sound parenting and professional helpfulness. I told her I'd pay for three months there and then she'd be on her own. No money, no car, no tuition—she would need to get a job. I was firm but supportive: She was welcome to come to dinner any time so long as she was sober.
>
> Beth got a job, got a junk car, stayed off opiates, put herself through college, and now she's getting her credential as a health professional. She got multiple scholarships after the first semester because of her grades. She initially bought into the whole AA cult and then saw what the deal was. We've had a lot of conversations about AA and the importance of believing you do have power over yourself. I am very proud of how she has matured. She's still a pistol but she has learned to harness her energy in a positive direction.

Cutting children loose is an extreme strategy—one often associated with old "tough love" approaches. But, in line with the Community Reinforcement and Family Therapy (CRAFT) approach, one Barry Lessin uses, Beth's mother put standards for their family in place and insisted that everyone—including her and her husband, as well as Beth—abide by them. Beth was always a valued member of their family and was welcome at home so long as she behaved in line with family standards. Moreover, Beth's mother judged—correctly—that Beth had the ability to meet the challenge, even as she had repeatedly failed at the standard, "I-have-a-disease" treatment.

Zach has developed a family-parental program within the Life Process Program to address family issues, including drug problems (see Appendix C). LPP is an on-line program. Turning to it means relying on your personal and family resources to address your children's problems. However, even if you turn to a professional (such as Zach) there is no escaping the obligation to think and work through your own family situation—no outside expert can do that for you. As Barry Lessin points out, this means that parents must retain calm good sense and apply their own values about good parenting, and the young person must be given the respect of being allowed to make his or her own decisions.

# The Limits of the 12-Step Approach

# 10

A A and its 12 steps are sacrosanct in America. Even many of the most trenchant critics of the disease theory of addiction—Carl Hart, Marc Lewis, Sally Satel, Johann Hari, Maia Szalavitz—don't challenge AA, recognizing that in doing so they will necessarily offend some people who feel they have benefited from the program. They show this restraint even though they may believe that its overall impact is harmful (see Maia Szalavitz below). AA *is* the template for the disease theory of addiction. Thus, Stanton's views are regarded as controversial, even when he is labeled a major addiction theorist. As described in *The Atlantic*:

> [Peele is] staunchly committed to his thesis that AA is not the only way to treat addiction, and alcoholism is not a chronic and progressive disease. Most addictions, he believes, are a product of culture and an individual's response to their personal experience.

At a minimum, for all the claims made on behalf of AA *et al.*, the dominance in America of 12-step programs and rehabs—the entire entrenched recovery movement—hasn't eliminated addiction. It hasn't even contained or curtailed addiction. Instead, there are many reasons to find that substance-related and addictive problems have worsened along with AA's and the disease theory's growth. We argue that AA's and the disease theory's resolute failure has occurred because the American recovery movement doesn't honor the principles of natural growth and development.

More specifically, let's consider:

- **The coerciveness of AA and 12-step programs and ideas.**
  According to Maia Szalavitz, "After 75 years of Alcoholics Anonymous, it's time to admit that we have a problem." Maia declares the need to "challenge the 12-step hegemony," since 90

percent of American addiction treatment programs employ the 12-step approach.

Of course, it's hard to object to AA and related 12-step groups. It's hard to object to a voluntary organization that makes itself available everywhere. But much AA attendance is court-mandated—an unconstitutional practice. When considering not only traffic and criminal court referrals, but also civil court ones (for example, due to divorce-court custody requirements), employee assistance programs (including those for doctors described in Chapter 6), and medical referrals and family interventions, hundreds of thousands of people annually are forced into AA and 12-step treatment.

- **How ineffective AA and the 12 steps are.** At the U.S. Nobel Conference on Addiction Treatment in 2015, Yale emergency medicine professor Michael Pantalon spoke on behalf of the motivational and brief practical approaches this book is about. At the same time, Pantalon pointed out:

> While 12-step programs have helped many, many people, they are not appealing to, or have not been effective for, countless others. Moreover, when you look at the 12-step meetings in a scientifically rigorous way, success is minimal, only about 5-10 percent.

But stating that 5–10 percent of AA attendees benefit from it ignores the natural development thesis of this book. As Szalavitz notes:

> Most people recover from their addictions without any treatment—professional or self-help—regardless of whether the drug involved is alcohol, crack, methamphetamine, heroin, or cigarettes. One of the largest studies ever conducted (NESARC) found that, of those who had ever qualified for a diagnosis of alcoholism, in the past year only 25 percent still met the criteria for the disorder. Despite this 75 percent recovery rate, only a quarter had gotten any type of help, including AA, and as many were drinking in a low-risk manner as were abstinent.

Since people get better on their own all the time, and so few people succeed through ubiquitous 12-step support groups and treatment programs, Szalavitz raises the radical idea that AA may be worse for many people than doing nothing.

- **AA has stymied the development of effective treatments and policies.** AA is so dominant in American thinking that it has effectively forbidden the development of alternative ways of thinking about and approaching alcoholism and addiction. This is a national tragedy.

- **AA can be harmful.** This negative impact is magnified in the U.S. by the incessant wheedling of people into AA and rehab and the churning by 12-step programs of vulnerable people who enter them and relapse time and again. The epicenter of this churning is Delray Beach, Florida, a haven for addiction treatment centers where graduates remain in the community even after leaving rehab, then relapse time and again. In the previous chapter, Beth's mother emphasized to her daughter that she had the power to change her life, and that AA's "powerlessness" message is wrong and harmful. Rather than helping her to recover in her three rehab stints, it was something that Beth had to overcome in order to become addiction-free.

### Case Study: "My Daughter Died After Repeat Visits to Rehab"

One woman, Sheila Hand, described how her daughter, Elizabeth, after returning to rehabs many times, died before her 30th birthday:

> "Elizabeth, then 24, was in Garrett House—a prison halfway house, part of the NJ Department of Corrections—following a spell in state prison for drug-law violations. She experienced problems related to heroin and other drugs throughout her adult life, and had previously attended several rehabs. Following her release from Garrett House, Elizabeth spent her last years in Florida (where she had previously been in rehab), which then had no legal syringe exchange programs. She died in 2014, aged 29, from endocarditis due to IV drug use with contaminated needles and related conditions."

- **AA convinces people their problem is lifelong.** AA is famous
  for its concept that people are permanently "in recovery," never
  recovered. Even in the cases where they hadn't used a substance
  for decades, they are taught that their addiction is growing
  stronger ("while you're in your AA meeting your addiction is
  in the parking lot doing push-ups"). That is, your addiction is
  a lifetime disease: You *are* an alcoholic, an addict. This was the
  message that Beth rejected, and that Elizabeth never could. The
  danger of believing that they were forever addicted was most
  obvious when they were exposed to their former addictions—
  through medical treatment, or voluntarily. The term "self-
  fulfilling prophecy" instantly springs to mind.

### Case Study: Why Did Philip Seymour Hoffman Relapse after 23 Years?

Philip Seymour Hoffman was abstinent for 23 years after having entered rehab at 22. Then he took some pain medications and
promptly progressed to rampant heroin use. As he was proceeding
toward death, he resignedly explained to people (he re-entered rehab,
then attended 12-step meetings) while he was using, "*I am an addict.*"

The process of recovery was the cause of Hoffman's death, as it was
for a host of rehab graduates (Amy Winehouse, Corey Monteith, Carrie
Fisher, and many grads of Drew Pinsky's "Celebrity Rehab") who died
soon after leaving rehab while promoting their recovery credentials. In
any real area of medical therapeutics, the rehabs (or AA) would have
been liable for malpractice. No one even considers such an idea when it
comes to 12-step programs.

## Why People Refuse—or Drop Out of—AA

AA and other groups may provide needed support for people at critical times. But such support doesn't have to come with the 12 steps and
disease label. Research shows that all forms of addiction support groups
offer equivalent benefits. But, of all forms of support, AA carries the
most baggage. As described by Yale physician Pantalon above: "They are
not appealing to, or have not been effective for, countless others."

AA groups are notable for their high dropout rates—50 percent after the first month and 90 percent and more within a year. Many people simply find AA meetings and their messaging uncomfortable and alienating. Zach was one such outcast, as he will describe.

But first, let's review the first three Steps:

**Step 1:** We admitted we were powerless over our addiction—that our lives had become unmanageable.

**Step 2:** Came to believe that a Power greater than ourselves could restore us to sanity.

**Step 3:** Made a decision to turn our will and our lives over to the care of God as we understood God.

It's our contention that these precepts of powerlessness and the need to turn yourself over to a greater power violate everything research—as presented in positive psychology—tells us: that leaving the past behind, empowerment, and confidence and belief in oneself are the keys to effective therapy.

Here is the experience Zach had at AA.

### Case Study: Zach's Attempt to Join AA

I introduced myself to the group, "My name is Zach. I used to have an addiction to heroin but I no longer do."

Some in the group quietly groaned, complete with eye-rolls; others were silent and looked away. Serious AA members declare that accepting my addiction label was a necessary part of the process, whether I believed it was true or not. But I wasn't prepared to lie.

So perhaps it was unwise to raise my hand during the open-sharing part of the meeting. The chairman invited us to share stories, thoughts, feelings, or "anything related to AA, alcoholism, or other experiences you wish to share."

I spoke again: "My name is Zach and, as I mentioned, I don't think I have an addiction or a disease. But I used to have a pretty serious problem (Zach was still only 25) and it's nice to be here with people making healthy life changes. I really appreciate the support. I have a personal concern about being here. I am not religious at all. I also don't wish to call myself powerless. I like to think I can take credit for the good things in my life just as much as I can take credit for the bad" [group laughter].

"Anyway, I like the idea of having a sponsor, somebody to call on when I need support. If anybody is willing to help me in that way, I would truly appreciate it." Seconds went by—though it felt like minutes—and nobody responded. Nobody talked at all. One more person eventually spoke, breaking an edgy silence. Then the meeting came to a close and, despite my protestations of disbelief, we held hands and recited the Lord's Prayer.

As we headed toward the exit, a man approached me, "Hey man, my name's Paul, and I like what you were saying in there. I'd love to be your sponsor. You wanna take my number?"

I smiled, "Great to meet you, Paul. Yeah, it would be great to talk to you sometime—you don't mind that I'm atheist and won't declare that I'm an addict or that I'm powerless?" I smiled awkwardly.

"No, of course not, I thought the same thing when I started. It took a while to understand the importance of working the Steps. You'll get there."

I missed the subtext of Paul's statement, which was, "You're just naive. You will soon find God." For some reason—perhaps it was because I was vulnerable and desperate for connection of any sort—I trusted him.

Some time later, Paul and I met at a local coffee shop. He walked in with a book in his hand, and sat down next to me. I joked, "So what's up, are you here to recruit me to the Watchtower Society or are you just selling Bibles?" Paul laughed.

"No, not exactly. But God is on my mind. Look, I know you're agnostic but I brought my copy of the Big Book." He held up the book as if I had never seen one (the Big Book is the centerpiece of AA literature) and announced, "There's a chapter here called, 'We Agnostics.' It's AA's way of explaining it's okay to be unsure of your spirituality."

I smiled skeptically. "Well, I'm an atheist. Does AA have a remedy for that?"

He rolled his eyes, "Give me a chance here, man! You might learn something." He read aloud: "We found that as soon as we were able to lay aside prejudice and express even a willingness to believe in a Power greater than ourselves, we commenced to get results, even though it was impossible for any of us to fully define or comprehend that Power, which is God."

The whole experience—the words themselves, the way that Paul was spoon-feeding them to me like an infant—drained my ordinarily deep well of tolerance. I had an epiphany of the magnitude Paul had hoped, but in the opposite direction. I realized once and for all that this program couldn't work for me.

I thought: "I want to be free of addiction, but I also want to be me—a vision Paul and AA evidently don't support." As demoralized as I was, I wasn't prepared to devalue myself further.

Paul finished reading, we finished our coffee together, and that was my last contact with him or AA. My rebound from the misdirection of addiction—and my reconnection with the joys of life—was free of treatment programs or support groups. I guess I have AA and Paul to thank for that.

Zach's response to AA is not unusual, as the many people who enter the Life Process Program and others who reject AA prove.

## Our World Demands Something Better

The people described in this book—children and adults and in-between—have succeeded in overcoming a variety of addictions and other issues in sustaining and sustainable ways. They have found the strength to overcome problems because they believed in themselves, their abilities, and their own value. Along with this existential confidence, which they were sometimes hard-pressed to maintain, they expressed personal values and found—and were helped by others to find—options and opportunities in life.

The societal changes that occurred in the 1960s are still a subject of debate. Did they liberate us, or start us on the road to waves of drug addiction, culminating in our latest opioid-death epidemic? The '60s began the process of stripping away the blinders that prohibited nearly everyone in mainstream society from using the vast array of available chemical experiences, a process today embodied by the legalization of marijuana. This process of new ways of relating to drugs (such as psychedelics) will continue to evolve in as-yet-unknown directions.

Already, there is now no way to avoid exposure to drugs, many of which we introduce to children as pharmaceuticals at increasingly early ages. What are children who take these drugs to make of their own experiences, their own lives?

It's the irony of the modern era: We have the freedom to believe what we want, to be who we want to be, to consume substances. Yet many of us are driven by fear to find a hiding place—Trumpism, addictive use of drugs or alcohol or some other addictive substance or involvement, an artificial identity as an addict. A number of best-sellers with apocalyptic titles such as *Suicide of the West* and *Civilized to Death* posit that, as the world and its population have become more content materially, we are no happier, and seemingly less so, than those who lived in the centuries before, when subsistence living was the norm. This thesis is supported by deepening addiction, depression, and suicide rates. What explains this?

Overarching everything in America is the loss of intimacy and community, a lack of connection to the world around us, and often a loss of connection to our own selves. *This disconnect to our own true selves is a central part of seeing ourselves and our children as diseased beings.*

# Recovery in the Real World 11

Nearly all of us pride ourselves on endorsing the science behind climate change, which we regard as undeniable. We (rightfully) fear the disastrous consequences of the powerful interests that are rejecting this reality. But the overwhelming mass of educated Americans bear a striking resemblance to climate deniers when it comes to mental health and addiction. And the consequences are real and tragic, as witnessed by our suicide and drug-death epidemics.

## We Already Know the Truths in This Book but Ignore Them, Part I: Suicide

In 2018, several prominent people committed suicide, including Kate Spade and Anthony Bourdain, whose case was mentioned in Chapter 6, when a journalist told Stanton that someone should have discussed Bourdain's early traumas with him when he became suicidal. Trauma-seeking therapy is now the most popular form of psychotherapy for depression. *And it isn't working.* Quite the reverse. While mental health commentators uniformly recommended that people instantly seek psychiatric help (which both Anthony Bourdain and Kate Spade did), the CDC issued a report, "Suicide Rising Across the U.S.: More than a mental health concern."

The alarming phenomenon the report presented: **"The U.S. suicide rate increased 25 percent from 1999 to 2016, even though the rates of psychiatric diagnosis and treatment also greatly increased."** While experts reported with depressing predictability that depression was a medical disease, the CDC instead found that "suicide is rarely caused by any single factor. In fact, many people who die by suicide are not known to have a diagnosed mental health condition at the time of death." The *New York Times* writer Benedict Carey was driven to present "How Suicide Quietly Morphed Into a Public Health Crisis," a piece that reeled under the confusion:

The rise in suicide rates has coincided over the past two decades with a vast increase in the number of Americans given a diagnosis of depression or anxiety, and treated with medication.

The number of people taking an open-ended prescription for an antidepressant is at a historic high. More than 15 million Americans have been on the drugs for more than five years, a rate that has more than tripled since 2000.

**But if treatment is so helpful, why hasn't its expansion halted or reversed suicide trends?** (Carey's words, our emphasis.)

"This is the question I've been wrestling with: Are we somehow causing increased morbidity and mortality with our interventions?" said Dr. Thomas Insel, former director of the National Institute of Mental Health and now president of Mindstrong Health, which makes technology to monitor people with mental health problems.

"I don't think so," Dr. Insel continued. "I think the increase in demand for the services is so huge that the expansion of treatment thus far is simply insufficient to make a dent in what is a huge social change."

Thus the neuroscientist and psychiatrist who headed the National Institute of Mental Health from 2002-2015, during the simultaneous meteoric rises in suicides and depression diagnoses and treatment, interprets that failure as *proof* that we should redouble our efforts to diagnose and treat more people for their mental diseases. In doing so, he expresses the obligatory mantra: "People deny their mental illness because of the stigma they unfortunately attach to their disease, denial they must be encouraged/forced to overcome and then pushed into treatment."

Recall in our discussion of disease stigma in Chapter 6 the research showing that young people who self-label their mental conditions are more likely to become depressed, and less likely to feel that they are capable of changing. When the reporter suggested that the way to have dealt with Anthony Bourdain was to uncover his life traumas with him, Stanton indicated that the best approach, per Martin Seligman's and Angela Duckworth's positive psychology models, as well as reams of data, was to direct the suffering person's attention to their purposes in life, their sustaining values, relationships, and goals, and to work with them to plan forward in fulfilling these positive visions of themselves and their lives.

This unquestioned acceptance of dysfunctional medical, disease panaceas is regularly rehashed at the *Times* itself. As the CDC made clear that most suicides can't be traced to a mental disorder, the *Times's* psychiatric expert Richard Friedman declared: "Suicide is a medical problem that is almost always associated with several common and treatable mental illnesses." The *Times* consistently purveys the mythical narrative, also disproved by research, that our opioid crisis is due to people receiving painkiller prescriptions who become addicted and die, even as painkiller prescriptions have declined dramatically over the past five years while drug deaths continue to accelerate. The *Times* reinterprets history to backdate this interpretation through the 19th century (see Chapter 2).

### Solving the Suicide Puzzle—Stanton's brother

The CDC report on suicide portrays it as a complex and human action, which Friedman and others insist on reducing to a medical problem that we can treat.

Stanton's brother, several years older than Stanton, Steven (not his real name) killed himself at age 59. He was—like Spade and Bourdain—a person with some social advantages, but deeper underlying discontents, none of which in Steven's case comprised mental illness.

Steven was an insecure person who accomplished quite a bit but who never felt comfortable in his own skin. He received a Ph.D. in physics from a prestigious university, but didn't land a position in academia. Instead, he worked at a variety of software companies over a spotty career. He married and had two children, then divorced and had a second marriage, which was substantial and loving.

In his late 50s, although he had a real family life and friendships, as did Bourdain and Spade, unlike them Steven had not created a secure professional identity. He finally took a trial job lasting six months, at the end of which he wasn't given a permanent position. He went home and gassed himself in his family garage. Meanwhile, a financial investment he had made in real estate failed.

Although he was economically challenged, Steven wasn't in real danger of losing his middle-class position (his wife worked). He *was* in danger of doubting himself and losing his tenuous hold on self-respect. This experience was so painful to Steven that he preferred to die instead.

Steven had friends and family and access to psychiatrists and mental health workers, as did Spade and Bourdain. He had no obviously diagnosable mental disorder. But he had lost his way financially, and then existentially, in his sense that he no longer felt he deserved to live.

## Answers to Suicide are Complex and Unworkable in America

In its report, the CDC—the universally respected health protection agency of the United States—detailed the needed steps for preventing suicide. They are the opposite of providing drugs to cure a disease.

### CDC Guidelines: How To Prevent Suicide

- Identify and support people at risk of suicide.

- Teach coping and problem-solving skills to help people manage challenges with their relationships, jobs, health, or other concerns.

- Promote safe and supportive environments. This includes safely storing medications and firearms to reduce access among people at risk.

- Offer activities that bring people together so they feel connected and not alone.

- Connect people at risk to effective and coordinated mental and physical healthcare.

- Expand options for temporary help (including providing financial help) for those struggling to make ends meet.

Steven could have been helped by a financial consultation and assistance, which seems simple enough. Yet the CDC's economic, skills, and community solutions for suicide—solutions at the heart of this book—were ignored. It's as though we don't care to help people who might kill themselves, preferring instead to ritualistically repeat our favored mantras.

## We Already Know the Truths in This Book but Ignore Them, Part II: Addiction

Americans have been taught to view recovery from addiction as a permanent state of being "in recovery," a term whose meaning everyone in the U.S. knows. The disease of addiction, goes this thinking, is never-ending. It can be held at bay only through daily struggle, like fighting the devil.

But that's not the developmental way of looking at things. It's also, as the data we have repeatedly cited show, not true. People develop greater self-control and maturity over their lives, change their priorities, and leave addiction and other life-defeating issues behind. It is the nature of being human. This was true for Margaret, Joseph, and Ozzie, whose identities we saw shift later in life; for DJ, Mark, and Gerard, who overcame childhood bumps in the road; and for Beth, Matt, and Zach, who overcame persistent, dangerous drug habits as they transitioned to adulthood.

## A Note about Developmental Psychology

Developmental psychology often is mistakenly equated with child psychology. They are not the same thing. Psychology recognizes that development, change, maturation, etc., take place throughout the lifespan. We are all always evolving. This fluid human presence in the universe is also a Buddhist notion, as Stanton and Ilse Thompson show in their book, *Recover!: An Empowering Program to Help You Stop Thinking Like an Addict and Reclaim Your Life.*

This empowered perspective is so obviously true that the Substance Abuse and Mental Health Services Administration (SAMHSA), the government agency charged with formulating drug and alcohol treatment policy, redefined recovery in 2011. It began by surveying the leading specialists in the mental health field:

> "The definition is the product of a year-long effort by SAMHSA and a wide range of partners in the behavioral healthcare community and other fields to develop a working definition of recovery that captures the essential, common experiences of those recovering from mental disorders and substance use disorders, along with major guiding principles that support the recovery definition."

The result was "Recovery Defined—A Unified Working Definition and Set of Principles," which SAMHSA meant to be a roadmap to recovery built on the best of current thinking. This definition is built on a conception of recovery as a developmental process.

## SAMHSA's Redefinition of Recovery

"Recovery is a process of change whereby individuals work to improve their own health and wellness and to live a meaningful life in a community of their choice while striving to achieve their full potential."

### SAMHSA's Principles of Recovery

- Is person-driven.
- Occurs via many pathways.
- Is holistic.
- Is supported by peers.
- Is supported through relationships.
- Is culturally-based and influenced.
- Is supported by addressing trauma.
- Involves individual, family, and community strengths and responsibility.
- Is based on respect.
- Emerges from hope.

SAMHSA's Recovery Initiative identifies four domains that support recovery:

- Health: overcoming or managing one's disease(s) as well as living in a physically and emotionally healthy way.
- Home: a stable and safe place to live that supports recovery.
- Purpose: meaningful daily activities, such as a job, school, volunteerism, family caretaking, or creative endeavors, and the independence, income and resources to participate in society.
- Community: relationships and social networks that provide support, friendship, love, and hope.

A person recovers by living a purposeful life in a social and community context—as described in this book. This is the consensus view of the people SAMHSA identified as the leading researchers in the addiction and mental disorder and mental health fields.

Lastly, and most important, the SAMHSA Committee never mentions "powerlessness"—the fundamental tenet of 12-step and disease-oriented approaches—but instead points in exactly the opposite direction:

> Recovery is person-driven. Self-determination and self-direction are the foundations for recovery as individuals define their own life goals and design their unique path(s) towards those goals.
> Recovery is built on the multiple capacities, strengths, talents, coping abilities, resources, and inherent value of each individual. Recovery pathways are highly personalized.
> Recovery involves individual, family, and community strengths and responsibility: Individuals, families, and communities have strengths and resources that serve as a foundation for recovery. In addition, **individuals have a personal responsibility for their own self-care and journeys of recovery.** (Our emphasis.)

There's a French saying for this never-ending rediscovery that SAMSHA has embarked on, the same path the data have led us to for decades: "*Plus ça change, plus c'est la même chose.*"

When the major governmental institution charged with addressing substance issues and mental health in America redefines the basic concept in its combined areas of concern—relying on the country's best-regarded experts in the mental health and addiction fields to do so—one might expect people to sit up and take notice.

And yet, a fair description is that nothing (or next to nothing) has changed in this country's approach to addiction and mental health. Here are four reasons:

- American concepts of addiction and mental illness are embedded in our culture.

- Other governmental agencies (the National Institute on Drug Abuse and the Surgeon General) fight directly against the idea that recovery is a self-directed process built around people's and communities' strengths. (See previous section on suicide.)

- A treatment industry predicated on our misconceptions remains incredibly profitable, despite its constant failures.

- A cadre of recovering people—actually a small, but highly visible, segment of those who face these problems—have staked their lives on promoting and preserving the status quo.

This last barrier is forbidding. As all data show, the percentage of people who recover relative to the number who are exposed to AA and the 12 steps is small, and those who recover through AA are far fewer than those who quit addictions on their own. Yet there are enough of them overall, they are so vocal, and their recovery tales are so woven into the fabric of American life that even the leading disease critics in America fear to take on the recovery behemoth. Meanwhile, those who quit addictions or alcohol problems on their own are either so wary of discussing this process (like Drew Barrymore), or so unwilling to label themselves as having been addicts or alcoholics in the first place, that they remain silent—or else take on the risk of being attacked.

### A Lost Girlhood Recovered—But No One Listens

One best-seller that fulfilled the American mantras of alcoholism, addiction, and recovery was Koren Zailckas's 2005 *Smashed: Story of a Drunken Girlhood*. Zailckas began getting drunk regularly in her early teens, and continued right through her college career. Americans loved hearing this story.

Then Zailckas quit alcoholic drinking when she graduated, got a job, and formed a stable relationship. She now writes novels about people who aren't alcoholics. When these things happened, she lost her audience. Why? She didn't go to AA and refused to label herself an alcoholic. "It just didn't feel true to me." "*Wrong answer*," those in the know declared. As a result, she gets responses like this one on Amazon: "She is so obviously an alcoholic that she really does a disservice to other young women because she leads one to believe that AA (and labeling oneself an alcoholic forever) is not necessary."

Stanton discussed this obligation in America of taking on an addict or alcoholic identity, and its dysfunctionality, when in fact we see that the best route is to avoid and to escape this identity. AA, it is true, is a community, and kudos to them for that. But they are a community built on an assumption of permanent human frailty and dependence—whether on drugs, alcohol, AA, or medicine. And so America is blockaded from approaches and solutions based on values and purpose and built around non-disease-identity communities. As a result, we are being defeated as a society in righting ourselves through normal social development.

# Raising Our Non-Addicted Next Generation

Although they don't form a club, it's not hard to find examples like Zach's and Koren Zailckas's of people who overcome addictions, often in early adulthood, sometimes later, often when they form stable, mature relationships, or, like Margaret or Rosabeth below, when they become parents. The data showing that people mature out as they proceed through their 20s and 30s, reviewed in Chapter 5, expresses this phenomenon. As a result, it is bad news for natural recovery that more and more Americans are either deciding not to have children or delaying parenthood. But such personal and family maturity and responsibility are still the best route to recovery.

## How to Raise a Child without Your Addiction

On the other side of this equation for parents who have had addictive experiences themselves is how they will break this chain of addiction with their children. To start with, nearly all will begin this freeing process by having conquered their own addictions. Nonetheless, the task of raising the next generation remains.

### Case Study: Harm Reduction and Drinking Like a Mother

Rosabeth had a long history of problem drinking—sometimes remaining drunk days at a time in her 20s, before she was married—and also of depression, having gone on and off antidepressants. But she never sacrificed her dedication to her work to her drinking. She also formed a good marriage, with Ray, a tolerant and supportive husband who was aware of, but not overbearing about, Rosabeth's drinking tendencies.

But because of her fears of her own and her family's past (several relatives had mental health and alcohol problems), Rosabeth was reluctant to have a child, which she knew Ray wanted. Indeed, as the eldest son of a large family, Ray provided a whole supportive clan with a rooting interest in their having a child.

Rosabeth became pregnant. She worried whether she had had a drinking bout after the baby had been conceived, even considered an abortion, but decided the fetus was okay. However, during her pregnancy, based on a trusted pediatrician's advice, she drank occasionally: "It's better to have a one or two drinks, rather than to build up an urge so that you drink full out even one night in your pregnancy."

And that's what Rosabeth did, cutting back her drinking to modest levels—which is today considered by some to be child abuse. Yet data consistently show that babies of moderate or occasional drinking mothers—even those drinking in the earliest trimester—have normal outcomes. This is a finding has been <u>reproduced for decades</u>, and ignored, even when presented in the most mainstream channels, like the *Harvard Medical School Health Blog*.

Rosabeth had a bouncing baby boy, Benjamin. She was a devoted mother, but she had a demanding job, which she also loved. That was fine too—Ray and Rosabeth had resolved not to be helicopter parents, and loved letting Benjamin explore the world, as appropriate, for himself.

It seems Benjamin just wasn't inclined to be a problem child. Rosabeth claimed that she was lucky that way, since she reckoned that her own genetic line was filled with emotional and addictive problems. But consider that Benjamin had a devoted mother and father and a large family who cared about, nurtured, and encouraged him to become a contented, independent person.

Will Benjamin develop the alcoholism and mental illness that marked his mother's family? While it's true that mental illness and addiction in a family make it somewhat more likely that children will develop these problems, the typical outcome is that, like Rosabeth, parents free their offspring of this legacy. They do so by reversing the conditions and outlooks that led to it, for themselves and their children.

Research consistently shows that, although at higher risk for drinking problems, the majority of children of alcoholics don't become alcoholics themselves. Indeed, Harburg and his associates in the Tecumseh, MI cross-generational study found that daughters of heavy-drinking fathers were *less likely* than other women to develop a drinking problem. Apparently, they learned a painful lesson from their fathers. They drank less because they associated with abstinent or light-drinking friends or partners.

## Case Study: A Senator Tells Us So

During the hearing for confirmation of Brett Kavanaugh as a U.S. Supreme Court justice, Minnesota Senator Amy Klobuchar—whose memoir recounted the painful story of having an alcoholic father— asked Kavanaugh if he had ever blacked out. He answered, "Have you?" Klobuchar declared: "I have no drinking problem. When you have a parent that is an alcoholic, you are pretty careful about (your) drinking."

Isn't that common sense when considering people given the room and support to develop normally? People who watched the hearing accepted it as such.

## The Bartender Interventionist

One night, Stanton and some colleagues were at a particularly well-run bar in Chicago. They fell to talking with the bar's manager, a young man who told them, "When I see someone 'drowning their sorrows' in booze, I'll take time to go up to them and to ask them how they're feeling, to show concern for them, and to suggest that they find a more positive activity—go see their family, a friend, or a movie." This was his version of a "brief intervention" that Yale emergency medicine professor Michael Pantalon has proven to be so effective, as described in Chapter 10.

The man continued: "My father was an alcoholic who abandoned our family. Years later I looked him up—it was too late to change his life, but I told him that I forgave him. And I have lived my life, now that I have children, to make sure that I'm not anything like him, including—especially—how I drink."

In a similar way, most people overcome their past traumas—in fact (per Seligman and Tierney, as described in Chapter 6) they learn and benefit from them. The research by Vincent Felitti on which Gabor Maté relies for his trauma-based theory of addiction identified adverse childhood experiences (ACEs) as causes of alcoholism and drug addiction. Felitti found that 3.5 percent of children with 4 or more such ACEs *"ever injected drugs"* and 16 percent *"consider themselves"* an alcoholic." Both of these outcomes, we have seen, implicate life-stage and social-cultural factors. While the 16 percent figure is distressing, it was only five percentage points higher than those with fewer ACEs.

Of course, we don't recommend family duress and parental neglect and abuse as ways to strengthen children. Yet trauma—from mild even up to severe trauma—does not create an inevitable, even a likely, legacy. Examples abound, like Bill Clinton and his alcoholic stepfather who beat his mother, and Barack Obama, who had a biological father who deserted the family, never contacted his son, and developed alcoholism himself and died young. Yet, not even the worst Clinton and Obama haters imagine their daughters to be anything other than doted-on children of privilege.

At the same time, let us note that a minority of addicted parents, who nearly always lack adequate social resources, are incapable of raising their children. Such parents show their family survival instincts, not by being able to achieve their own recovery, but by struggling to do so and sometimes by permitting—or wanting—their children to be raised by relatives or foster parents. Stanton worked as a public defender representing such parents, who are kept in touch with their children through family court, sometimes having visitation rights and trying to regain custody, sometimes having their parental rights taken from them.

This is unfortunate, even under less-than-ideal familial circumstances. As one foster parent told us:

> I've had 17 foster kids, a majority from such families. Sometimes, family members recovered enough to resume parenting, which is the ideal outcome, but usually after many years, and with some repeated failures. The kids, by the way, having been exposed to this parental behavior, are generally the most likely to avoid alcohol and drugs themselves. Yet even in the most difficult cases, I've learned that it is important for the kids and their birth parents to maintain as much contact as they reasonably can. Even if full reunification can't happen, birth families usually are helpful in raising their children if given a chance.

The drive to separate children from families is one more example of the need for harm reduction, meaning to accept the nonperfectionist goal of striving for achievable outcomes in the absence of ideal ones.

For her part, Rosabeth, a person with considerable personal and family resources, overcame disturbing life experiences and addictive problems of her own to be an effective parent. She—along with a well-chosen husband—seemingly had placed her son on a positive life track. Her story demonstrates, as the data indicate, that parental attitudes and choices are the most important influences in childhood substance use and overall mental health.

## Recovery Nation

Stanton was interviewed in a podcast by two hosts celebrating *Recovery Nation*, an organization that offers self-help resources to people struggling with addiction, although Stanton is not on board with the idea of restricting one's life to a recovering identity. One of the hosts spoke about teaching her children that they were born addicted due their family history, and never to drink or take drugs. Stanton doesn't usually talk about his family life in discussing addiction and mental health issues. But in this case, he told his podcast hosts: "Both my wife and I had brothers who committed suicide. Neither of us ever sat our three children down and told them, 'You know suicide and depression run in our family, so you need constantly to guard against them.'"

Stanton often appears in public forums with people with serious addiction histories. Of course, by the time these individuals make such public appearances, they are leading stable, productive lives. Stanton always asks them, "How do your children deal with alcohol?" In one such debate, the former head of treatment at Hazelden answered that his two children were moderate, take-it-or-leave-it drinkers, which is typical with prominent recovery spokespeople Stanton encounters.

Stanton replied, "That's remarkable—you short-circuited your family heritage!" (The man's father drank alcoholically and had been abusive.) "How did you accomplish that?" Hazelden's former chief clinician answered, "I threatened to beat them if they drank like I did."

Stanton offered this response in place of the mocking, unhelpful one given by the treatment professional:

> "First, I think you created an emotionally and financially stable home for your children. Second, I think you loved and encouraged them, and provided them with all the opportunities you could to allow them to fulfill themselves, telling them, 'You can be whoever you want to be.' Finally, although you made them aware of the need to be mindful of their drinking, you didn't burden them with an

alcoholic identity that would always be lurking in their lives and that they would have to struggle to escape."

These are the pillars of childrearing for encouraging a child's self-determination and integrity that are the foundations for avoiding addictions and debilitating mental health issues, regardless of a family's addictive heritage. All parents, not just those with family or personal histories of substance problems, face the same challenges in raising their own children.

We take a values approach. We believe that nearly all people have critical values that, ultimately, can rule out addiction for them. Of course, even in wonderful families, children sometimes run into difficulties. But the values with which to confront such problems can be, and usually are, present in the child and family (as they were ultimately for David and Nic Sheff), along with community, school, and religious groups.

## 12 Values that Prevent Addiction

These 12 bedrock values fight addiction.

1. **Purpose,** above all. It's not what addictive things or obstacles children encounter (there is bound to be something), but their guiding light propelling them forward that guarantees they will avoid or overcome addiction.

2. **Achievement.** Valuing accomplishing things, making a positive contribution.

3. **Caring about self** (self-esteem). Rejecting things that would harm them.

4. **Caring about others** (empathy/compassion). Addictions are harmful to people whom the child, or adult, cares about. Concern for loved ones and other people overrules addiction.

5. **Responsibility.** Addictions impair people, making it difficult for them to fulfill responsibilities. Knowing the child must fulfill his or her obligations thus rules out addiction.

6. **Awareness/mindfulness.** Enjoying thinking, being aware and mindful, is the opposite of the mindlessness of addiction.

7. **Adventure.** Addictions are sought because of their

predictability, so that children who enjoy the challenges of life aren't likely to become addicted.

8. **Pleasure and fun**. Addictions aren't fun, but rather are barriers against fear, so that seeing the world around one as enjoyable is the opposite of addiction.

9. **Social, political, religious commitments**. Engagement opposes addiction. Uncle Ozzie's labor activism that caused him to quit a quarter-century, four-pack-a-day cigarette addiction is one example of such a commitment.

10. **Financial health**. Addictions such as smoking, drugs, alcohol, gambling, shopping, *et al,* burn money. Being concerned about financial health and not wasting money and personal resources is an antithesis of addiction.

11. **Efficacy, agency, empowerment**. Feeling that one can make a difference is the opposite of the ineffectuality that leads to addiction—this is the keynote to all successful therapies. (We place efficacy so far down the list not because it isn't fundamental, but rather because it grows from enacting all other values in life and from seeing that you as a parent—and ultimately the child—control their own destinies. We turn to this in the next chapter.)

12. **Maturity.** Having a secure adult identity—one that causes a person to see themselves as a capable, potent, contributing member of society with responsibilities toward others—is a bulwark against addiction. (Remember Joseph, who rejected his addict identity when he became a respected member of his community, and Rosabeth, who stands for all parents.)

# Developing Purpose, Efficacy, and Independence

13

## Purpose, Purpose, Purpose

We list purpose and achievement first among the values here. There is some controversy in doing so, because achievement on its own has achieved a bit of a bad name. In Chapter 7 we described the alarming results from asking UCLA's entering students if they "felt overwhelmed by all I had to do." In 1985, 18 percent said they did; in 2016 the figure was 41 percent, prompting the New York Times to ask in 2017, "Why Are More American Teenagers Than Ever Suffering From Severe Anxiety?"

Alissa Quart wrote *Hothouse Kids: How the Pressure to Succeed Threatens Childhood*, a book that, for obvious reasons, resonated with many people. Kids find that the demands placed on them exceed their confidence in their ability to produce the results others want for them, which they have internalized. The result of this discrepancy between demands and personal resources is anxiety.

We believe that this split between achievement and contentment is a false dichotomy. Instead, we believe that achievement, as a part of purpose, is fundamental to human contentment.

## The Nearly Century-Long Terman Study

You've read teasers, like "How to lead a long and fulfilling life," often selling some product or course. But that topic has been investigated thoroughly in the longest-running study of the course of human development ever conducted, the Terman Study at Stanford University.

Begun in 1921 to study geniuses (Lewis Terman developed the original IQ test), this research has evolved into an examination of the factors that lead to success and happiness over the lifespan.

The findings of this 95-year study are remarkable—direct and clear-cut—yet still surprising.

It turns out that an easy, stress-free life doesn't make you happier and definitely won't help you live longer.

Analyzing large groups of people over many decades allows researchers to uncover connections between cause and effect that short-term studies naturally miss. (It's really hard to know if what I did in my 20s actually made me happy in my 70s unless you catch me at both stages of life.)

So who tended to live the longest, most fulfilling lives? **The people who actively pursued their goals, and were highly engaged in that pursuit.**

In fact, many of those who worked the hardest turned out to live the longest. According to The Longevity Project (part of the Terman Study), actually achieving your lifelong dreams doesn't matter. Pursuing those dreams is what counts:

> We did not find that precisely living out your dreams matters much for your health. *It was not the happiest or the most relaxed older participants who lived the longest. It was those who were most engaged in pursuing their goals.* Those who were the most successful were the ones least likely to die at any given age. In fact, those men who were carefree, undependable, and unambitious in childhood and very unsuccessful in their careers had a whopping increase in their mortality risk. (Our emphasis.)

Of course "success" means—and definitely should mean—different things to different people. That's why determining what success means to you, and then actively working to achieve your definition of success, is the key. Living a laid-back, carefree, stress-free life may sound great—but as the study shows, "happy-go-lucky" people don't thrive. Persistent, conscientious people thrive.

## Assisting People to Find Purpose

In the Life Process Program, people learn skills and attitudes, and use their beliefs and personal assets, including relationships and communities, to leave addiction behind.

But underlying progress against addiction is the feeling clients develop that their lives are purposeful, that they have goals and meaning with which their addiction interferes, and so they are motivated to leave addiction behind. Purpose is like a true north, one that allows people to overcome bumps and curves in the road because, ultimately, they know where they are headed. They have sources of meaning in life that will always be more important than resuming their addiction.

Purpose is not something that can be GIVEN. It is something to be uncovered amidst a person's values, sometimes with careful guidance and help.

### Case Study: Pursuing Purpose within LPP

Here is an example of interaction in which Zach gently worked with a client to help discover the client's sense of purpose. Any information that would identify the client has been changed to protect his privacy.

The client was skeptical when he first began LPP, but didn't know what else to do or where else to go.

After going through a series of preliminary questions and responses, the client said he was seeking to extend his free time activities into more meaningful arenas. Zach, in his role as coach, responded in some detail:

> You mentioned early in the program that you didn't think it was a good idea to take advice from others about what *should* motivate you. I agree, and you have done some valuable reflection on your own since then. I'm happy to offer observations about your answers to the questions and perhaps you can build from there.
>
> You feel that intelligence is a strong skill of yours; also independence. You're not totally averse to being part of a system or having a consistent routine, but you also mentioned that you are uncomfortable being told what to do and how to do it for very long.
>
> You are taking some impressive steps and putting in hard work to conform to standards at work, in your social life, and with your partner. It sounds like you've been working hard to do what's expected of you:
>
> - **At work:** as part of achieving a promotion in the long run;
>
> - **In your relationship:** the other day you had a meaningful conversation with your girlfriend and truly listened to her in a way that made you want to rethink the way you interact with her.

But I'm hearing you say, loud and clear, that something is missing. Am I right about that?

The way you've described your personality and signature skills suggests to me that you might benefit from becoming innovative as a practice. Have you ever thought about creating something (perhaps some content) that *you* get control over? Something you can offer to people, but which doesn't necessarily obligate you to them?

You're a reader, you love telling stories, and you've enjoyed taking risks in the past, so this could be something like starting a podcast or writing a book, or doing something as daring as trying stand-up comedy.

Or you could write out a curriculum for a class that you teach outside of work (or online). There really are a lot of options here, and maybe none of those seem appealing, but you can imagine similar pursuits.

Such involvements—or something else you choose—may be of great benefit to you. You deserve to do things:

- that capture your attention and match your personality;
- that you can do while working your (more routine/scheduled) day job (of course, any new involvements could be just hobbies but could also turn cash-positive);
- that involve some risk, which you said is important to you, but with no enormous pressure to keep it going. As you say, you wish you had pursuits that you could drop anytime without hurting anyone, including yourself.

There really is no limit to how far you could take it if you chose to do so.

For any feelings that your personality is a "curse" you *do* seem to have a gift for seeing the world in a way very few people do. And since you thrive on doing your "own thing," then you may find great benefit in generating your own interesting experiences while also having a consistent routine to keep you grounded.

The client reviewed various options he has entertained for writing, and resolved to move forward. This client is now working on a memoir, and beginning a video blog for students who want to write poetry, on their own, outside of the college classroom. He's nearly done with LPP, and things aren't perfect, but he's moving in the direction of meaning/purpose and believes he can sustain it.

As for children, other elements that we list—fun, adventure, intimacy, community—are also critical contributors to a fulfilled life. However, *achieving contentment while avoiding anxiety results when children (and adults) work within their values to pursue meaningful goals, utilizing skills they have developed.* There is no alternative.

## Efficacy and Empowerment

There is a science of empowerment (also called-self-efficacy). Motivational interviewing (MI) has been adopted in virtually all therapies (except when it is ruled out by the dictates of the 12 steps) as the most effective type of addiction treatment. A review of every systematic study of alcoholism treatment conducted by William Miller, who developed MI, and Reid Hester showed MI to have produced the best results, combined with "brief interventions": minimal treatment in which people are provided information, periodic check-ins, and encouragement to find their own solutions.

In Chapter 10, on the ineffectiveness of AA, we reviewed the work of Yale Medical School emergency medicine professor Michael Pantalon. Pantalon's research group at Yale found brief motivational approaches to be, by far, the most effective means for addressing addiction. Their approach involves a "recovery coach"—a trained helper who does not impose a 12-step recovery model but rather points the person to his or her own resources: "Rather than confrontationally telling someone what he or she has to do, through motivational intervention **we ask the individual to tell us why they might, of their own free will, choose to change**. The results are often stunning." (Our emphasis.)

Motivational interviewing is presented throughout this book. It involves referring people to their own values as the source for their motivation to change. Essential to this approach is the idea that the individual is the agent of his or her own recovery. (The same as holds for the SAMHSA redefinition of recovery reviewed in Chapter 11.) The bottom line for MI is self-efficacy. That is, people's belief that they can realize their desires and goals in life; that they are empowered, rather than powerless.

In the case described above, Zach demonstrated this motivational approach by listening carefully to the client, organizing and feeding back to the man what he had been describing about himself and his life in such a way that helped him to discover his own vocation.

## On Being a Parent—Inspiring Independence

Recognizing people's own values and understanding how motivational interviewing succeeds is to embrace your own efficacy as a parent, your critical role in whether a child becomes addicted. These values focus on the keynotes of purpose, responsibility, and connection with others, while living in and enjoying the here-and-now. These values, and those underlying MI, also mean that you recognize the integrity and independence of your child as his or her own human being

One obstacle to good parenting is fear. We discussed in Chapter 9 David Sheff's discovery of his impotence as a parent, which was overtaken by fear—justified, of course, by the potentially lethal or otherwise life-destroying consequences of his son Nic's drug addiction. But what is the answer to such fear? He and all parents might want to avoid their children taking street meth—even though Adderall provides them with the same chemical. But Nic also had a drinking problem. So no alcohol. And the elder Sheff seemingly wants young people to avoid marijuana. That can be your goal, as unlikely as all of this avoidance is to occur.

But there are seemingly endless things for young people to be afraid of growing up today.

## Overselling Trauma—The Fearful Society

Today's parents often operate as agents of fear. Fear of going outside, of the dangers of the street, surely of the dangers of drugs and alcohol. They worry, understandably, about the damage young people do to themselves, stemming from emotional problems, suicide, and addiction.

### Case Study: Overprotecting a Child

Eugene and Deborah were two people who had overcome trauma in their own lives. Deborah's mother died when she was five, and her father was an unreliable alcoholic. As soon as Deborah graduated high school in the Midwest, she moved to New York (where she had relatives), got her own apartment with a friend, got a job, and went to college at night. She graduated with a communications degree and became the head of public relations for the company she was already working for.

She met Eugene while managing a health promotion campaign. He had designed a phone app that assisted people to track their health habits and to find referrals when they encountered problems. The product was a clever combination of technology and human savvy. Eugene had developed these skill areas in response to the duress of his own upbringing. After his parents divorced he lived with his father and stepmother. He finally revealed to his own mother that his stepmother was abusing him—separating him from her own two children, denying him food at meals, and refusing to allow him to participate in after-school activities. He was 13.

His mother had the strength and good sense to immediately initiate Eugene's return to her home, which was more spare economically, but where Eugene was of course treated as a full participant along with his biological sister. He was content and he thrived—a bit of a nerd but highly skilled technically and well-liked by other kids. When Deborah met Eugene later in their lives, she instantly told her best friend, "I'm going to marry him." Deborah had learned to recognize and to value a reliable man, in the absence of having one in her own background.

Deborah and Eugene had a daughter, Veronica, who was as privileged as a child can be. Her parents earned very good livings, and they doted on her almost as a direct function of the care they had missed in their own childhoods. At times friends noted that Veronica's parents acted as though they never wanted her to experience any discomfort—to lead a perfectly untraumatized, unchallenged existence. People noticed that they were carrying Veronica from place to place; they almost seemed not to want her feet to touch the ground!

This created increasing adjustment difficulties for Veronica and her parents. Although Deborah and Eugene were kind and generous themselves, they seemed to be blind to—or at least ignored—Veronica's treatment of others. For instance, whenever Deborah and Eugene hired a caretaker to look after Veronica while they went out, Veronica became angry and lashed out at the sitter. One evening they came home to find the babysitter in tears due to the screaming and insults of a seven-year-old.

Although they were apologetic and paid the sitter extra, Eugene and Deborah proved incapable of creating any consequences for Veronica's misbehavior. As a result she had few friends at school and preferred her parents' company, shutting out anyone else who entered their sphere. Her parents gave up on leaving her behind. Even as a teenager, she went to dinner and shows with her parents. "How will she separate herself to go to college?" their friends wondered.

Problems like these are impossible to ignore forever. In her teens, her parents placed Veronica in a special discipline-oriented private school. But, as Zach's work demonstrates, unless the underlying home dynamic is altered, school-imposed discipline is stopgap and will provide only limited personal transformation. And Eugene and Deborah still strove to interject themselves into every conflict, every challenge, Veronica confronted in life—even at the school. They couldn't stop themselves.

Among the greatest challenges, perhaps the greatest, faced by parents is allowing children to act independently and to become their own person. We have discussed fear as an underlying motivation in addictions of all sorts, causing people to seek refuge from challenges they don't feel up to meeting. The greatest remedy for this feeling of self-doubt and confusion is for children to experience life in the raw, directly and on their own terms, and to deal with the consequences for themselves.

The end state of this process of responsibility and connection and independence is maturity, a state at the opposite end of the spectrum from addiction. True to the developmental process, maturity is a naturally occurring event in most people's lives. Today, permitting independence is often parents' greatest challenge.

### Case Study: Joanne and Her Daughter, Closeness and Separation

All parents face the dilemma of creating a close, loving relationship while understanding that the relationship cannot grow closer forever, and in fact must become more distant. The goal is to help the child form his or her independent identity.

Joanne was a mother who felt that necessity acutely. She had grown up with a single mother. She and her mother lived in limited circumstances in a well-off neighborhood, and Joanne always felt like the poor relation. Sometimes, in order to measure up to those who were better off than her, she went overboard. For example, trying to be appealingly thin, she developed an eating disorder.

But she got good grades, and had jobs on weekends and summers. She had to work to pay her own way through college. With this background, Joanne resolved to use college as a ladder to move upward in life. She married an attractive and ambitious man who went to work in the financial industry, and who provided her with a lovely home in a fashionable suburb.

However, that solution to life's challenges didn't work for Joanne. Her husband had very different values from hers, which became apparent after they had a daughter, Lana. Joanne's values also differed from the lifestyles of many her prosperous neighbors, who failed to appreciate her interest in working to help others. When Lana was five, Joanne divorced.

It was a difficult divorce; her husband contested every cent. Although Joanne was a capable, independent person, she worried about whether she would be able to provide the kind of life she had wanted for Lana. In the meantime, using her limited spousal support, she enrolled in a program to become a therapist herself.

Joanne was very close with her daughter. But she always had a purpose in mind. As Joanne put it, "There is no conflict between closeness and independence with a child. The more love and security a child feels, the better able to separate they are." Although she was always available to Lana, Lana readily engaged with others and separated from her mother—including her visitations with her father (making a good thing of necessity) and going to school, sleepovers, and summer camp. Lana knew how to pack her own suitcase.

Still, Joanne worried about Lana's going to college, which for Joanne had to mark a major demarcation in their relationship. How could she afford to send Lana to a good school she had been accepted to in another state? Joanne resolved to make do, and Lana also worked and contributed to her college expenses.

Joanne had a close friend who was more cautious and protective of her daughter, who was the same age as Lana. When it came time for the friend's daughter to go to college, she wouldn't allow her to go very far away. "There are just too many dangers out there, like drugs and sex." In fact, Joanne was aware that Lana had consumed alcohol and used drugs. But she had discussed her drug use with her daughter. Lana had made good choices throughout her school and social life, so Joanne was confident that substances would never dominate Lana's life.

The friend's daughter seemed to accept the situation of remaining in her hometown. She married her high school boyfriend and dropped out of a local college she was attending. She had a child with the man, then they separated. The young woman's life spiraled downward, and—paradoxically, given her mother's desire to protect her from sex and drugs—she became mired in drug use.

Joanne, of course, felt deeply for her friend's situation, and did all that she could to support her. But their divergent experiences caused her to reflect:

> "I choose not to operate out of fear. Of course, I was worried about everything bad that could happen to Lana, which involved choices beyond my control, like who Lana would date and her course of study and career. But I saw all along that she made good choices in friends, in school activities, in being physically healthy. And I was always aware that she needed to grow and to achieve her independence. I made every decision about her life with that goal in mind."

There is always uncertainty in this process, which is why so many parents seemingly operate out of fear. It would be an oversimplification, for instance, to say that Joanne's friend's daughter became enmeshed with drugs because she didn't go away to college. Many other events, some of which occurred by chance, had to intervene.

But at some point parents have to accept and embrace this uncertainty as a necessary part of parenting—they can't control their children's fates. All they can do is to provide the soundest possible foundations for their children, to recognize that, ultimately, their children's lives are their own, and to work as steadfastly as possible to foster independence.

## Fostering Purpose, Self-Empowerment, and Joy

Children can find and follow their own calling if they are allowed to do so. Lana did so: she was as motivated as Joanne to help other people, and entered a helping profession on her own. She also took responsibility for her life. She was forced to in many ways by the relative hardships (minor as these were in the grand scale of things) she endured with her mother. But too many young people feel incapable of meeting the demands they face—let alone finding joy in them. This tendency is amplified when they don't own their goals and instead operate through external motivations and the desire to please others.

Encouraging independent effort and purpose in children is the subject of Stanford psychologist Carol Dweck's work. Dweck provides a guide for how children gain grit (or perseverance), contentment, and success in her book, *Mindset*, written in the light of her research on how children come to view their personalities and skills, and thus their options in life. Dweck found through a series of experiments that praising children's intelligence harms their motivation—their ownership and enjoyment of their own efforts.

How can praise be harmful? Children love praise, especially for their intelligence and talent. However, although it gives them a boost, like other self-defeating motivations and satisfactions we have reviewed, praise works only for the moment. As soon as they hit a snag, children attuned to praise lose confidence and their motivation sags. They develop an internal logic that says: "If success means I'm smart, then failure means I'm dumb."

Dweck's research shows the way to empower children to develop their full potential is not to praise them for their talents and performance, and instead to reinforce and support the children's own efforts. The difference, Dweck finds, between lauding raw talent and encouraging self-directed effort is the development of two opposing frames of mind: "fixed mindset" and "growth mindset." People with fixed mindsets are desperate for approval and interpret failure as an attack on their self-esteem. They avoid challenges, obstacles, and criticism in order to maintain a positive self-image, which for them means praise.

Children who are acknowledged and rewarded for their efforts, rather than for their successes, develop growth mindsets. People with growth mindsets see themselves as lifelong learners. They believe their talents and abilities can be sharpened and they accept challenges, and even value failure as a form of feedback and an opportunity to improve. Children with growth mindsets look forward to the future because they are optimistic about their ability to grow and gain further satisfaction. Thus, like those tracked from youth to seniority in the Stanford Terman Study, they are likely both to feel fulfilled and to enjoy their life journeys.

Dweck emphasizes that it isn't sufficient for a parent or teacher to claim a growth mindset for a child without the adults' continuing efforts along with their children's—as Joanne and Lana demonstrated. Mindset itself is not black and white, a fixed attribute. We all exist along a spectrum; we can all move in the direction of greater flexibility, growth, and joy. These motivations, as we have seen, are related to addiction, which is an effort to permanently fix satisfaction without having to endure the fear and challenge of uncertainty and failure.

*  *  *  *  *

We have reviewed psychological theories that point us in the non-addictive direction. Martin Seligman tells people not to regard their problems as being determined by their pasts or biological destinies, and instead to aim to strengthen their future well-being. Angela Duckworth adds that "gritty" people believe that they control their future and so work at what they care about. Carol Dweck provides a framework for developing grit through a healthy acceptance of uncertainty. Taken together, these psychological theories tell us that there are no external forces that cause addiction, nor external rewards that guarantee satisfaction. There is only a life to be lived fully in the here-and-now.

Appendix B, "Parents' Addiction and Development Manual," provides a more detailed exploration of developing independence and purpose with children.

# Overcoming Addiction 14

While this isn't a treatment manual per se, throughout this book we have developed a series of principles around natural recovery and child development that lead us to clear paths to overcoming addiction. These include recovery either in the long run—that is, growing up—or in here-and-now efforts to change: on one's own, through a group, or with a treatment provider.

### 10 Factors in Overcoming Addiction and Embracing Life

- Recognize that addiction isn't a lifetime disease.
- Develop the skills needed to gain life rewards.
- Resolve emotional problems and become less anxious, depressed, and afraid.
- Don't lose sight of—in fact, build on—your existing strengths.
- Develop further skills and life assets—such as a family, work, status, security—that you don't want to lose.
- Become engaged in relationships at all levels of intimacy and in larger communities.
- Look for positive options in life—including fun, adventure, and meaning.
- Mature beyond a selfish focus on your own needs.
- Gain and acknowledge control of your life—a sense of personal agency—so that you feel that you can get what you need in the world.
- Reaffirm—keep front and center—your purpose in life and your values that oppose addiction.

In our Life Process Program of coaching for addiction, we emphasize that these tasks of living are achievable for most people, despite possible side trips and off-ramps. Such deviations from perfection, even if to some degree regrettable, aren't to be rejected as despised parts of yourself. Instead you should try to avoid repeating while acccpting them as part of your complete and complex existence.

LPP focuses above all on people's conceptions of themselves and what is possible in their lives. This is the same approach that Zach has developed in his years of work with children. The process of change with both groups of people is the same: they learn to become oriented toward greater goals; to treat themselves like a person who is worth *having* such goals; and to be confident that they can create positive outcomes—to achieve these goals—for themselves.

Trauma and disadvantage don't eliminate this possibility. When Stanton speaks to groups of people who have faced a variety of challenges, he says, "Do you ever feel that you are the fortunate ones? You can appreciate the value and joy of a life lived fully, of not being weighed down by self-defeating thinking and problems. You can also empathize with people who face problems, an empathy that others are afraid to feel. Or maybe they refuse to be aware of this side of life, which is real and present for so many people. So, in crucial ways, you have the advantage on other people."

## Relapse and Purposelessness

The Life Process Program includes a segment on relapse prevention, the essential insight of which contradicts a fundamental tenet in the 12-step philosophy and which is a basis for harm reduction. AA and the disease theory teach their recruits, "one drink or drug is too much; a thousand drinks or drugs aren't enough." The opposite insight about relapse prevention is that, having had a bad moment, or night, or weekend, doesn't dictate a relapse to your former level of addiction. You maintain the same motivation, skills, and commitment to leading a different sort of a life after this bad period.

Stanton witnessed the performance of a 12-step preacher named Ryan Leaf, a former football star who failed at professional football, had an extended period of painkiller addiction, then got arrested, went to prison then rehab, and entered recovery. He now lectures people on addiction. In the course of his talk, he describes a colleague who was recovering from alcoholism, had a drink, and shortly thereafter died. For Leaf, "You have a choice—about whether you take the first drink." Implied in his statement is: "After that first drink, there is no choice." In AA, if you have a sip of alcohol, let alone a drink, let alone a night of drinking, you lose all credit for your sobriety, even if it's been fifty years since your last drink.

What a dangerous, self-defeating philosophy! Even readers whose knowledge is limited to popular psychology magazines and websites recognize the power of the "self-fulfilling prophecy"—that if you convince yourself that something is inevitable, you make it so. Thus, a person who follows the 12-step philosophy learns, "One drink, one drunk," and internalizes "In for a penny, in for a pound (dollar)"—if you drink or drug, you might as well go all out. LPP and other responsible treatment approaches instead instruct people that they can pull out of whatever tailspin they're in at any point and return to their former state of abstinence, controlled use, recovery, living a full life—however they conceive their life change.

We have emphasized natural recovery in this book; if you don't find that sufficient, you can sign up for the Life Process Program or any other support group (preferably SMART Recovery) or treatment you wish to. Natural recovery grows out of your ordinary progress and maturity in life. As we've emphasized, people like Joseph, who declined to abuse a prescription for painkillers after quitting his heroin addiction, or Ozzie, who could no sooner imagine returning to smoking than cutting off his hand, are not actively practicing relapse prevention; they are *living* it.

### Case Study: Sweetie's Purposelessness and Relapse

Stanton received a late-night phone call from a woman he hadn't spoken to for some time. Sweetie had had a tough life (she was both privileged and abused) and remained alcohol dependent for 20 years, from her teens through her thirties.

Then she quit drinking and a wide range of prescription meds. She created her own cognitive behavioral therapy for accomplishing this. Although Sweetie had bypassed formal education while drinking, she had a dizzying range of skills and natural beauty that led her to modeling, along with musical, writing, and artistic skills.

But she wasn't a motivated person. She noted about herself, "Even when I was with a group of friends dancing, or roller skating, or going to a show, I always wanted to go out drinking to make the evening complete."

In her call to Stanton, Sweetie related her life since quitting her substance addictions for almost a decade: "I never found something that I could get involved in and succeed at. And, to tell the truth, none of it really interested me. I returned to my husband [whom she had left after she recovered]. He's been supporting me financially, but we don't get along at all. In fact, I've begun drinking again, and seeing old lovers, and we're totally alienated, even though we live together."

Stanton asked, "Can't you find groups of people with whom you can play your music, or paint, or find other ways to pass your time? Do you seek meaning in these other relationships?"

"What do you mean, 'meaning?' I see these people because they're fun, and they take my mind off of my life and misery at home."

Just as purposefulness is a more-or-less lifetime cure for addiction, purposelessness is a void in life that allows people to slide back into one addiction or another.

## Meaning, Purpose, and Joy in Adulthood

Although maturity often occurs naturally with age, it entails much more than just getting older. The mature person is someone who lives with integrity. He or she takes responsibility. Mature people, moreover, do not act primarily for economic or social gain, but act consistently in line with their values.

But in case this all sounds too earnest, maturity and purpose are not grim accompaniments to a life lived in a harness of worthiness! They go hand and hand with joy. As Stanton and Archie Brodsky wrote in *Love and Addiction*:

> The antidotes to addiction are joy and competence—joy as the capacity to take pleasure in the people, activities, and things that are available to us; competence as the ability to master relevant parts of the environment and the confidence that our actions make a difference for ourselves and others.

Martin Seligman's positive psychology likewise goes beyond treating pathological symptoms and suffering toward a psychology that understands the importance of building character strengths and living a good life. Seligman draws a critical distinction between mental illness and mental health in his book *Learned Optimism: How to Change Your Mind and Your Life.*

> Curing the negatives does not produce the positives. Strangely, one can be both happy and sad. . . . The skills of becoming happy turn out to be almost entirely different from the skills of not being sad, not being anxious, or not being angry. . . . When you lie in bed at night and contemplate your life and the lives of the people you love, you are usually thinking about how to get from +2 to +6, not how to get from -5 to -2.

We disagree with Seligman to the extent that we find that, for many of our Life Process Program clients, addressing emotional problems is a necessary—at least a helpful—concurrent effort. Nonetheless, for both overcoming addiction and achieving happiness, we shift our focus to increasing well-being and joy rather than focusing only on life problems.

Through the lens of positive psychology, psychologists have been rethinking the meaning of the good life. This reassessment parallels how we are rethinking addiction. That is, psychology and psychiatry have been locked into mechanistic models that reduce people to automatons driven by abstract brain mechanisms over which they have no control.

This view is taken by Nora Volkow, director of the National Institute of Drug Abuse. In an article entitled "Addiction is a Disease of Free Will," Volkow claims (in the liberal *Huffington Post*, among many other places) that "addiction is not just 'a disease of the brain,' but one in which the circuits that enable us to exert free will no longer function as they should. Drugs disrupt these circuits. The person who is addicted does not choose to be addicted; it's no longer a choice to take the drug." The *New York Times*, in its frequent features about addiction, backs to the hilt this "hijacking the brain" model of drug use and addiction. ("In your mind you're okay. But one is too many, a thousand is never enough.")

Is this vision of addiction true? Is Volkow's and the *Times'* idea of humanity what our treatments, our lives, should be built around? Volkow and her cohorts act as though only the most basic feelings are available to humans—seeking pleasure or avoiding pain. But, as Seligman and his colleagues emphasize, life involves more than that. Think about the greatest joys in your life. Were they purely physical pleasures or avoidance of pain? Or were these deeper satisfactions, like something that comes from achieving a valuable goal, or forming a deeper relationship with or helping another person, or developing a skill at a challenging activity? And, did this joy come about easily, or did it take effort and even sacrifice?

Joy is a fundamental value and tool against addiction. And it, like avoiding and overcoming addiction through purpose, requires people to find meaning in their lives. Purpose and meaning likewise underlie Angela Duckworth's concept of grit, the same kind of perseverance identified by the Terman Study as the source of both longevity and lifetime satisfaction. Time and again, we are struck—in our own lives, in the lives of successful people, and even in the lives of fictional characters—by these truths.

## A Tree Grows in Brooklyn

In Chapter 3 we referred to a classic American novel, *A Tree Grows in Brooklyn*, which features Francie, one of three children in an impoverished family in Brooklyn as World War I loomed. Raised by a father who died of alcoholism at 35—whom she nonetheless adored and who was often highly nurturing—and an incredibly hard-working mother who cleaned the tenement houses in which they lived, Francie was, with her aunts, part of a supportive extended family which dared America to break it.

When Francie was seven, she and her younger brother were left to go alone to receive their smallpox vaccinations. Nervous about the upcoming shots, Francie and her brother played in the muddy lot next to their building before going to be inoculated. While she was being given her injection, the doctor spoke to the nurse about how dirty Francie was—how filthy poor families were—as though Francie wasn't there.

Francie responded to the doctor and nurse, "My brother is next. His arm is just as dirty as mine, so don't be surprised. And you don't have to tell him. You already told me." The professionals were shocked that Francie had been paying attention and was able to speak for herself—that a seven-year-old knew that she deserved better treatment from them. Francie's family made sure her self-respect and autonomy survived poverty and disparagement.

Francie's teachers likewise despised her and favored the better-off students. She dropped out of school to contribute to her family at age 14, when she lied about her age and got a series of jobs involving processing information—which she was prepared to do since her mother had read Shakespeare and the Bible every night to her and her brother, and since she went regularly to the local library. She took summer college courses, where she got needed help (after all, she never went to high school) from an older student.

Francie entered the University of Michigan at age 16—as did the real-life author, Betty Smith. After completing her memoir-novel decades later, Smith traveled to New York by bus for her book's release. She went out to buy a newspaper in the morning so she wouldn't have to tip the bellboy. When she returned, the desk clerk told her, "There are a lot of people looking for you—something about a book."

Recall from Chapter 3 that Francie pledged to live her life completely, to enjoy even its dreary and painful moments. Betty Smith achieved both joy and competence. She, like Francie, was a person with grit who persevered through life's challenges. And, while at it, she avoided (as did her brother) her father's alcoholism.

## The Glass Castle

Another woman who came from an unpromising background, but who likewise received unusual nurturance from her down-and-out family, is Jeannette Walls, author of the best-selling memoir *The Glass Castle*. Walls's family led an itinerant life around the Southwest, following her alcoholic father, who never could hold an engineering job very long, despite his talents, which extended into the literary realm. At night he debated the meaning of words in the dictionary with Jeannette, then wrote a letter to the dictionary's publisher contesting the listed definitions. (They usually responded with free books.)

The children often went to bed hungry, and they would pick sandwiches out of school trash cans the next day. Yet, when they remained somewhere long enough to get report cards, they excelled due to their brilliant father's tutelage and their mother's artistic skills. When their mother landed a teaching job she wasn't up to, the sisters graded her papers so she could keep the job. After graduating high school, despite their father stealing their squirreled-away savings, Jeannette and her sister moved to New York, where her sister became a commercial artist. They were joined by their brother, who became a cop.

Jeannette got a job writing for a local Brooklyn newspaper. She felt that she had landed the best position in New York City! Eventually, the paper's editor confided that there were even better writing jobs in New York. When Jeannette objected that those jobs required a college education and she had no money, he explained scholarships to her. Jeannette applied to and attended Barnard and graduated with honors. She eventually became the events columnist for *New York* magazine.

And Jeannette, her sister, and her brother didn't become alcoholics.

In another case where individuals and families exceeded the unpromising limitations of their origin stories, Christine Baker Kline, a novelist whose books include the bestselling *Orphan Train*, recalled her father's way of approaching life with her and her sisters:

### A Father's Legacy, Excerpts
by Christine Baker Kline

Dad was always going out on a limb, befriending people who didn't necessarily seem to want new friends, trespassing on private property, pushing the boundaries of acceptable behavior in quest of adventure. His philosophy was that you don't need money or plans, only a willingness to be present in the moment and to go where inspiration takes you.

Raised dirt poor in rural Georgia by a millworker mother and a father who often went to the bar rather than home after work, Dad learned early on that his quickest route up the social ladder was through charm and smarts. He got himself to college—the first in his family—on a football scholarship, then used seminary to spring-board to a doctorate in a foreign land.

This spontaneity meant that we missed flights, lost luggage, drove on perilous roads late at night, stayed in some cold-water hovels, and sometimes went hungry. But it also yielded beautiful surprises: an undiscovered beach, a fisherman's hut with a breathtaking view, a hillside breakfast of goats' milk yogurt and fresh honey that I still re-member 35 years later. It led to his daughters' sense of the world not as a huge frightening place but as a wonderland ripe for discovery.

Even now, in his late 70s, he lives each day with a kind of purpose-ful recklessness, asking provocative questions and seeking new expe-riences in the belief that he can break through to something better, more meaningful, more satisfying. . . .

There's no doubt that my dad's endless curiosity has shaped who I am. I often find myself—to my own kids' embarrassment—chatting with strangers in lines, accepting spontaneous invitations, and seek-ing out-of-the-way adventures.

I think the most important thing I learned from my dad is that when you go out on a limb there's a risk it will break, but you'll get a whole new perspective on the world. And if you're really lucky, it can feel like flying.

These three children of alcoholics—Betty Smith, Jeannette Walls, and Christine Baker Kline's dad—all of whom were raised in poverty, em-barked on lives of adventure, meaning, accomplishment, and legacy. We have described how the odds are stacked against kids who experience poverty and abuse. Yet these people transcended those obstacles.

Each of the three had extraordinary personal and family resources in doing so. Jeannette Walls, after all, had an exceptional father, however flawed, and her brother and sister to share her experience. Francie had a father who was devoted to her, despite his own life-destroying behavior, along with her mother and her mother's sisters. Christine Baker Kline had her father's life urges, which he taught her in the here and now, which she kept in front of her always as a life model.

Among the real, down-to-earth models in this book, we have the ex-ample of a single mother, Joanne, who guided her daughter Lana for-ward despite many limitations they faced. Joanne herself underwent youthful anorexia and drank somewhat excessively in the aftermath of her divorce, so that Lana herself had to deal with a less-than-perfect, if always loving and well-intentioned, mother. At the same time, we need to be aware that Joanne and Lana lived in a prosperous community that provided them with an array of social services, counseling, and educational benefits. Joanne and Lana didn't have to go it alone.

There is no overcoming the advantages of the help of others, from families, parents and other role models, and communities. As noted earlier, Stanton works with Bryan Cressey, a Chicago healthcare management and investment guru. Cressey founded Above and Beyond Family Recovery Center, a group that works with people with addiction in a disadvantaged urban area to address their issues with family, work and education, and simply their human needs through a non-disease-oriented treatment and support program. Bryan believes that his hard work and good fortune obligate him to help others. His experience also tells him that addiction is addressed only through giving people hope about, and opportunity to succeed throughout, the entire scope of their lives.

# Conclusion
## The American Delusion

# 15

Americans have a fantasy—that we can sidestep cultural, community, and personal problems and find a medical solution for addiction and mental disorders. This fantasy grows from American faith in medical technology (a faith that in some areas of medicine may be well-founded), from American exceptionalism and faith-healing, from unscrupulous snake oil salespeople and rehabs, and from a medical theocracy that rules not only our health lives, but our personal visions of ourselves and of our collective future as a society.

This fantasy represents magical thinking that we might recognize as such if we were to observe it in some isolated forest tribe. It is wrong, unhealthy, counterproductive and self-feeding. By neglecting individual lives, especially those in inner cities and pockets of poverty in Appalachia, New England and elsewhere, but also of the scions of socially and economically well-off families, we fertilize the breeding grounds for addiction and emotional problems.

There are no shortcuts to confronting these issues, no ways to say, "We realize that these are problems; we'll deal with them once we've overcome addiction and mental illness."

The general outlines of these problems are well known:

- Substantial segments of our society are underwater and stand no chance of breaking through to the surface.

- Even our privileged young people, destined to inherit the earth, are often ill-suited for meeting the considerable emotional demands they face, and depression and anxiety are everywhere evident in America.

- We become more distant from one another in terms of our ability to find and express human intimacy.

- We invest less, emotionally and economically, at the community level of society.

- We experience life ever more at a distance, locked in homes and electronic devices and separated from streets and direct experience.

And, as we showed in Chapter 11, although we as a society have taken the measure of our problems and understand how to solve them, we ignore the group, community, and cultural solutions shown to make a difference. We cannot help ourselves. As indicated by National Institute of Mental Health Director (from 2002-2015) Thomas Insel's doubling down on the psychiatric and antidepressant therapy he espoused in the face of ever-deepening plagues of depression and suicide, we are addicted to the American way of doing business. This addiction to diseasification is even more apparent under Nora Volkow, the head of the National Institute on Drug Abuse for the duration of our two-decades-long opioid crisis.

## Community, Community, Community

There was an exception in the aftermath of the suicides of Kate Spade and Anthony Bourdain to the incessant recommendations that we call 800 suicide-prevention numbers as the solution for our epidemic of suicides. ABC news ran the obligatory headline, "Calls to suicide prevention hotlines spiked after celebrity deaths." But the article was more complex:

### Suicide Prevention is More than Talking Somebody Out of Taking Their Life

We should think about suicide prevention much like we think about prevention of heart disease, suggested Dr. Christine Moutier, a psychiatrist who serves at the chief medical officer for the American Foundation for Suicide Prevention.

Just as we don't combat heart disease by only focusing on people who are on the verge of a massive heart attack, neither should we put off caring about suicide until people are on the brink of ending their lives.

"In our line of work, in our world, this kind of moment happens on a smaller scale all the time," said Moutier. "When a community is hit with suicides, there's a readiness to take action in game-changing new ways."

She pointed to her own history at the UC San Diego School of Medicine, where she was first a resident and later a professor of psychiatry and assistant dean. *In the span of 15 years, 13 physicians—most of them on faculty at the academic medical center (tragically ironic, perhaps)—took their lives,* she said.

Through a depression-awareness and suicide-prevention program she helped lead, **the community experienced a shift toward being there for and helping one another, she said. "The entire culture changed," Moutier explained, and UCSD went from having "too many physician suicides to almost none."** (Our emphasis.)

Johann Hari has made the strong case that the absence of human community and connectedness is at the root of our current epidemic of mental disorders in his best seller, *Lost Connections.*

## Truth Seeking

Our focus here is not about how to change the world—as crucial as those efforts are. It is about changing our lives, the lives of our children, and the small parts of the world that we touch. We need to create a positive universe for ourselves. That endeavor may well be increasingly necessary and difficult, judging by the data we have reviewed about the mental health and addiction-proneness of children and young adults and the decreasing, unhappy life spans of Americans who are deprived of hope.

Life—and addiction—are changeable for everyone, and despair isn't good, or necessary, or inevitable, no matter our circumstances. There is hope. And we all have the power to find and to follow it.

But, mainly, we, the authors, seek to tell the truth, the scientific truth, as the greatest help we can provide. Indeed, our main mission is to make clear how the scientific truth is identical to the social and existential truths of the matters that America laments and flails against with blind gestures and destructive results. As one participant in our Life Process Program said about the LPP approach to addiction, "It's only common sense!"

Hail to common sense, in our own lives, with our children and families, and with American and other societies in the world community.

# Appendix A
## Readers' Exercises by Chapter

These exercises are designed to help you think through the problems that you face, or that may be faced by your child. You may want to write answers in a notebook, or just go through the material to help clarify your thinking. Not all questions may apply to your specific situation, so feel free to skip those. Because many readers will be mainly concerned about preventing or treating their children's addictions, many of the questions relate to that situation, but the same concepts apply across the board.

### Chapter 1: Addiction as a Developmental Process

Addiction is not a brain disease, and most people outgrow it, given the right circumstances. We examine roots of vulnerability to addiction—and resilience—for you and/or your child.

#### Your World

**A. Reflection**

1. Do you know people who have overcome addictions or negative alcohol or drug habits (including smoking, caffeine, medications)?

2. Do these people now use substances in controlled or moderate or appropriate ways?

3. Describe what that means or looks like.

4. What addictions or negative habits have you overcome?

5. What life difficulties do you currently face?

**B. Action**

1. Of the people you know who have overcome addictions, what enabled them to do so?

2. How did their life situations change to point them toward recovery?

3. If you have overcome an addiction, what enabled you to do so?

4. What would such changes look like in your life now? How would you produce a similar change in your current circumstances?

5. How are you addressing each of your life difficulties?

## (For Parents) Your Child's World

### A. Reflection

1. How much adversity is present in your child's life?

2. What are the pressures and expectations in your child's life?

3. What are the developmental challenges of your child's current stage?

4. Are there addictions in your area that are common to your child's general age group? You can include such things as video games and dieting in addition to drugs and alcohol. Be as specific as possible (e.g., online multiplayer video games or vaping tobacco products).

5. What challenges do you see coming up in the next few years?

6. What does it look like to be healthy or successful at your child's age?

### B. Action

Your child will benefit from a coherent understanding and explicit naming of what the realities of his/her world are. Ask your child a question about each of the above bullet points, to get his or her descriptions. You and your child will both benefit from an open discussion of the life issues they face, including possible addictions.

## Chapter 2: The Addiction Experience

People become addicted to experiences produced in a variety of ways at different life stages, experiences that they often outgrow. These experiences fulfill people's needs in dysfunctional ways that most people can learn to overcome and replace with better sources of positive feelings.

## Your World

### A. Reflection

1. Have you or people close to you taken painkillers? Did you or they become addicted?

2. Why did or didn't you or they become addicted? How did the painkiller experience affect you?

3. How did your values and life alternatives influence this reaction?

4. What addictive experiences and involvements would you identify in your own life?

5. What were the circumstances that made you susceptible to the addiction?

### B. Action

1. Create a list of addiction-causing experiences and situations in your life.

2. Create a list of situations and alternatives you have used and can use to avoid addiction.

3. Describe how your neighborhood and workplace may be encouraging addictions.

4. Describe what you, if you were a political leader, would do to counteract addictions where you live and work.

5. Challenge your thinking. Describe what you feel is unchangeable about a person.

6. Think about ways that you can model calm and caring—rather than fear—in response to drugs.

## Your Child's World

### A. Reflection

1. Do you teach your children that drugs or alcohol cause addiction? Do you teach your children that they control their own lives more than drugs can?

2. Do you discuss unhealthy involvements of all kinds with your children? How?

3. Has anyone in your family struggled with any sort of addiction? What is your family's story about what happened?

4. How does your family talk about that person?

5. How concerned are you about your child's risk of addiction?

6. What do you think will prevent addiction in your child? What do you think leads to recovery?

**B. Action**

1. Point out and discuss addictive behavior and why it is unhealthy.

2. Encourage emotional literacy. Examine emotions you and your child feel. Discuss what emotions look and feel like, how to label them, and how to respond to them in constructive ways.

## Chapter 3: Expanding Life Experience

Lifelong addictions are rare. Enhancing your life experience reduces the addictive side of your life.

### Your World

**A. Reflection**

1. Describe life experiences you can draw on. What is valuable to you in your life? What are your sources of enrichment?

2. What is the most adventurous thing that you do, or have done in the last six months?

3. Have you talked to anyone new in this time frame?

4. Does your child see you engage in activities that are enriching for you? What kinds of enrichment are available to your family? What about in your community more broadly? Include any activity that builds community or has value.

5. How would you define a good life? Do you feel that you are living a good life? Does your child see you embodying your values?

**B. Action**

1. What new, fun, or valuable things can you become involved

in—such as community, religious, political, physical activity (e.g., hiking or athletics), friendship, etc.?

2.   What new things—involving going new places or seeing new people—can you do immediately in your home, neighborhood, town or city?

3.   What adventures can you realistically conceive of yourself undergoing?

### Your Child's World

### A. Reflection

1.   Is your child trapped in a very narrow world—school, electronic devices, home?

2.   Do you see your child's life as more locked in than yours was at the same age?

3.   Do you think that your child fears new experiences?

4.   What do you think of as your child's most valuable involvement?

5.   What does your child do that he or she feels is most valuable?

### B. Action

1.   How can you limit your child's down time and encourage involvement in positive, engaging activities?

2.   How can you address any fears that your child has about trying new or challenging things? (Hint: are you encouraging these fears?)

3.   Identify realms where your child feels a sense of mastery and competence, or a sense of being needed. Figure out ways to promote or support those realms without taking them over.

4.   What new or adventuresome things can you do with your child, or can you support without being directly involved?

5.   Be adventurous and imaginative and hopeful in speaking to your child about his or her future.

## Chapter 4: The Life Process of Children

Children, like all people, prefer to be agents in their own lives. That can mean being successful; if not, then being in control; and if not in control, then at least being able to predict what will occur, even if it's bad. Children need basics for proceeding in life and solving problems and bad patches in their lives: motivation, options, rewards, connection. These are related to the components of addiction in Chapter 1 and addictive process list from Chapter 2. Tie these together in thinking, speaking, and action with your children.

### Your World

**A. Reflection**

1. Do you interpret life difficulties your child (or anyone) encounters as a disability or popular mental health diagnosis?

2. Think about how you came to "know" about this label and why you believe it.

3. Describe the consequences, good and bad, that flow from this diagnosis/labeling.

**B. Action**

1. Describe this same condition strictly in normal, everyday terms, avoiding all diagnostics and labels.

2. Think about what the difference is between diagnostic/labeling versus not.

3. What positive consequences can you see from the non-labeling approach?

### Your and Your Child's World

**A. Reflection**

1. When does your child settle for less-good outcomes?

2. What limits your child in this way?

3. What fears are operating for your child?

4. Where do these fears stem from?

5. Do you or others (like teachers and counselors) regard these

limits and fears as disease states that are part of your child's permanent brain structure?

6.   When and how do you, and they, express this?

7.   What are the consequences of this for your child?

## B. Action

Apply the five questions, listed below, to find solutions in areas where your child may struggle—such as schoolwork, athletics, engaging with people and making friends, or simply going outside or acting independently. At the same time, apply the five questions to an area where they are doing well:

1.   What motivates your child?

2.   How does he or she assert self-control?

3.   What options are open to your child?

4.   What meaningful rewards flow from these options?

5.   What opportunities for connection are there (or can you create) in these situations?

## Chapter 5: Children and Addiction

**Critical issues**:

- How can we get more teens and young people to avoid problematic drinking and drug use by maturing at an earlier age?

- What is the consequence of telling young people with alcohol or drug problems that they are lifelong alcoholics or addicts?

- How can we build on the natural ameliorative tendencies of age to get even more people to recover from their drinking and drug problems?

**The Reality of Childhood/Youthful Drug Misuse**:

- No one is destined to be addicted.

- Early childhood recreational substance use may have downsides, perhaps severely negative ones, but such experiences are not lifetime sentences.

- The route out of early substance problems is to embrace as full—and as fully rewarding—a life as possible.

- This goal is not enhanced by calling a child (or anyone else) an addict, and we shouldn't do so.

### Your and Your Child's World

## A. Reflection

1. Why do so many children develop substance-use disorders and mental health issues?

2. Is this different from years gone by?

3. What are the differences between now and then?

4. Are the differences good or bad?

5. Is your child's life easier or harder to navigate than yours was at his or her age?

6. Are you pessimistic about how well children are prepared to deal with the world today?

7. What are the consequences of the problems you see?

8. Ideally, how should the world change to produce mentally healthier children?

9. Can your child live a successful, emotionally healthy life in a world with the problems that you have identified?

10. What do you think treatment for an emotional disorder or a substance problem must include?

## B. Action

1. What can you do to bring good things into your child's life that were present in your life but less present today in children's lives?

2. What can you do to help institutions you are a part of—for example, as a parent at a school or day-care center—to reduce what you have identified as the worse-off elements for children today?

3. How would you find successful professional help or therapy

or other curative settings for your child when he or she faces emotional problems/addiction?

## Chapter 6: Diseases, Disorders and Self-Fulfilling Prophecies and Chapter 7: Beyond Labeling

The question is whether—in our efforts to engage children, accommodate their learning styles, and support them in realizing their potential—diagnoses of disorders help or hinder. The disease-oriented approach in treatment for addiction is not helping and is probably making things worse. Diagnoses are often dehumanizing because they reduce nuance and complexity. They have negative consequences because of their associated stigmas.

Disease diagnoses are particularly problematic when applied to ever-changing children. The catastrophizing viewpoint inherent in such diagnoses essentially prescribes pessimism, which is a focal symptom of depression and anxiety. More important, *it demoralizes the victims or sufferers and makes them more pessimistic about their ability, and less likely, to change.* These problems are likewise true of trauma-based therapy, which focuses people on their low-points and worst-case scenarios, rather than reviewing positive options and aiming for these.

### Your and Your Child's World

**A. Reflection**

1.  How were you feeling when you solved a problem or dealt with an addiction (e.g., smoking) in your life? Were you feeling strong, or down about yourself?

2.  Do you think that encouraging your child and focusing on strengths and successes, or harping on problems, is most likely to help?

3.  Why do you think so many people fail in rehab programs?

4.  Why do you think that people keep sending their children to such programs, despite so many bad outcomes?

5.  Can you imagine how you would be feeling when confronted with a serious problem of your child's that would cause you to resort to such a program?

**B. Action**

1.  Create a therapeutic report on your child:

    - Describe your child in ten words; make eight of them positive, and the others neutral.

    - Describe how your child's unique qualities benefit your family.

    - Describe areas where your child's qualities cause difficulties.

    - Try to understand why those things are difficult for him/her; present the child's perspective.

    - Think of concrete ways that various environments can be tailored to address those difficulties and grow your child's strengths.

2.  How can you be positive, on your own part or for your child, when a serious problem arises?

3.  Map out a plan for progress for yourself or your child. Make it optimistic, but realistic.

4.  Visualize the specific steps needed to follow this program.

## Chapter 8: Behavioral Addictions and What They Show Us

Psychiatric diagnoses no longer use the terms "addiction" or "alcoholism," "addict" or "alcoholic" in connection with use of substances. Even regular use of substances is not defined as a disorder without meeting several problem criteria. Strange to say, the term "addiction" has been retained and applied to so-called behavioral disorders—so far, in American psychiatry, to just one—gambling.

In the World Health Organization diagnostic manual, compulsive sexual activity and gaming are addiction-type diagnoses.

The truth is, addiction is not in the thing, but in our lives—in the processes and the consequences of our activities and involvements.

If a child refuses to play with other kids or to read or to get exercise because of compulsively playing video games (as described in Chapter 6), this is an addictive problem—that is, an attachment to a self-destructive, self-feeding process that prevents engagement in life. The problem isn't the video games, but the fact that gaming overrides everything else. This is the essence of all addictions.

## Your and Your Child's World

**Reflection**

1. What serious addictions have you had in your life, to non-substance activities as well as to substances?

2. Which of these persist to the present?

3. Why, exactly, are problems caused by these involvements?

4. What psychological satisfaction do you get from them? (Consult addictive criteria in Chapter 2.)

5. Is there any activity your child engages in that has addiction-like qualities, as listed above (e.g., gaming/phone/social media)?

6. What satisfactions do these activities provide for your child?

**Action**

1. List other ways you or your child could gain the satisfactions currently gained through addictive activity.

2. Do you know this because you or your child have done these activities and gotten these satisfactions, or have considered them as possible positive activities before?

3. Consider scheduling these or similar activities into your regular daily, weekly, and monthly schedules, then track your or your child's addictive involvements.

4. Does thinking about these things as being addictions make it easier to confront them, or more daunting to do so? Might they be easier to overcome without thinking of them as addictions?

5. Try to direct your thinking toward understanding what you get from these activities and finding substitutes for these "benefits."

6. Reflect on addiction as a developmental process and consider the addictions you've listed above that you've overcome—thinking about how you did so, and believing that you can do so again with other addictions, as can your children.

## Chapter 9: Abstinence and Harm Reduction, in Adolescence and Recovery

Abstinence isn't required for remission (a.k.a. recovery)—only the absence of substance-use *problems*, according to the diagnostic manual for the American Psychiatric Association, called *DSM*. This makes the *DSM* a harm-reduction document.

After a year of the absence of such problems, the individual is certified as having achieved long-term remission ("recovery"). That is, DSM recognizes addiction or its equivalents as time-limited conditions.

Harm reduction (HR) is an approach to drug use and addiction in which abstinence isn't the end-all goal; instead, improvement of the person's situation—and of their overall life—is targeted.

### Your and Your Child's World

**Reflection and Action**

1. Do you believe that a person can resolve a drug or alcohol problem without abstaining, either continuing to use that substance in a controlled way (e.g., reducing drinking to non-problem levels, or taking pain killers as needed after having been an opioid addict, or smoking marijuana occasionally after having been addicted to it), or else using another psychoactive substance (e.g., drinking or using marijuana after having been addicted to heroin or meth)?

2. Have you done so?

3. Can adolescents and young adults learn to drink in a positive, socially acceptable manner?

4. At what age do you think this is possible? (Answer according to your belief, aside from the fact that the drinking age in the U.S. is higher than anywhere else in the Western World.)

5. How would this happen, in your view?

6. Put another way, we might ask: Who will teach your child to drink? A high school kid? A college fraternity or sorority member? A fellow military service person? Someone your child meets on the street? Or do you believe that you are able to teach your child how to drink in a socially acceptable manner?

7. Can drinking be done in a socially acceptable way in a college setting?

8. Will this socially acceptable use ever be possible with drugs like marijuana, now that marijuana is legal in many places?

9. Can adolescents use drugs in non-alarming ways, ways that won't impair their current functioning or future lives? How would you determine if your child was using drugs in a non-destructive way?

10. How would you react/did you react, if/when you discovered that your child smoked marijuana, drank, or took a stimulant, like a friend's Adderall, in order to study?

11. If your child had an actual, diagnosable drug problem, after they quit, would you insist that they never consume drugs, or drink, ever again, for the rest of their lives?

## Chapter 10: The Limits of the 12-Step Approach

Debunking: Strong evidence suggests that AA is not effective, can be harmful, and often alienates people who don't accept its religious grounding (e.g., a higher power). In any case, most people, even those who have apparent substance-use problems, refuse either to attend AA or a 12-step group in the first place, or else quickly quit such groups.

### Your and Your Child's World

### Reflection and Action

1. Do you believe that people can/should be ordered to attend a 12-step group, for instance, after they have been found driving while intoxicated?

2. Have you ever attended a 12-step group meeting? Did you enjoy/benefit from it, or did you find it strange or off-putting?

3. If you haven't attended one, imagine doing the first three steps:

    • Step 1: We admitted we were powerless over alcohol—that our lives had become unmanageable.

    • Step 2: Came to believe that a Power greater than ourselves could restore us to sanity.

- Step 3: Made a decision to turn our will and our lives over to the care of God as we understood Him.

   How does that feel to you?

4. Can you imagine people—even if they have a substance use problem—reacting negatively to these steps and rejecting doing them?

5. What should happen to them then?

6. Do you think it is psychologically beneficial to say/think that (a) you are an alcoholic or addict forever, (b) you are powerless?

7. What possible downsides are there to saying/believing these things?

8. Would you give different answers to these questions depending on the age of the person—for example, if they were 18 versus 45?

## Action

1. How would you feel about sending your child to a 12-step based rehab?

2. What kinds of skills, feelings about themselves, outlooks on the world would you hope they would gain in rehab?

3. Do you think this would be likely with the 12 steps and what you have heard about rehabs?

4. What dangers would you be worried about for them there, both in terms of who they associated with, and in terms of the lessons they learn?

5. What is the worst outcome you have heard about/can imagine from a young person going to rehab?

6. What could you do to prevent such worries and dangers?

7. Would you want to speak with your child about what he or she learns in rehab, to understand how they interpret and use it?

8. Can you imagine any other way to approach a drug

or alcohol problem you discovered, or thought, that your adolescent/young adult child had?

## Chapter 11: Recovery in the Real World

Professionals working in recovery in both mental health and addiction have joined together in formulating new, more holistic, less drug-linked criteria and goals for recovery, looking at the person in their life context. The Substance Abuse and Mental Health Services Administration (SAMHSA) convened a panel of experts across both fields to redefine recovery.

This new definition and approach doesn't view recovery as lifelong, but rather focuses on the individual embarking on a new journey in life. This journey is client-directed, empowering them, and has four key components: health, home, purpose, community. This creates a whole new narrative, one that runs counter to much of the mainstream discourse around addiction and mental illness.

### Your and Your Child's World

**Reflection**

1.  Do you know people—in your family or a friend or someone in your community—who have redirected their lives and emerged from addiction or a mental disorder, much as did Drew Barrymore in Chapter 5? Answer the following questions about that person—or some other figure you have heard of who regained a positive life after overcoming an addiction or mental disorder.

2.  What did their recovery involve? What tells you they are recovered?

3.  What changes did they initiate in their lives?

4.  How did their attitudes and outlooks change?

5.  What people and communities were involved in this change?

6.  Did they achieve more intimacy with their families, or create families?

7.  Did they gain education or change jobs or get more involved in their existing work and skills?

8. What did you make of their journey, as much as you witnessed of it?

9. Can you imagine that some people reject this recovery story—as for example those who claim that Drew Barrymore is actually an example of "denial"?

10. How would you help to explain to such a skeptic why such nontraditional recovery stories are real, valuable, achievable, and should be the focus of our helping efforts?

**Action**

1. Think about what your recovery story would look like, if it extended into the future in a positive way. Review all of the elements in the above questions for key points to cover in your own current and future recovery.

2. Let's talk about your child's recovery story from any disorder or addictive problem he or she might be said to have. Imagine the positive elements and skills you included in your therapeutic report for your child in the Chapters 6-7 exercise.

3. Do you believe these recovery stories—yours and your child's?

4. Have you had a love addiction, or more than one? Was this very hard to recover from? Use your recovery from a love addiction to describe what is necessary for all recovery stories; or, on the other hand, apply what you have learned from successful recoveries you have had to a lingering love addiction you may still harbor.

## Chapter 12: Raising Our Non-Addicted Next Generation

Parenthood is not only a source of meaning and purpose that reduces the likelihood of addiction for ourselves. It is an opportunity to improve our own lives while avoiding transferring our problems to our children. In this way, history is not destiny. That is, a personal or family history of addiction is more likely to be a beacon for avoiding such errors with our children than it is to recreate our problems in our children's lives.

This is a value-driven book, and we include 12 Values to Prevent Addiction: Purpose; achievement; caring about self; caring about others; responsibility; valuing money; awareness/mindfulness; adventure; pleasure and fun; social, political, religious commitments; efficacy, agency, empowerment; maturity. These are examples of values you may enact in raising your own children.

## Your and Your Child's World

### Reflection

1.  Describe your strongest values, and give examples of them in your life.

2.  Think about how such values have sustained you and guided you through tough times.

3.  Have you ever had to defend these values against others' opposition, even against people close to or intimate with you?

4.  Have you ever failed to honor your values? (Everyone has.) Think about, and describe how this occurred and why. Now, alerted to this danger, how would you deal with such situations in the future?

5.  Select four of the values in the list we have offered. Have you displayed these, and do you display them, in your life? Provide examples.

6.  If you have had addictive experiences, or your family tree is replete with them, do you feel that this heavily preordains your child to be addicted or alcoholic, or even guarantees that he or she will be?

### Action

1.  Do you live a value-driven life? Would you like to? How would you go about doing this, or doing it more?

2.  Do you discuss values with your children? How do you/would you do so? Give examples.

3.  How do you display and exemplify the values you cherish to your children? Give examples of when you did so, or when you failed to do so.

4. If you have an addictive background, how do you think about the concept "self-fulfilling prophecy"? Define it. Have you ever seen it operate? How will you counteract this in your and your child's case?

5. What kind of message can you convey to encourage your child to select his or her own destiny? Think about what values you want to display, what kind of support want to give them, to make sure that they will lead the most fulfilled and constructive lives that they can, no matter what past addictive problems you have had.

## Chapter 13: Developing Purpose, Efficacy, and Independence

Having a purpose in life, feeling able to control your life (efficacy, agency, or empowerment), and independence are the fundamental values/abilities that allow people to avoid and escape addiction, no matter what circumstances they face. Having purpose in life has been found to be the single best predictor of longevity and health, both physical and mental. In our world, self-efficacy and independence are the most challenged aspects of children's lives, as parents often are driven by fear and the urge to protect their kids from experiences they themselves underwent and benefited from.

### Your and Your Child's World

**Reflection**

1. Do you struggle around your child's desire to achieve, and worry whether to burden him or her with high-achievement motivation?

2. Where does this feeling come from; is it part of your own background?

3. At the same time, do you admire highly successful people?

4. What attitudes toward success do you express to your child?

5. Do you view the world as dangerous, much more dangerous than it was when you were a child?

6. What level of fear do you convey to your child about life? Why is this necessary?

7. What would help the most to allay your fears for your child? Would it be your confidence in their ability to handle their own lives, an ability that you have seen them gradually develop and display?

8. Do you feel that your child is capable of being as strong a person as you are?

**Action**

1. Think about how you can help someone, like your child, find their own purpose, one that reflects their strengths and wishes.

2. Encourage the person to express their own motivation, rather than imposing yours. (Hint: Ask questions, including ones you don't propose to answer for the other person.)

3. Can you let your child try, fail, and try again without intervening?

4. What is the most independent thing you would allow your child to do for himself or herself now? In two years? In five years? In ten years? Ever?

5. What are three ways you display love to your child? How do you display confidence in them? Do these two qualities reinforce or repel one another?

6. How do you show your child you respect them?

7. How do you deal with your child's weak areas—do you take over tasks your child finds difficult, or can you let them struggle on their own, encouraging them while they continue to try?

8. Can you say to yourself, "My child's path is his/her own, and not mine to control"?

## Chapter 14: Overcoming Addiction

People overcome addictions, not by solely, or even principally, thinking about and addressing the object of their addiction, but by considering, working on, and improving the entire fabric of their lives.

This process involves the following ten steps: (1) recognize that addiction isn't a lifetime disease; (2) develop the skills needed to gain life rewards; (3) resolve emotional problems and become less anxious, depressed, and afraid; (4) build on your existing strengths; (5) develop further skills and life assets—such as a family, work, status, security; (6) become engaged in relationships at all levels of intimacy and in larger communities; (7) look for positive options in life; (8) mature beyond a selfish focus on your own needs; (9) gain control of your life—a sense of personal agency; (10) keep your purpose in life and your values that oppose addiction front and center.

## Your World

### Reflection

1. In what areas of your life do you exert good control and self-control?

2. In what areas are you weakest, least in control?

3. Has this ordering, in terms of your hierarchy of control, always been true for you? When and how was it different?

4. Are you a person who can be counted on? How so, or why not?

5. Do you consider yourself mature, as an actor in the world, with friends and family, with people you work with or know in your community?

### Action

1. Can you try to export the control from one area of your life, where it is strong, and import it to another, where it is not?

2. What do you need to do better, more regularly, to be considered a responsible person?

3. How can you display greater maturity? With which people do you feel this is most necessary? In which areas of your life do feel this greater display of maturity is most needed and would be most beneficial?

4. Describe when you acted most maturely and responsibly—was this a genuine expression of you that can be at the center of your existence?

5.  Are you optimistic about yourself and the world you live in? What steps are necessary for you to take to gain this type of optimism and sense of security?

## Chapter 15: Conclusion: The American Delusion

In a sense, everything in this book is common sense, dealing with day-to-day existence, embracing values that you have been taught—and admired—your whole life. There are no magic solutions out there for you, for curing your addictions or enriching your life. There is only being true to your purpose and who you want to be. All else can be brought under your aegis if you hold true to these things.

While this isn't always easy, don't be sidetracked by external agents people try to convince you will solve your problems, make you feel good, or turn you into a valued person.

Seeking such magical solutions, rather, is the core of addiction.

## Final Questions:

1.  Describe how the search for simplistic solutions for you and your child can be alluring, but actually addictive in itself.

2.  What are examples of when you have sought or accepted magical solutions in your life?

3.  What are examples you have seen other people become invested in?

4.  What culture-wide examples of magical solutions can you imagine, or describe?

5.  List explanations you have heard, that many people accept, and that perhaps you believe for addiction or mental illness, and turn them around to see what their flaws and negative effects might be.

6.  Do you believe that you, and ultimately your child, can ultimately decide what is true about and right for yourself/themselves?

7.  What kinds of skills, learning, and experience will allow you or your child to accomplish this?

8.   What kinds of support and inputs will enable you to improve
     your ability to come to the best understanding of, and to make
     the best decisions for, yourself?

We offer our best wishes and hopes for you and your children, on your
and their lives.

# Appendix B
## Parents' Addiction and Development Manual*

B

### By Dr. Noriko Martinez, Zach Rhoads, and Stanton Peele

Parents and children struggle to understand and master the destructive potential of addictions of all kinds. But addiction does not have a mind of its own; it is woven into people's lives. And while there is no magic-bullet solution, addiction can be avoided, controlled, and escaped. You can help your children explore life on their own while serving as their guide through developmental stages. In this way, your children will have full access to the many mansions that are part of a fulfilling life.

Doing so may help your child avoid addiction entirely; it may help your child escape a current addiction; or it may give you the framework and understanding you need to take your own steps toward helping your child.

**1. The first step to preventing addictions of all sorts is to understand what is happening in your child's life now. What is your child's context?**

#### A. Reflection: Your Child's World

Parents are present for each moment when their children are little. And parents teach their children how to see their worlds by telling stories together about things that happen. When a dog walks by and the child exclaims, "Dog!" the parent then expands, "Oh look, it's a big yellow dog! Look at its fluffy tail!" And then later, when the child is reporting "I saw a dog," the parent adds detail, "Yes, we were on a walk together, and we saw a big yellow dog with a fluffy tail, remember?" In this way the parent models and helps strengthen the child's developmental next-steps in storytelling (respecting his/her stage of development per

---

* This manual was developed in conjunction with Dr. Noriko Martinez, a child and family therapist, a Loyola University instructor, and the parent of three children.

Chapter 4, "The Life Process of Children").

Parents build out the story with the child, helping children decide what is important and what isn't, and what feelings make sense. "When we saw that dog, it was so cute! We laughed when it licked your nose." Or "When we saw that dog, it was so scary! We thought it might bite you." These stories parents and children tell together will help to shape how the children will see similar things the next time around.

As your child grows and forms a world that is more and more separate from yours, it can take more work to fully grasp their world and help them develop stories about it. But even teenagers benefit from adult help in paying attention to the world around them and developing their stories. The things you pay attention to give them ideas about what *they* should pay attention to, and the way you understand things helps *them* to understand what is important, why, and how.

The goal in this section is to take the time to be clear about the stories you tell about your child's life, to them and yourself. What matters to your child? Where is your child going at this stage in life? At the same time you will build a bridge to understand your child's life story. What is your child's perspective on the world? Are his/her stories compatible with your own views?

*The goal is for your child to develop fully into a strong, independent human being.* The following questions will help you explore this process, so that you may help your child build resilience, even in the face of adversity. Here are some critical elements in such stories.

### How much adversity does your child face?

A life with no adversity has plenty of food, shelter, clothing, medical care; no major changes like moves, divorces, deaths; no experiences of danger like hurricanes, car crashes, or serious illness; no fighting or unhappiness among family or friends. In other words, there's no such thing. The question here is about how your child balances (or doesn't balance) the good things in life with the difficulties. These adversities take some attention and kids need a way to understand them.

### What are the pressures and expectations in your child's life?

Children in different cultures, times, and locations face different expectations and demands. There are different kinds of chores and expectations regarding contributions they can make to the family; keeping up grades; meeting social or religious expectations; achieving academically and in other performance areas. For example: Does your child have to wake up early to tend to animals? Is your child expected to achieve at a high level in school in order to go to a competitive university? Does your child need to take care of younger siblings?

### What are the developmental challenges of your child's current stage?

Building your child's story requires that you recognize where your child is in life. Every developmental stage has its challenges, and you should remind yourself of what the tasks are at your child's current age and stage. At the same time, parents sometimes forget what kids are capable of, and then expect too much or too little from them. Below is one chart of development. But your thinking can move into different areas. For example, is your child learning to ride a bike? Losing molars? Learning how to dress in a way that won't be made fun of? Dealing with puberty?

| Stage | Your child's task | What it might look like | Your role |
|---|---|---|---|
| Infancy | Trust that his/her needs will be met<br><br>Exposure to people | Crying, fussing, communicating happiness or unhappiness<br><br>Alert looking around followed by lots of sleep | Meeting all your baby's needs as soon as possible<br><br>Comforting your baby when you can't meet his needs<br><br>Interacting with him, or having him with you as you interact with the world |
| Toddler-hood | To feel in control<br><br>To learn to make choices<br><br>To learn to know what he wants | Strong opinions that can change swiftly<br><br>Strong "No!" even when she means yes<br><br>Extreme reactions to minor disappointments | Avoid saying no as much as possible<br><br>Providing opportunities to make choices that are safe, acceptable to you, but have some consequence |

| | | | |
|---|---|---|---|
| Childhood | To learn how to do all kinds of things<br><br>To learn the rules of their world | "Teaching" you things<br><br>A strong desire to fit in with friends and to follow the rules<br><br>A need for sameness as a kind of fairness | Showing respect and being impressed at all your child's knowledge and abilities<br><br>Giving lots of encouragement |
| Tweenager | To try out adolescence | Experimentation with stereotypical adolescent behaviors<br><br>Sometimes acting childish, sometimes teenager-ish | Giving your child opportunities to try out responsibilities under your guidance, e.g., sitting far away or even in another theater when you go to the movies<br><br>Being flexible in treating your child more like a child or more like an adolescent |
| Teenager | To try out adulthood<br><br>To develop an adult identity | Questioning rules and authority<br><br>Having a sudden disdain for you and your ways<br><br>Trying out different identities | Giving your child freedom to be different from you and different from one moment to the next<br><br>Protecting your child from bad outcomes |
| Young Adult | To establish independence | Beginning attempts at independent, self-sufficient life | Showing your confidence in your child's abilities to make her own life |
| Adult | To become respected peers of parents<br><br>To understand full cycle of life | Watching your aging<br><br>Looking for ways to give back to society | Model process of aging<br><br>Allow child to have meaningful input into your decisions |

## What challenges do you see coming up in the next few years?

You are always planting the seeds to help build stories for what is to come in your child's life before these events surface. For example, with a baby in diapers you can start to talk about what life will be like when they become diaper free. This is an early example of your helping them imagine their own positive future. Before you actually teach toilet use, you are building the beginning of a story that your child will live out while providing tools of understanding before your child needs them. You can be mindful about what seeds you plant by thinking through what is coming up next for your child.

This is especially important prior to adolescence, when milestones of development are separation and independence from parents. Stories you build together ahead of time—for example, about how you will be ready to help out in an emergency, or the difference between making stupid mistakes and being a bad person—can resonate through adolescence even as your child creates independent space for themselves.

### How does your child react to mistakes?

In a balanced developmental process, children will learn that mistakes are inevitable byproducts of conscious decision-making. The child will act; things will happen that they did not know would happen; and they will observe these results and learn from the mistakes. They will use this experience to make decisions about how to act next—this is a cycle that will be repeated throughout life.

You, an adult, understand that mistakes create opportunities for growth. You can model this idea to your child by inviting him or her to accept mistakes as a part of life. Most importantly, you can teach them that their worst failures can also be their greatest successes from a different perspective.

Zach spoke with Carol Tavris*, a social psychologist and coauthor (with Elliot Aronson) of the book, *Mistakes Were Made (but not by me!)*. He asked her how parents ought to help kids respond to mistakes. Here is her response:

> The most important lesson for kids is that failure is essential if we're ever going to learn anything at all. We're going to make mistakes; we're going to fail; we're going to not get it the first time; we're going to be clumsy; we're going to just not understand; we're going to not draw a pretty picture the way the talented kid in the corner can do; we're going to not understand some math problem; we're going to *not get it*.

---

* https://www.youtube.com/watch?v=E_soRYeNjPE

We're going to fail. We. Are. Going. To. Fail. And that does not mean that you are stupid, or that you will always fail, or that there is something the matter with *you*.

Carol Dweck has done important research showing that children who think that mistakes mean that they're stupid tend to give up after they make a mistake, because they feel that the mistake "is *ME*." Children who understand that failure is just a part of learning and that success is due to effort, rather than natural intelligence, are more likely to continue trying. As a child in one of her studies said, "Mistakes are our friend."

Dweck and others have found that parents who praise their children for their efforts ("You worked hard on that project, Janine, and it really shows!") rather than praising them for "natural talent" ("You're just a natural at art, Janine, and it really shows!") help the children accept the necessary mistakes and failures they need to improve.

That's the attitude we most need to convey to our children. Because although we say in our culture that everybody has a chance to do everything, in fact, underlying that is the idea that either you're born smart and talented or you're born stupid with no ability. And nothing can be more defeating to tell children than that.

When children are aware that even the best people make mistakes (bad choices), they are better able to distinguish between their mistakes and their own self-image. Rather than "I screwed up, I'm a bad person," the story about themselves is something more like "When I—a good, competent person—act incompetently or do something that hurts others, I remain a good competent person. My action remains a hurtful or incompetent action that I want to—and can—improve." In this way, they are able to separate the ability to see themselves as good and competent people who, in this particular case, did something wrong. But they are always able to improve themselves or the situation.

The single greatest antidote to addiction is to welcome change, while also experiencing and dealing with the uncertainty and difficulty of making the change. This is the opposite of seeking the certainty of an addiction. You can move forward by appreciating your world and your ability to deal with the slings of fortune that it throws at you.

### *What does it mean to be healthy or successful at your child's age?*

No one's story is entirely foretold in the first chapter; your child is not supposed to be an adult yet—that comes later. So it is important to include what your child should be striving for. How will you and your child know if your child is on the right track? The question of "doing it right" must take into account the child's developmental stage, while keeping in mind that sometimes "failing" at one age is setting a person up for greater success at a different age. The 12-year-old you wish was more socially active may become a major intellectual or poet or artist or software engineer. The 7-year-old who won't go along with all your rules can become the 25-year-old who maintains a moral compass. In fact, you can take any challenging characteristic or behavior and look for the seed of something good that you can nurture.

## B. Action: Your Child's World

### Noticing, naming, framing, responding

Your child will benefit from a coherent understanding and explicit naming, framing, and responding to realities of his/her world.

Once you have put some thought into all of the realities of your child's life, then it's time to put them into a story. To develop your stories of your child's world, you should first put yourself in your child's shoes as much as possible. Our worlds expand as we age, but as children, it is fine to have a limited awareness of the impacts of things outside of our own lives. When parents divorce, a child's perspective entails things like not understanding how mom and dad can be separate, worrying about what it means for their stuff and their schedules, wondering who they are allowed to talk to about it, etc. The story must start from their perspective.

Second, you should be honest, while using age-appropriate language and being succinct. You do not need to fill your stories with detail, but you do want to include the truths of your child's world. Do not underestimate your child's competence to deal with hard realities. In fact, you teach them whether they can handle it by how you talk to them. If you are calm, you create the assurance that you and your child will handle it together, and your child will feel calm and confident. The two of you are already building a story about how you can manage things together and, further down the line, how your child can handle whatever life tosses at him or her. (And there will be plenty.)

A good story to build together is one that is clear and rational, contains the truth of challenges and the possibility of overcoming them, and expresses the values that are important to you and your family.

**Example:** A father is upset because his mother has Alzheimer's and no longer recognizes him. His 8-year-old daughter sees him coming home from the nursing home and senses his upset. She asks him what he's upset about. Many parents would try to shield their children from the realities of aging and illness. Instead, her father can say something like this:

**Father:** Well, my mother has a brain disease, and she has gotten pretty sick.

**Daughter:** Is she going to die? (Kids often get right to the point, and it's fine to go there with them.)

**Father:** At some point she will certainly die, but probably not for a little while yet.

**Daughter:** Could my mother get the brain disease too? (Kids often worry about death of parents or of themselves when they hear about death, and it is better to be honest.)

**Father:** She could, some day. Many people do get this brain disease when they are older. You'll be older too, then, because that wouldn't be for a long time.

**Daughter:** That sounds scary.

**Father:** It is, and it's sad, too. (He may start to cry, and that's OK, because that is a genuine feeling in response to something sad.)

You don't have to shield your kids from reality. So long as you have a way to talk about it clearly and honestly, then your kids can safely understand and deal with any situation. That is part of the reason it is important to think through your own story first, so that you can tell it clearly when your kids ask. When parents realize that they don't have to construct elaborate, sugar-coated stories for their kids, and instead can be real, they are relieved. It is much easier to present the truth than elaborate euphemisms, and when parents are calm and reasoned, children won't be traumatized by challenging information. Most of the time, they come up with their own ways of understanding that parents can learn from as well!

## 2. Identify what your child is being taught about addictions.

### A. Reflection: The role of addictions in your child's world

Your child's lifelong relationship with any mood-altering drug will be shaped, in part, by the stories your family has developed around such drugs. The purpose of this section is to develop an understanding about the stories circulating in your community and in your family that teach your child what it means to use a substance or engage in an "addictive" activity: when is it appropriate (if ever)? How dangerous is it? Why do people do it? What happens to people who use? What does it mean to become addicted? What happens to people when they become addicted?

You can think about how different the stories can be if you answer those same questions about different substances and activities. For example, how do those questions sound when you apply them to alcohol? Heroin? Gambling? Video games? Your similar or varied answers inform the stories of those substances and activities that you want to tell your children and that, in turn, they will base their ideas on.

However, some of the common stories that are shared in the culture at large are misleading and contribute to more problematic responses to substance use—we've demonstrated this throughout the book. Your own views and values around addiction may or may not align with larger cultural ideas. Either way, your child will need to coalesce these views into a single story. You can help your child fit these different—even seemingly contradictory—worldviews into their own narrative.

*How many people in your life have used substances (legal or illicit) and are not currently addicted to them?*

The first task is to review whether you know stories about people taking drugs without becoming or remaining addicted. If you don't have stories like this, then the narrative around any substance will be more frightening and the apparent ways of using the substance will be more limited: for example, how a child, then an adult, views taking a painkiller following a knee or other operation. Remember, the majority of people who take drugs do so responsibly and without ever becoming addicted. Of the people who do develop problems with drugs, most outgrow their problems over time.

Remember, addiction is not limited to drugs. Nowhere is this realization more relevant and true than in child development (which we'll discuss in the next sections).

### *Are there addictions in your area that are common to your child's general age range?*

You can include such things as video games and dieting in addition to drugs and alcohol. Be as specific as possible (e.g., online multiplayer video games or vaping tobacco products). These are the substances and activities that other kids may be talking about, and that adults around your child may be mobilized to try to limit. Once they have been identified as addiction risks, there is often a rise in alarming stories about dire outcomes as a result of the addiction. By identifying cultural fears around addiction, you can help your child separate mythology from truth, and you can concentrate on what really makes a difference for your child.

### *How do people engage with substances (or activities) in non-addictive ways?*

As this book clarifies, substances and activities are not themselves the core of addictive behavior. Nonetheless, some substances have more stories of "normal" or "healthy" use than others. For example, although food addictions can be an issue, there are plenty of examples available (although fewer than there once were) of normal and healthy eating. But every child needs to formulate an idea of non-addictive, healthy eating behavior.

On the other hand, there are fewer stories about normal and healthy heroin use. But, of course, nearly everyone will use painkillers, and so you need to have a positive story about pain medications. Understanding the positive, acceptable use of painkillers is part of identifying what a relationship with this substance should be. For all such substances and activities, you need to establish *what a healthy relationship with those substances/activities looks like.*

*What is the story of that substance (or activity)?*

Many substances have common narratives about their effects. You may have heard marijuana causes people to be forgetful, relaxed, and hungry; that it is a gateway drug that leads to more serious drug use later; or that marijuana is a miracle drug that can cure many illnesses and isn't addictive. Then there's the idea that kids who are given freedom to decide the amount of time they spend on video games will spend every hour playing violent games that will desensitize them to violence. Or, some say, video games are the new social hangout and improve dexterity and reaction time.

What is your position on these things?

*How does your family talk about people who are addicted? What components of that story are about fixed traits of the person, and what parts are about changeable states or circumstances?*

As discussed in Chapter 13 and in Zach's conversation with Carol Tavris, Carol Dweck presents evidence that a "growth mindset," the idea that people can grow with effort, promotes better life outcomes. The story that personal effort leads to growth and change is a powerful motivator throughout life and leads to growth and change.

When addictions are understood as unchangeable characteristics about a person, on the other hand, there is little belief or motivation that people—your child—can avoid or overcome addiction. Usually people's stories are not so starkly one or the other. The point with these questions is to look for the nuances in your family's stories to see where there is optimism about a person's agency and ability to change versus stories that see change as unlikely and a person as helpless. You can emphasize the aspects of your story that support the growth mindset.

*Has anyone in your family struggled with any sort of addiction? What is your family's story about what happened? How does your family talk about that person?*

Scary stories about substance use may promote dysfunctional relationships with substances. The goal here is to identify which parts of your stories might convey fear or hopelessness to your child.

Start by thinking through the stories, and then consider them from your child's angle to identify pieces of the stories that may seem alarming, that may depict the substance user as bad or damaged, or that make the trajectory of use seem terrifying and inevitable. Rather than, "your grandmother's drinking caused problems in her life so alcoholism runs in the family," explore her life space. The conversation may sound more like, "Let's talk about some reasons your grandmother may have drunk despite its hurting her."

**B. Action: Challenge your own thinking.**

As parents, our instinct is to protect our children from anything we see as harmful. Sometimes we know that our fear is unreasonable; but it is easier to accede to fear than to calm it. We may know that stranger kidnappings are incredibly rare, and yet we take every imaginable step to protect our children against them. We have our own stories about who we think our children are that make us anxious. But some of those stories do more harm than good, and may in fact lead to the very things we worry about.

You may return to the same stories you have been using if you decide they are worth keeping. But it is good to examine them occasionally to make sure they still hold true. You may have discovered throughout the book that many of the "facts" that shape stories about addictions are themselves larger cultural stories that you can choose to give up. We aren't going to tell you what stories to tell, but do rely on your own personal experiences (for example, with painkillers) rather than on pre-packaged DARE and media Temperance Tales.

### The Fatal Glass of Beer

"The Fatal Glass of Beer," about a country lad who takes his first sip and plummets straight to the gutter, was a popular Temperance Tale. After Elizabeth Warren announced her presidential candidacy, she sent out a New Year's Eve Instagram livestream from her kitchen: "Hold on a second—I'm gonna get me a beer," she said as she walked off camera to return with a bottle, which she matter-of-factly cracked open, then drank from the open bottle. Her husband snuggled lovingly with Warren, "Enjoy your beer."*

---

* https://m.youtube.com/watch?v=sWehvtOL_VI

Since Warren is 69, grew up in rural Oklahoma, became a Harvard Law Professor and is now a United States Senator, we can assume that beer is a regular, pleasurable part of her existence. This is a story many of her viewers could relate to, an example of positive substance use most people take for granted, a behavior she modeled for her children and now for millions of viewers.

### What do you believe is unchangeable about a person?

It may seem obvious, but in order to change, you first have to believe that change is possible. While it is true that some change is impossible (I will never be any taller, or sprout wings. . .), sometimes we limit ourselves and our children because we give up on change too quickly. And sometimes, when we strive for distant possibilities, we get much further than we would have expected. Start by looking for what you think is unchangeable. Challenge yourself to find examples of people you know who changed in ways that surprised you.

### Are you concerned about the specter of addiction in your child's world?

Regardless of the views you express, there is a larger conversation about addiction throughout society, a view that addiction is uncontrollable, and therefore something to be greatly feared. As a parent, it is hard not to focus on that fear. In response, we start scaring our children with stories of drugs or by modeling fear, or else we avoid the topic altogether, with the result that our children rely on stories they hear from whoever will talk to them. That often ends up being other kids, and their stories can be deeply flawed in their own ways. At the same time, children are hearing opposite, unbelievable stories via the media and from drug education programs like DARE. If you are going to start talking with your child about addiction, you will need to face your own fears about drugs and addiction. Reading the stories presented in the book can support an attitude toward addiction that is less fear-based and more measured.

### Develop your own story: What substances/activities do you want to introduce your child to (on the assumption that they will be introduced at some point, and you'd rather it be with you)?

After reading the many stories from the book, perhaps you have some idea that the most common stories about substances are at a minimum mistaken, and moreover are often damaging. It is your job as a parent to have a story about drugs and about addiction ready so that you can introduce these early, and with confidence. A healthy story about addiction includes honesty and is not based on fear. Substances/activities that people become addicted to are not frightening bogeymen that cannot be named or dealt with. They are not mysterious and elusive dangers that call to us like the mythical sirens that lured sailors to their deaths. People may become addicted to many things, but those things don't have to be addictive.

How will you explain this to your child? Think about all of the things that might come up: alcohol, tobacco, cannabis, gambling, smartphones, food, sex and relationships. How can you talk about these things with your child in an honest, age-appropriate way? List for yourself the substances and activities that you want to address, focusing perhaps on those that are most pressing (look back at your answer to the question about what addictions are common in your area for children in the age range of your child).

## 3. Growing protective factors.

### A. Reflection: Life experience you can draw on

As described in Chapter 3, addictions occur far less often for people who have fulfilling, constructive life paths. When you strengthen those life paths, it is harder for addictions to take root or keep a stronghold. In this section the goal is to have a clearer sense of what a constructive life path might be in your family. As with everything else you have been asked to think about so far, this can look quite different across families. In one family, a constructive life means having a stable job and home; in another, it means following religious principles; in yet another, it means finding and following a passion. In the end, while a person's own perspective will determine whether that person feels good about the life path taken, that perspective draws heavily from what their family and friends say. Your child will hold ideas that grow out of your ideas as well as the ideas of friends, teachers, extended family, and community. When you can be clear about bringing things back to your values, then your child is able to make value-based choices in his or her own life.

This is in contrast to trying to control your child's behavior solely through punitive discipline. While rules and consequences will play a role in your household, they are scaffolding to prevent major problems while the protective factors are still growing. That is, until your child has developed a sense of making choices based on strong values, rules and consequences can help keep your child safe. But they will not teach your child to think through and make choices.

Keep in mind that children learn from what their parents model more than from what their parents say—although you should try to keep the two things in synch. If you want your children to live meaningful lives that align with your and their values, then you have to enact, as well as to speak, such positive values. This means that you have to be able to answer easily and simply when they ask questions about you and your life, and why you do the things you do. Thinking through these things collaboratively can be useful. Putting them down in writing will help you focus your energy to build a meaningful life for you and your child, as well as to have the words when teachable moments arise.

This doesn't mean that you must have all of the answers, as long as you can be open to thinking through and exploring answers together with your child. It's not concrete knowledge, itself, that aids in development. It is in confronting new experiences with anticipation and excitement about the unknown and the challenging. When your child asks you a question, sometimes the answer is "I don't know." That's fine. Kids will thrive having a shared and healthy respect for uncertainty. Respect for uncertainty requires an appreciation of novel experiences, confidence in one's ability to learn from novelty, and mindfulness, or living in the present.

### Mindfulness, or Living in the Present

- Appreciation of new things and experiences requires openness to noticing them, which puts them in the present and brings awareness of context and setting.

- The capacity to allow uncertainty and notice new things makes daily activities less routine and more stimulating.

- The more children notice about something, the more they engage with, explore, and understand it, which keeps them in the present moment.

- When children are in the present and engaged with the world, they can't help but make choices that improve health and happiness.

Pursuing goals is the foundation of a healthy life. This active pursuit and a growth mindset create the awareness that things can always change, and that negative experiences or behaviors and traits don't need to last forever. This mindset is a permanent anti-addiction asset.

### *What do you value?*

This list includes activities, goals, and even things. What do you care about? How do you know you are being a good person, or living a good life? See if you can get underneath these particular things, activities, or goals to find the general values that run through them. Perhaps you value making difficult choices; living a disciplined life; taking care of those around you; striving for your best in all things; promoting peace and kindness; or being in the present. You will find many values that resonate for you. Part of your thinking process will be about knowing when you are acting in line with your values. This is how you use your values—and teach your child to use theirs—to guide your and their choices.

Recall our list of "12 Values that Prevent Addiction" (Chapter 12) to guide your thinking as you identify your values:

- Purpose
- Achievement
- Caring about self
- Caring about others
- Responsibility
- Valuing money
- Awareness/mindfulness
- Adventure
- Pleasure and fun
- Social, political, religious commitments
- Efficacy agency, empowerment
- Maturity

***Does your child see you engage in activities that are enriching for you?***

As discussed throughout this book, a key outlook for fighting addiction is pursuing a meaningful life. Are you clear that you prioritize living your values and pursuing things that you find meaningful? Perhaps your work is meaningful and fulfilling; does your child know that? Or perhaps a key value for you is being a good friend, and you devote time to connecting with people.

Use these questions to identify what you are doing that is meaningful to you, what values these actions connect with, and how much your child sees and understands this process.

- What kinds of enrichment do you make available to your family?
- How do you get involved in your community or with other people?
- How would you define a good life?
- Do you feel that you are living a good life?
- Does your child see you embodying your values?

## B. Action

***Identify realms where your child feels a sense of mastery and competence, or a sense of being needed. Figure out ways to promote or support those realms without taking them over.***

As described in Chapter 4, children want to feel predictability, and they want to feel that they can impact the world around them. If they can do that only through acting out and getting punished, then they will act in that negative way. On the other hand, if they can have a sense of their value in the world (building on the last set of exercises), and they can see their value in the eyes of their parents, then they will not be prone to seek negative attention. Just as you identify and pursue meaningful activities in your life, it is important to direct your family to finding and supporting activities that your child finds meaningful.

- What activities does your child engage in independently?
- What opportunities are there currently for your child to make meaningful decisions?

- Where can you add more such opportunities?

Consider also the sources of current or possible enrichment that you identified. For those that your child already is involved in, notice the nature of the involvement and see whether you can increase the sense of purpose and mastery there. For the ones that your child is not involved in yet, consider what the "on ramp" looks like to support your child's becoming involved as appropriate and possible.

### *Develop emotional literacy.*

One major requirement for kids as they mature is to learn about emotions. What causes emotions? What do emotions look like? How should emotions be expressed? What should someone do in response to emotions? These are all things to be learned, which can take time and effort. This learning process is grounded in your values about what is important and what being a good person and living a good life involves. Your job as the parent includes helping your child attain the tools to understand these things.

There are many teachable moments for emotions. Consider these from least to most emotionally "hot": talking about situations, people, characters in movies or books; processing emotions in the moment, before they become overwhelming; processing stronger emotions when only one person is overwhelmed (you or your child); processing stronger emotions when both of you are overwhelmed. The basic arc of teaching emotions follows.

## Rules for Teaching and Learning Emotions

1. **Establish safety.** If everyone is already calm and feeling close, this step has already been accomplished. When people are worked up and having a hard time listening to each other, then the first thing is to reconnect and soothe. As a parent, if you are upset or angry, you may need to take a time out for yourself to calm down first. You should speak your choices out loud: "I have lost my mind. I need some time to find it. Give me five minutes to calm myself, and then I'll be ready to figure this out together." If you are calm, but your child is upset, you can hug, you can express sympathy, and you can say things like, "I really want to help, but it's hard to help when you're yelling like that."

2. **Label.** Naming feelings puts a handle on them, making them easier to grasp. The process of labeling the feelings should be a shared activity, where the goal is to find a label that includes a cause, a feeling, and a result. The person who has the feeling generally gets to be the final judge of whether the label is correct. But as the parent, you have to be as open as you can to your child's interpretation of both your and their emotions. An example of labeling that includes the cause, feeling, and result might be, "Geez, you just fell off your bike, that seems scary! I'm glad you came over for a hug!" The cause is the fall, the feeling is "scary," and the result is seeking comfort and care. An example of trying to figure it out together: "That look on your face makes me think you're mad. Are you? What happened?" And then after the child explains: "Oh, your sister pushed you, and you feel like it was on purpose, that would make me mad, too! What did you do?"

3. **Establish togetherness.** Whatever the feelings are, you want to be clear with your child (and with yourself!) that you two are on the same side, figuring it out together. This overlaps with safety and labeling. In the last example, when the parent says, "That would make me mad, too," that is an expression of togetherness. It is saying, "I see you and what you are experiencing, and I can get in that experience with you."

4. **Figure out what to do about the feeling.** Do you need to work at solving a problem together? Or perhaps imagine what should happen next? Again with that example, when the parent finds out that the child punched the sister in return, the aim is problem solving. Managing feelings is a skill that people learn over time, and they need to be able to make mistakes and learn from them. This flows naturally from that understanding that mistakes are opportunities,. A parent might say, "Uh oh, punching usually leads to more hurt and anger. You must have been really angry to have punched your sister. Maybe we can figure out something else to try next time you're that angry."

While the above are listed as numbered steps, you may find that you have to circle back frequently when in an emotionally hot moment. When you are discussing characters in a movie ("That character seems really sad! Do you think it's because of what happened? What do you think he should do?"), you run through this process in a simpler and more detached way. When two people are both upset, you may need to return to safety, labeling, and togetherness. Sometimes you may try ideas that make your child feel like you haven't really understood the feeling. Or your child will have ideas that make you feel like your child hasn't understood your feelings! And then emotions may run hotter, which means you have to return to earlier steps. This process dovetails with seeing mistakes as opportunities, and seeing that we can always grow and change.

### 4. Support a natural development process.

Over the course of these exercises so far, you have been trying to be clear about your child's world and your values. A core need for all people is to be an effective agent in the world: to see that they can make things happen. Because of your importance to your child, he or she will want to make things happen with you. Your child wants to know that you are responsive, hopefully in a positive way, but at least in a predictable way.

Some key concepts to remember: **People need motivation, self-control, options, rewards, and connection**. As you are supporting your child's development, the goal is to provide them with opportunities to grow their awareness of each of these.

### A. Reflection: What do your child's needs look like?

What looks like manipulation or power struggles can actually be a child's attempt to achieve motivation, self-control, options, rewards, or connection (see Chapter 4). Think of a recent example when you and your child had a difficult interaction, and work to fill in as much detail as you can. What actually happened? What came right before? What was your response? What happened afterward? Then take the perspective of your child: where do you see your child's need for motivation, self-control, options, rewards, and connection? What is motivating for your child? How does he experience self-control? What options are available? Realistically, what does your child see as possible responses in that situation? Avoid using your wiser adult perspective to see what would have been a better choice. What is the meaningful reward related to the scenario? Remember that getting any kind of predictable response (even the "soggy potato chip") can be a reward. And how did your child experience connection in that interaction?

## B. Action: Support choices that feel better.

A soggy potato chip is better than no potato chip, but when they are available, your child will choose the crisp potato chip. Once you have identified what your child needed in that moment, your job is to find a realistic alternative that can fill that need in a more constructive way. If it includes positive attention from you and other adults, it will feel better, and your child will choose it. Your child will need your help in learning to see and make that choice, however. Experiencing it one time will not be enough. In fact, sometimes you will find that your child seems to become more controlling or manipulative. This is because the new possibility feels uncertain and unpredictable. Your child is thinking, "Is this really an option? Or is it just an illusion?" (although not in those words). Your child might get nervous or feel uncomfortable, unsure of whether this new response from you is reliable. So you will have to be consistent with alternatives even through this initial bumpy patch. Bumpy patches can also pop up again in moments when your child feels overwhelmed, or with other changes or upsets, when your child reverts to something that feels more certain. As long as you can continue to see it as a way to feel some sense of predictable reward and self-control, then you can return to figuring out how to meet that need in other ways.

There is converging evidence from a few different areas (behavioral work with children; counseling with couples) that the golden ratio of positive to negative interactions in a relationship is five to one. That means that for every negative interaction, you need to have five positive interactions in order for the relationship to stay balanced. The point here is that you do not need to be perfect. You will do your best to support good choices and a strong relationship, but sometimes you will make mistakes. These are opportunities for you to grow as a parent and as a person as well. They are opportunities to model that people can make mistakes in relationships and still make things right. In order to keep your relationship balanced, you simply plan to look for five positive interactions whenever you do have a conflict or a parenting mistake.

# 5. Developing your child's story

As described above and throughout this book, your child wants to have an impact on you. There is nothing better for developing agency and efficacy than to impact another mind. Even more valuable is feeling that you can impact how that other mind sees you. As a parent, your view of your child may be the one with the greatest impact, so your view is the one that your child wants most to impact. We often get stuck on things we wish were true about our kids ("My child wants to play piano, I'm sure of it!") or things we dread are true ("My child is going to do terribly in school, just like I did"), and fail to be open to what actually is true. And yet, despite these alternative realities, we can still find beautiful stories to tell about our children that help them feel truly understood.

## A. Reflection: What stories already exist about your child (and you)?

You are already telling your child stories about him or herself. A good story helps support development, as discussed in the fourth step. It reflects your child's motivations, attributes self-control to your child, demonstrates active choices, identifies clear rewards, and is embedded in connections.

### *What labels do you apply to your children?*

Include diagnoses but also other labels like athletic, kind, distractible, troublemaker, etc. How much do you think those reflect your child's "true" character? Can you remember examples from your child's past that show the truth of that label? Can you think of times when your child defied or went beyond those labels?

### *What labels get applied to you that feel frustrating or inaccurate?*

What labels get applied to you that you find helpful, or comforting? How so? What makes the difference between helpful and frustrating labels? Is it who they come from? How much they resonate, or how "true" they feel?

Now, thinking about your answers to (2), look back at your answers to (1). Which of those labels do you think are going to feel good to your child? Which of those labels fit with supporting development?

## B. Action: Develop a grounded story about your child.

What words can you use to describe your child? Come up with at least 10, and try to frame them as positive or neutral. Consider the story of DJ in Chapter 4: Zach took a step back to see DJ differently, focusing on what kind of person he was rather than what he was doing wrong. He found DJ's unique abilities and used those as a way to connect DJ with his schooling. Take a step back from your child to consider how strangers might see your child, and also consider things that you have seen consistently over your child's lifespan. What makes your child who he or she is? How can your child's unique qualities benefit your family? What are areas where his qualities cause difficulties for him or the people around him? Try to include an understanding of why those things are difficult for him that represent his perspective. For example, rather than, "She gets too rowdy indoors," look at her perspective, "I don't get to move around as much as I want to." What are concrete ways that your child's various environments can be tailored to address those difficulties and grow those strengths? What does the story look like with the context changed?

### *The reality of youthful drug use*

You and your child will come to your own conclusions about how best to navigate the experience of development and how to address issues surrounding drugs and all kinds of addictions. But you may benefit from a summary of our views as discussed in detail throughout the book.

### Four Addiction Truths

1. No one is destined to be addicted.

2. Early childhood recreational substance use may (or may not) have downsides, perhaps severely negative ones, but such experiences are not lifetime sentences.

3. The route out of early substance problems is to embrace as full—and as fully rewarding—a life as possible.

4. This goal is not enhanced by calling a child (or anyone else) an addict, and we shouldn't use that label.

Maintaining a cultural abstinence-only philosophy regarding drugs may lead to us losing communication with the young people we need to reach most. In a world where drugs are ubiquitous, a sensible question is not, "How do we keep our kids away from drugs?" but, "How do we keep our kids safe while preparing them for this world?"

Some children will come into contact with drugs. Don't panic: 80–90% of kids ages 12–17 choose to refrain from *regular* drug use, and the vast majority of teen drug use does not lead to negative use. If we expect to retrench substance abuse, we must make clear to children that there is a huge difference between use and using with negative consequences or relying on a drug to deal with experience, and between occasional and regular use.

Drug use does not equal addiction, but people can develop addictions when they build their lives around drug use (or many other things), depending on how balanced the rest of their lives are. The best antidote for keeping your children safe from the harms of addiction is by working with them, and allowing them to explore for themselves, as they enter each stage of development, as we've addressed in the previous steps.

One way to be sure that your child's habits are developmentally appropriate is to consider the following:

- What are the signs of success in your child's life?
- What would be indicators that something is going wrong?

And if you determine your child does have an addiction, you may refer back to the anti-addiction strategies in Chapter 14, and consider the approach that we take in our Life Process Program in the following Appendix C.

# Appendix C
## The Life Process
## Program/Family Program

Stanton and Zach work with the Life Process Program (LPP), an on-line non-12-step addiction treatment option based on values, purpose, skills, relationships, community, meaning, responsibility, and maturity. LPP provides an easily accessed alternative option to the standard 12-step treatments and AA.

Stanton developed the Life Process Program out of his own work and refined it over several years of operation in a prestigious, CARF-accredited* residential rehab. Now LPP is available completely online and is accessible for people around the world. It combines exercises based on videos, reading material, and clients' experiences, reflective questioning of clients, and an ongoing self-narrative in which clients explore their past decisions and alternative scenarios—all of which is accompanied by online coaching as well as video sessions with coaches.

### Program Foundation

1. **The Life Process Program, as its name indicates, is based on the concept that improvement in addictive areas of people's lives requires them to improve their key life "pillars"** (see Chapters 2, 11): Health, Home, Purpose, Community.

2. **LPP doesn't apply labels like "addict" or "addiction"** (see Chapters 6-7)—but instead explores with the person the functions that their negative behaviors (addictions) serve ("Why do you drink/take drugs/get involved in unhealthy relationships?").

3. **LPP is client-centered, nondirective, and non-judgmental** (as opposed to AA, see Chapter 11)—it accepts

---

* Commission on Accreditation of Rehabilitation Facilities

and works with people's own perceptions of themselves and their situations. All change emanates from the client, and is under their control.

4. **LPP is empowering** (see Chapters 2, 11). LPP doesn't view people as diseased, disabled, or dishonorable, but rather sees them as whole human beings capable of controlling and redirecting themselves.

5. **LPP is harm reduction** (see Chapter 9). LPP accepts clients' own goals around consumption, whether to moderate use or to abstain. (Of course, in areas such as sex, love, eating, etc., abstinence is not a possibility at all.)

6. **LPP is accessible within people's homes and fits into their daily lives,** helping them to improve these, rather than removing them from and replacing their existing lives and relationships.

## Program Overview

**Eight Modules:**

LPP comprises eight comprehensive written modules containing videos and reading material. This includes over 50 written exercises that help clarify clients' thinking about their lives, including their emotions and life situations, as follows:

- Self-reflection—regarding your own health/addiction profile
- Values—ordering your deepest priorities
- Motivation—translating thinking into action
- Rewards—the "whys" that make change real
- Resources—what you already have going for you, along with the skills you need to develop further
- Support—finding help all around you
- Maturity—uncovering the adult in you
- Greater goals—purpose, purpose, purpose (Chapter 13)

**Coaching:**

- Clients work with a trained and experienced addiction professional (they may choose to work with a male or female coach) who provides advice, feedback, and guidance while responding to submitted exercises.

- Clients can have 1-1 coaching sessions with their LPP coach via Internet audio and video.

## LPP Philosophy

### Definition of Addiction

*Addiction is the following process:*

- A person becomes engaged in an experience in order to fulfill emotional and identity needs.

- This has the kick-back effect of detracting from the person's ability to live a balanced life.

- Despite the negative consequences, the person becomes increasingly dependent on that activity or experience for satisfaction.

*Addiction is **not** a disease*

Understanding that addiction is not a disease shifts the focus away from chemical sources of addiction. It is not a molecule that locks a person's brain into addiction; it's the way people turn to drugs, alcohol, or any kind of engaging experience as a way of resolving emotional issues such as anxiety and depression, of offering them the feeling that they are worthwhile, of providing an artificial sense that they control their lives.

*Addiction **is** a life process*

Addiction is a way people become engaged in an experience as a way of dealing with their lives.

*People become addicted to an experience (not a drug)*

It's not the thing to which people are addicted that determines their involvement in an addiction. It is how they engage with their overall lives, relationships, and feelings.

## Solution to Addiction Problems

LPP enables people to enhance their life-space and life gratification—to find better sources for the needs that they're trying to fulfill through the addiction, but to do so in the course of living ordinary, non-addicted lives. LPP does this by helping people identify the satisfactions the addictive experience provides for them and to find other kinds of experiences and satisfaction to replace addictive ones.

## LPP Options

While LPP helps people explore their addiction to an experience, most clients identify their problems in relation to drugs, alcohol, or other specific involvements. Clients can choose from the following programs: *Alcohol/Drugs/Food/Sex/Pornography/Gambling/Love and Relationships.*

Finally, LPP offers a Family Program to provide resources and support for children and families.

## Life Process Family Program

Zach has developed a track for families in Stanton's Life Process Program: The Life Process Family Program (LPFP). The Family Program provides critical resources and immediate support for caregivers whose children are experiencing developmental, behavioral, and addiction problems.

## Purpose

The Life Process Family Program helps parents and other caregivers develop their ability to make positive decisions for themselves, children, and the entire family, especially involving addictive issues—perhaps the child drinks outside the home, smokes, takes drugs, eats poorly, is preoccupied with pornography, has an unhealthy involvement with some form of technology like video games or social media, or creates unhealthy relationships. Children with these problems may become so involved with a negative substance, activity, or person that they feel incapable of dealing with life issues like making friends, going outside and exercising, and completing schoolwork—all of which the LPFP addresses.

## Vision

The LPFP promotes constructive collaboration between caregivers and children. Trained and experienced LPP family and addiction coaches help caregivers foster the most positive qualities in children while avoiding the useless and often damaging effects of criticizing and punishing them.

## Goals

Parents are often told their child's addiction problem is a disease for which they must seek medical treatment or join a support group with the goal of total, lifelong abstinence. People receive this message in school and from the media, government organizations, and treatment providers. But abstinence is often not possible, as in the case of shopping addiction, gambling, eating, love and sex, and social media, communication devices, and video games. *Lifetime* abstinence may also be unrealistic for a young person in the case of alcohol or drugs.

Addiction is not a life sentence; most things that overwhelm young people or that they struggle with as children become more manageable as they mature and develop a grounded sense of themselves. Participants in the LPFP learn how to help children who become preoccupied with drugs, food, relationships, or technology, in a collaborative way that doesn't necessarily rule those things out of their lives altogether for all time. If a child's involvement is especially destructive, then stability—not abstinence—is the foremost consideration, which LPFP also helps parents to establish with children. Underlying all intended life improvements in addictive behaviors for the child are broader issues of purpose, achievement and engagement, communication, relationships, self-contentment and belief in themselves, and ultimately maturity and responsibility for themselves.

## Philosophy

Addiction is not a result of a drug's effects. It is an expression of a person's whole life, and is embedded within that life. In particular, we cannot separate any form of addiction from the family in which the person with the addiction resides. Telling children they are powerless over their addiction will make it even more likely that they will continue to act this way, that parents will accept their behavior passively, and that neither party will take responsibility for their lives and their addiction.

Instead, LPFP clients learn to communicate and collaborate—to live and to love together.

This doesn't mean that adults are responsible for the child's addiction. But they are a part of it; certainly they are impacted by it. Parents and children together create the family's emotional state, communication style, acceptance of responsibility, shared goals, and the ultimate maturity of the child. The Life Process Family Program thus addresses all of these factors as critical elements in the addiction.

LPFP involves more than simply filling in answers and pondering readings. Participation means engaging the entire family. Of course, some issues a child faces may occur at such an early age that children can't be involved directly. But they may be old enough to respond to questions and exercises themselves, or else at least to react to parents' responses and suggestions. When they are too young to do this, then parents may translate what they encounter in ways that children can understand as a part of their place in the addiction and recovery process.

### Comparing LPFP with Other Programs

Other programs help families, including children, work through addiction problems. One of the most prominent examples is CRAFT, which we cite in Chapter 9, and highly recommend in Appendix D. The Life Process Family Program shares many values with CRAFT, including the concept of collaboration with children rather than relying on punitive consequences. But the LPFP extends beyond the parameters of CRAFT—and other programs—in crucial ways.

### Differences between CRAFT and Life Process Family Program

| CRAFT | Life Process Family Program |
| --- | --- |
| Focuses on child's drug and alcohol use while protecting other family members | Considers the child's substance use and family interactions and well-being as a unit |
| Harmful drug and alcohol use is the root of the adolescent's problems | Unsolved problems in adolescence happen when the child's skills are not adapted to the demands of situations they face |
| Getting child or family member to consider treatment is the end goal | The goal is to engage the child in a fluid, collaborative effort to set and achieve goals that will solve problems for both the child and parents going forward |
| Drug and alcohol treatment will help the child learn how to live a safer, fuller life | Addiction is a detour in a developmental process; kids can learn skills, harness motivation, and gain resources without leaving their normal home environment |

# D

## Appendix D
## Additional Resources

We hesitate to recommend addiction programs to children and families. Unfortunately, many addiction therapy programs and support groups in the United States accept the disease model whose limitations and drawbacks we have identified. As we have shown, the disease model can be counterproductive in both the prevention and treatment of addiction—especially so with regard to children.

We recommend solution-focused organizations—rather than addiction-related ones—for children and families. By this we mean programs that apply concepts of problem-solving, harm-reduction, self-efficacy and self-control rather than focusing on a child's or family member's addictive "illness."

Thankfully, there *are* groups whose methods empower families and children to narrate their own life-stories (these groups rarely label themselves addiction groups). The following programs embody these concepts; all are devoted to improving human development and addressing the dimensions of growth that, when balanced, ultimately lead to an addiction-free life.

Stanton has long been suggesting resources in appendices of his books. If you don't find a resource in our list that suits your needs, you can visit Stanton's website for a longer, comprehensive list (http://www.peele.net).

You may also find new and reliable resources on Zach's podcast, "The Social Exchange" (http://www.thesocialexchange.libsyn.com). Zach engages with his audience about their interests, and in each episode interviews an expert (often a well-known researcher or author) with practical—and sometimes cutting-edge—advice for listeners.

### Ross Greene's Lives In The Balance

https://www.livesinthebalance.org/

Lives in the Balance is a non-profit organization founded by clinical child psychologist and author of The Explosive Child, Dr. Ross Greene. This educational program helps parents and educators engage children in a model called Collaborative & Proactive Solutions (CPS) (as partners) to get ahead in life, and to ensure that all parties listen and act according to the wants and needs of each person involved. The Lives in the Balance website provides a user-friendly guide to solving problems collaboratively with children.

## The Fitzgerald Institute

https://www.thefitzgeraldinstitute.org/

The Fitzgerald Institute is a program for parents and educators wanting training about their own children and/or the children they work with. It was founded by Jeanine Fitzgerald, author of The Dance of Interaction. Jeanine and her daughter Erin Fournier travel the country (and internationally) engaging families, schools, and communities about how to prepare children for this world. Most importantly, they train children on how to become part of these collaborative partnerships.

In the realm of drug- and alcohol-related treatment, we recommend the following:

## Community Reinforcement and Family Training (CRAFT)

https://www.robertjmeyersphd.com/craft.html

CRAFT is a framework for people and their loved ones to work through addiction-related problems—as described in Chapter 3. Dr. Robert Meyers first introduced CRAFT to the public in his book Get Your Loved One Sober — Alternatives to Nagging, Pleading and Threatening.

## Center for Motivation and Change

https://motivationandchange.com/

The Center for Motivation and Change (CMC) is built on, and expands upon, the CRAFT framework, as described in CMC's founders' book, Beyond Addiction: How Science and Kindness Help People Change (by Carrie Wilkens, Jeffrey Foote, Nicole Kosanke, and Stephanie Higgs). CMS offers both residential and outpatient treatment using a motivational approach to addictive substance use and behaviors. It accepts people's ability to change permanently.

## The Harm Reduction Therapy Center

https://www.sfcenter.org/resources/center-harm-reduction-therapy,
415-574-0966

The Harm Reduction Therapy Center, created by Patt Denning and Jeannie Little, is in many ways the pioneer of harm reduction psychotherapy for substance users, and continues to maintain a panoply of individual and group services in the San Francisco Bay Area.

## Families For Sensible Drug Policy

http://fsdp.org

Families for Sensible Drug Policy (FSDP) is a global coalition of families, professionals, and organizations representing the voice of the family impacted by substance use and the harms of existing drug policies. FSDP empowers families by educating and advocating for a new paradigm of comprehensive care and progressive solutions for family support based on science, compassion, public health and human rights. They do so by collaborating with stakeholders to advance comprehensive public health approaches, best healthcare practices, reality-based education and family-friendly drug policy reform.

## Center For Optimal Living

http://centerforoptimalliving.com/

The Center for Optimal Living, directed by Dr. Andrew Tatarsky, is an outpatient, harm reduction treatment group located in New York City that practices individual and family therapy for people facing substance-use issues, other risky or addictive behaviors, and a range of mental health issues. The Center recognizes a range of possible outcomes for substance use in response to clients' problems, goals, and choices. It seeks to promote positive change through the principles of compassion, collaboration, and empowerment.

## Practical Recovery Psychology Group

www.practicalrecovery.com

San Diego-based Practical Recovery, founded by Tom Horvath, Ph.D., offers non-disease, fully personalized harm reduction treatment, which has as primary focus building up a meaningful life for client. Practical Recovery serves both local clients, and clients from around the world, who come for an innovative treatment format, the IIOP (individualized intensive outpatient program).

## St. Jude Retreat/The Freedom Model

https://www.soberforever.net/, 888-424-2626

St. Jude Retreat is a residential and outpatient program that practices The Freedom Model, a non-disease approach focused on people's ability to escape addictive behavior and thinking and to create a totally free consciousness.

# References

## Epigraphs

Lindsay Crouse. "Who Says Allie Kieffer Isn't Thin Enough to Run Marathons?" *New York Times*, October 27, 2018. https://www.nytimcs.com/2018/10/27/sunday-review/allie-kieffer-weight-marathons-body.html

## Introduction: Why We Are Writing This Book

Stanton Peele. https://www.amazon.com/Stanton-Peele/e/B000APH1ZW

More susceptible to addiction. Maia Szalavitz, "The social life of opioids: New studies strengthen the ties between loss, pain, and drug use," *Scientific American*, September 18, 2017. https://www.scientificamerican.com/article/the-social-life-of-opioids/

but incorrect. Marc Lewis, "Why the disease definition of addiction does far more harm than good," *Scientific American*, February 9, 2018. https://blogs.scientificamerican.com/observations/why-the-disease-definition-of-addiction-does-far-more-harm-than-good/

is commonplace. Gene Heyman, "Quitting drugs: Quantitative and qualitative features," *Annual Review of Clinical Psychology*, Vol. 9:29-59, March 2013. http://www.annualreviews.org/doi/abs/10.1146/annurev-clinpsy-032511-143041

## 1: Addiction as a Developmental Process

Stanton Peele and Archie Brodsky, *Love and Addiction*. New York: Taplinger, 1975; Watertown, MA: Broadrow Publications, 2014.

Vietnam Veterans Three Years After Vietnam: How our study changed our view of heroin. Lee Robins, John Helzer, Michie Hesselbrock, and Eric Wish, "Vietnam Veterans three years after Vietnam: How our study changed our view of heroin," Problems of Drug Dependence (Proceedings of the Thirty-Ninth Annual Scientific Meeting of the Committee on Problems of Drug Dependence), 1977. https://onlinelibrary.wiley.com/doi/full/10.1111/j.1521-0391.2010.00046.x

Vietnam Veterans' Rapid Recovery from Heroin Addiction: A fluke or normal expectation?" Lee Robins, "Vietnam Veterans' rapid recovery from heroin addiction: A fluke or normal expectation," *Addiction*, Vol. 88: 1041-1054, 1993. http://www.rkp.wustl.edu/veslit/robinsaddiction1993.pdf

following message. Douglas Quenqua, "Rethinking addiction's roots, and its treatment," *New York Times*, July 10, 2011. https://www.nytimes.com/2011/07/11/health/11addictions.html

415 scientific reports of recovery. William White, Recovery/Remission from Substance Use Disorders: An analysis of reported outcomes in 415 scientific reports. Philadelphia: Philadelphia Department of Behavioral Health and Intellectual Disability Services and the Great Lakes Addiction Technology Transfer Center, 2012. http://www.williamwhitepapers.com/pr/file_download.php?fn=2012+Recovery-Remission+from+Substance+Use+DisordersFinal&ext=pdf

research found. Catalina Lopez-Qunitera, D.S. Hasin, J. de los Cobos, A. Pines, S. Wang, B.F. Grant, and C. Blanco, "Probability and predictors of remission from life-time nicotine, alcohol, cannabis or cocaine dependence: Results from National Epidemiological Survey on Alcohol and Related Conditions," *Addiction*, 2011 Mar; Vol. 106(3): 657–669. https://www.ncbi.nlm.nih.gov/pmc/articles/PMC3227547/

In a separate analysis. C. Blanco, R. Secades-Villa, O. Garcia-Rodriguez, M. Labrador-Mendez, S. Wang, and R.P. Schwartz, "Probability and predictors of remission from lifetime prescription drug use disorders: Results from the National Epidemiologic Survey on Alcohol and Related Conditions," *Journal of Psychiatric Research*, Vol. 47: 42-49, 2012. https://www.ncbi.nlm.nih.gov/pubmed/22985744

Maia Szalavitz asked. Maia Szalavitz, "Most people with addiction simply grow out of it: Why Is this widely denied?" *Pacific Standard*, October 1, 2014. https://psmag.com/social-justice/people-addiction-simply-grow-widely-denied-91605

Szalavitz emphasizes the treatment solution. Maia Szalavitz, "Addiction doesn't always last a lifetime," *New York Times,* August 31, 2018. https://www.nytimes.com/2018/08/31/opinion/addiction-recovery-survivors.html
(fn) a list. Ruth Fowler, "10 people revolutionizing how we study addiction and recovery," *The Atlantic*, October 6, 2011. https://www.theatlantic.com/health/archive/2011/10/10-people-revolutionizing-how-we-study-addiction-and-recovery/246202/

quit a "massive" cocaine habit. "Mets Hernandez admits 'massive' cocaine habit," *Los Angeles Times*, September 6, 1985. http://articles.latimes.com/1985-09-06/news/mn-23679_1_keith-hernandez

ordinary developmental process. Marc Lewis, "Addiction and the brain: Development, not disease," *Neuroethics*, Vol. 10(1): 7-18. https://link.springer.com/article/10.1007/s12152-016-9293-4

now drinks alcohol moderately. Maia Szalavitz, "It's time to reclaim the word 'recovery'," Addiction Treatment Forum, December 22, 2014. http://atforum.com/2014/12/its-time-to-reclaim-the-word-recovery-by maia-szalavitz/

Stanton Peele and Ilse Thompson, *Recover! An empowering program to help you stop thinking like an addict and reclaim your life*. Boston, Lifelong Books, 2015.

"A Really Good Thing Happening in America." David Brooks, "A really good thing happening in America: A strategy for community problem-solving does an extraordinary job at restoring our social fabric," *New York Times*, October 18, 2018. https://www.nytimes.com/2018/10/08/opinion/collective-impact-community-civic-architecture.amp.html

childhood adversity measures. Stanton Peele and Alan Cudmore, "The seductive (but dangerous) allure of Gabor Maté," Psychology Today Blogs, December 5, 2011. https://psychologytoday.com/blog/addiction-in-society/201112/the-seductive-dangerous-allure-gabor-mat

Angela Duckworth, *Grit: The power of passion and perseverance*. New York: Scribner, 2016.

who go to leading colleges. Benoit Denizet-Lewis, "Why are more American teenagers than ever suffering from severe anxiety?" *The New York Times Magazine*, October 11, 2017. https://www.nytimes.com/2017/10/11/magazine/why-are-more-american-teenagers-than-ever-suffering-from-severe-anxiety.amp.html

Maia Szalavitz has pointed out, "Addictions are harder to kick when you're poor: Here's why," The *Guardian*, June 1, 2016. https://www.theguardian.com/commentisfree/2016/jun/01/drug-addiction-income-inequality-impacts-recovery

## 2: Addictive Experiences

recognized by the American psychiatric establishment. Stanton Peele, "Addiction in society: Blinded by biochemistry," *Psychology Today*, June 9, 2016. https://www.psychologytoday.com/articles/201009/addiction-in-society-blinded-biochemistry

does not lead to addiction. Elly Vintiadis, "Is addiction a disease? The current medical consensus may very well be wrong." *Scientific American Blogs*, November 8, 2017. https://blogs.scientificamerican.com/observations/is-addiction-a-disease/

David Courtwright, *Dark Paradise: A history of opiate addiction in America*. Cambridge, MA: Harvard University Press, 1982.

Virginia Berridge, *Opium and the People: Opiate use and policy in 19th and early 20th century Britain* (rev. ed.). London: Free Association Books, 1998.

(fn) "Is Addiction a Disease? The current medical consensus about addiction may well be wrong." Elly Vintiadis, "Is addiction a disease? The current medical consensus may very well be wrong." *Scientific American Blogs*, November 8, 2017. https://blogs.scientificamerican.com/observations/is-addiction-a-disease/

"People Are Dying Because of Ignorance, Not Because of Opioids." Carl Hart, "People are dying because of ignorance, not opioids," *Scientific American*, November 1, 2017. https://www.scientificamerican.com/article/people-are-dying-because-of-ignorance-not-because-of-opioids/

"The Social Life of Opioids: New studies strengthen ties between loss, pain and drug use." Maia Szalavitz, "The social life of opioids: New studies strengthen the ties between loss, pain and drug use." *Scientific American*, September 18, 2017. https://www.scientificamerican.com/article/the-social-life-of-opioids/

"Why the Disease Definition of Addiction Does Far More Harm than Good." Marc Lewis, "Why the disease definition of addiction does far more harm than good," *Scientific American*, February 9, 2018. https://blogs.scientificamerican.com/observations/why-the-disease-definition-of-addiction-does-far-more-harm-than-good/

Stanton noted at the time. Stanton Peele, "Prince's death and the opioid addiction/overdose myth," *Psychology Today Blogs*, June 26, 2016. https://www.psychologytoday.com/us/blog/addiction-in-society/201606/princes-death-and-the-opioid-addictionoverdose-myth

opioid hysteria websites. opioids.thetruth.com

published a critique. J.V. Pergolizzi, R.B. Raffa, G. Zampogna, et al., "Editorial: Comments and suggestions from pain specialists regarding the CDC's proposed opioid guidelines," *PAIN Practice*, September 7, 2016. http://onlinelibrary.wiley.com/wol1/doi/10.1111/papr.12475/full

extended study of prescribed opioid users. "Postsurgical prescriptions of opioid naïve patients and association with overdose and misuse: Retrospective cohort study," *BMJ* 2018:j5790. http://www.bmj.com/content/360/bmj.j5790

Marcia Angell. Marcia Angell, "Opioid nation," *NYRB*, December 6, 2018. https://www.nybooks.com/articles/2018/12/06/opioid-nation/

don't become addicted. Paul Hayes, "Many people use drugs—but here's why most don't become addicts," *The Conversation*, January 8, 2015. http://www.iflscience.com/health-and-medicine/many-people-use-drugs-here-s-why-most-don-t-become-addicts/

Survey depicts a day in a drug user's life, and it's pretty normal. Chloe Aiello, "Survey depicts a day in a drug user's life, and it's pretty normal," Cnbc.com, December 29, 2017. https://www.cnbc.com/amp/2017/12/29/survey-depicts-a-day-in-an-drug-users-life-and-its-pretty-normal.html

2016 National Survey on Drug Use and Health. R. Ahrnsbrak, J. Bose, S.L. Hedden, et al., *Key Substance Use and Mental Health Indicators in the United States: Results from the 2016 National Survey on Drug Use and Health.* Rockville, MD: Substance Abuse and Mental Health Services Administration, 2017. https://www.samhsa.gov/data/sites/default/files/NSDUH-FFR1-2016/NSDUH-FFR1-2016.htm

shown not to work. Scott Lilienfeld and Hal Arkowitz, "Why 'just say no' doesn't work: A popular program for preventing teen drug use does not help," *Scientific American*, January 1, 2014. https://www.scientificamerican.com/article/why-just-say-no-doesnt-work/

Stanton Peele, Archie Brodsky, and Mary Arnold, *The Truth About Addiction and Recovery*. New York: Simon & Schuster, 1991.

Stanton Peele, *7 Tools To Beat Addiction*. New York: Three Rivers Press, 2004.

Stanton Peele and Ilse Thompson, *Recover!: An empowering program to help you stop thinking like an addict and reclaim your life*. Berkeley, CA: Da Capo Press, 2014.

Michael Pollan, *How To Change Your Mind*. New York: Penguin, 2018.

what concerned him. Michael Pollan, "My adventures with the trip doctors," *New York Times Magazine*, May 15, 2018. https://www.nytimes.com/interactive/2018/05/15/magazine/health-is-sue-my-adventures-with-hallucinogenic-drugs-medicine.html

far more typical on the margins of society. Stanton Peele, "Why liberals love the disease theory of addiction, by a liberal who hates it," *Pacific Standard*, September 26, 2014. https://psmag.com/social-justice/liberals-love-disease-theory-addiction-liberal-hates-91098

McGovern said. Rhoda Fukushima, "The life and death of George McGovern's daughter," *Chicago Tribune*, June 24, 1996. http://articles.chicagotribune.com/1996-06-24/features/9606240120_1_alco-holism-relapses-death

52 such deaths per 100,000 in 2016. Centers for Disease Control and Prevention, *Drug overdose death data*. Washington, DC: Department of Health and Human Services, 2017. https://www.cdc.gov/drugoverdose/data/statedeaths.html

identifying every one of these opioid deaths. Brianna Ehley, "The immigrant doctor who's solving West Virginia's opioid crisis," *Politico Magazine*, May 2, 2018. https://www.politico.com/magazine/story/2018/05/02/west-virgin-ia-opioids-immigrant-doctor-solution-218118
among middle-age male users. SciPol, "The opioid crisis is surging in black urban communities," *SciPol* (Duke University), March 9, 2018. http://scipol.duke.edu/content/opioid-crisis-surging-black-urban-communities

critic. Marcia Angell, "Drug companies & doctors: A story of corruption." *New York Review of Books*, January 15, 2009. https://www.nybooks.com/articles/2009/01/15/drug-companies-doctorsa-story-of-corruption/

Opioid Nation. Marcia Angell, "Opioid nation," *New York Review of Books*, December 6, 2018. https://www.nybooks.com/articles/2018/12/06/opioid-nation/

Chris McGreal, *American Overdose: The opioid crisis in three acts*. New York: Hachette, 2018.

aversion to pain. Stanton Peele, "Why do we now have a prescription drug use problem?" *Huffington Post*, May 30, 2011. https://www.huffpost.com/entry/why-do-we-now-have-a-pres_b_858687?ec_carp=602228221496122974

Carl Hart, *High Price: A neuroscientist's journey of self-discovery that challenges everything you know about drugs and society*. New York: Harper, 2013.

wet housing. Susan E. Collins, Seema L. Clifasefi, Elizabeth A. Dana, et al., "Where harm reduction meets housing first: Exploring alcohol's role in a project-based housing first setting," *International Journal of Drug Policy*, 23(2): 111-119, 2012. https://www.ncbi.nlm.nih.gov/pmc/articles/PMC3726334/

in Time by Maia Szalavitz. Maia Szalavitz, "The wet house: Homeless people with alcoholism drink less when booze is allowed," *Time*, January 20, 2012. http://healthland.time.com/2012/01/20/the-wet-house-homeless-people-with-alcoholism-drink-less-when-booze-is-allowed/

interviews with the residents and staff. Collins et al. https://www.ncbi.nlm.nih.gov/pmc/articles/PMC3726334/

### 3: Expanding Life Experience

remarkable discovery. Gene Heyman, "Quitting drugs: Quantitative and qualitative features," *Annual Review of Clinical Psychology*, 9:29-59, 2013. https://www.annualreviews.org/doi/abs/10.1146/annurev-clinpsy-032511-143041

according to Liz Phair. Liz Phair, "Stray cat blues," *New York Times*, November 4, 2010. https://www.nytimes.com/2010/11/14/books/review/Phair-t.html

He described. "Ask Keith Richards: Do you still enjoy playing old songs?" *YouTube*, https://www.youtube.com/watch?v=GNTdj09LSzU&app=desktop.

Wikipedia biography. *Wikipedia*, "Richard Harris." https://en.m.wikipedia.org/wiki/Richard_Harris

Stanton Peele, Archie Brodsky, and Mary Arnold, *The Truth About Addiction and Recovery*. New York: Simon & Schuster, 1991.

Stanton Peele, *7 Tools To Beat Addiction*. New York: Three Rivers Press, 2004.

online version. Life Process Program. www.lifeprocessprogram.com

## 4: The Life Process of Children

Ross Greene, *The Explosive Child*. New York: Harper Paperback, 2014.

According to Greene. "Kids do well if they can." http://www.informationchildren.com/kids-do-well-if-they-can/

Rudolph Dreikurs, *A New Approach to Discipline*. New York: Dutton, 1990.

Leon Vygotsky, *Mind in Society: The development of higher psychological processes*. Cambridge, MA: Harvard University Press, 1978.

zone of proximal development. B.G. Lyons, "Defining a child's zone of proximal development," *American Journal of Occupational Therapy*, 38:446-51, 1984. https://www.ncbi.nlm.nih.gov/pubmed/6465269

## 5: Children and Addiction

2016 National Survey on Drug Use and Health. Center for Behavioral Health Statistics and Quality, *Results from the 2016 National Survey on Drug Use and Health: Detailed Tables*. Rockville, MD: SAMHSA, 2017. https://www.samhsa.gov/data/sites/default/files/NSDUH-DetTabs-2016/NSDUH-DetTabs-2016.pdf

she confessed. "Barrymore: 'I'm not sober,'" *World Entertainment News Network*, September 24, 2009. https://m.chron.com/entertainment/article/Barrymore-I-m-not-sober-1749954.php

dark and fearful place. Today, "Drew Barrymore: I was in a 'dark and fearful place' before Santa Clarita Diet,'" *Today.com*. https://www.today.com/video/drew-barrymore-i-was-in-a-dark-and-fearful-place-before-santa-clarita-diet-1193547843720

Childhood Drug Addiction: Drew Barrymore. Orchid Recovery Center, "Childhood drug addiction: Drew Barrymore," *Orchidrecoverycenter.com*, November 24, 2008. http://www.orchidrecoverycenter.com/blog/childhood-drug-addiction-drew-barrymore/

*Psychology Today.* Stanton Peele, "Drew Barrymore: Sober winemaking newlywed," *Psychologytoday.com*, June 5, 2012. https://www.psychologytoday.com/blog/addiction-in-society/201206/drew-barrymore-sober-winemaking-newlywed

continue drinking. Stanton Peele, "United States changes its mind on addiction—It's not a chronic brain disease after all." *Lifeprocessprogram.com*, November 20, 2009. http://www.peele.net/blog/091120.html

U.S. Surgeons General. Stanton Peele, "The solution to the opioid crisis," *Psychologytoday.com*, May 16, 2017. https://www.psychologytoday.com/blog/addiction-in-society/201703/the-solution-the-opioid-crisis

gaming addiction was classified as a disorder. World Health Organization, "Gaming disorder," *Who.int*, September 2018. https://www.who.int/features/qa/gaming-disorder/en/

## 6: Diseases, Disorders and Self-Fulfilling Prophecies

Maia Szalavitz, *Unbroken Brain*. New York: Picador, 2017.

Marc Lewis, *The Biology of Desire: Why addiction is not a disease*. New York: PublicAffairs, 2016.

Surgeon General's 2016 Report on the opioid crisis. Stanton Peele, "The solution to the opioid crisis," *Psychologytoday.com*, May 16, 2017. https://www.psychologytoday.com/blog/addiction-in-society/201703/the-solution-the-opioid-crisis

Marc Lewis. Marc Lewis, "Why the disease definition of addiction does far more harm than good," *ScientificAmerican.com*, February 9, 2018. https://blogs.scientificamerican.com/observations/why-the-disease-definition-of-addiction-does-far-more-harm-than-good/

Stanton. Stanton Peele, "Open letter to Nora Volkow," *peele.net*, April 6, 2008. https://www.peele.net/blog/080406.html

2018 addiction series. PBS, *NOVA: Addiction*, October 17, 2018. https://www.pbs.org/wgbh/nova/video/addiction

"Dealing with Addiction." PBS, *Dealing with Addiction*, December 20, 2017. https://www.pbs.org/wgbh/nova/video/addiction

opioid deaths—both painkillers and heroin—topped record levels yet again. NIDA, *Overdose Death Rates*, August, 2018. https://www.drugabuse.gov/related-topics/trends-statistics/overdose-death-rates

Number of prescriptions for opioid painkillers drops dramatically in U.S. NBC News, "Number of prescriptions for opioid painkillers drops dramatically in U.S.," April 20, 2018. https://www.nbcnews.com/health/health-news/number-prescriptions-opioid-painkillers-drops-dramatically-u-s-n867791

opioid OD deaths still rose. CNBC, "West Virginia dispensed 31 million fewer pills—but opioid OD deaths still rose," January 22, 2018. https://www.cnbc.com/amp/2018/01/22/west-virginia-saw-drop-in-opioid-painkillers-prescribed-deaths-rose.html

"Why Our Drug Epidemic Is Worse than Ever." Stanton Peele, "Our drug epidemic is worse than ever," *Psychologytoday.com*, January 5, 2017. https://www.psychologytoday.com/us/blog/addiction-in-society/201706/our-drug-death-epidemic-is-worse-ever

"Why the Future is Always on Your Mind." Martin Seligman and John Tierney, "We aren't built to live in the moment," *New York Times*, May 19, 2017. https://www.nytimes.com/2017/05/19/opinion/sunday/why-the-future-is-always-on-your-mind.amp.html
diagnosed with ADHD and medicated increased by over 40 percent. Susanna Visser and Stephen Blumberg, "Trends in the parent-report of health care provider-diagnosed and medicated ADHD," *Journal of the American Academy of Child & Adolescent Psychiatry*, 53:34-46, 2014. https://www.sciencedirect.com/science/article/abs/pii/S0890856713005947

due to dopamine deficiencies in the brain. Ellen Littman, "Typical ADHD behaviors: Never enough? Why your brain craves stimulation," *ADDattitude*, (no date) accessed December 4, 2018. https://www.additudemag.com/brain-stimulation-and-adhd-cravings-addiction-and-regulation/
raise a culture-wide concern. Rachel Bluth, "ADHD numbers are rising, and scientists are trying to understand why," *Washington Post*, September 10, 2018. https://www.washingtonpost.com/amphtml/national/health-science/adhd-numbers-are-rising-and-scientists-are-trying-to-understand-why/2018/09/07/a918d0f4-b07e-11e8-a20b-5f4f84429666_story.html

"Generation Adderall." Casey Schwartz, "Generation Adderall," *New York Times*, October 12, 2016. https:/www.nytimes.com/2016/10/16/magazine/generation-adderall-addiction.amp.html

Research on the effects of self-labeling. T. Moses, "Self-labeling and its effects among adolescents diagnosed with mental disorders," *Social Science and Medicine*, 68(3):570-78, 2009. https://www.ncbi.nlm.nih.gov/pubmed/19084313

Additional research. Dara Shifrer, "Stigma of a label: Educational expectations for high school students labeled with learning disabilities," *Journal of Health and Social Behavior*, 54(4):462-80, 2013. https://www.researchgate.net/publication/259207993_Stigma_of_a_Label_Educational_Expectations_for_High_School_Students_Labeled_with_Learning_Disabilities

any clinical picture of a kid is limited and time-bound. The Secret Teacher, "We are too quick to label children who aren't perfect," *Guardian*, June 20, 2015. https://www.theguardian.com/teacher-network/2015/jun/20/secret-teacher-too-quick-label-children-arent-perfect-adhd-dyslexia

Stanton Peele, *Diseasing of America*. San Francisco: Jossey-Bass, 1989.

## 7: Beyond Labeling

estimates appear to be increasing. "CDC finds mental health woes in one in five U.S. kids," *Cbsnews.com*, May 7, 2013. https://www.cbsnews.com/news/cdc-finds-mental-health-woes-in-one-in-five-us-kids/
MedicineNet. "Mental illness in children," *Medicinenet.com*, September 6, 2018. 1975; Watertown, MA: Broadrow Publications, 2014.

"Why Are More American Teenagers than Ever Suffering from Severe Anxiety?" Benoit Denizet-Lewis, "Why are more American teenagers than ever suffering from severe anxiety?" *New York Times*, October 11, 2017. https://www.nytimes.com/2017/10/11/magazine/why-are-more-american-teenagers-than-ever-suffering-from-severe-anxiety.amp.html

began asking incoming college freshmen. HERI, "CIRP freshman survey," heri.ucla.edu. https://heri.ucla.edu/cirp-freshman-survey/

it surged to 41 percent. Cooperative Institutional Research Program, *The American Freshman: National Norms Fall 2016*. Los Angeles: UCLA Higher Education Research Institute, 2017. https://www.heri.ucla.edu/monographs/TheAmericanFreshman2016.pdf

Angela Duckworth, *Grit: The power of passion and perseverance*. New York: Scribner, 2016.

## 8: Behavioral Addictions and What They Show Us

Stanton Peele and Archie Brodsky, *Love and Addiction*. New York: Taplinger, 1975; Watertown, MA: Broadrow Publications, 2014.

American Psychiatric Association, *Diagnostic and Statistical Manual of Mental Disorders* (5th ed.). Washington, DC: American Psychiatric Association, 2013. https://cchealth.org/aod/pdf/DSM-5%20Diagnosis%20Reference%20Guide.pdf

World Heath Organization, *International Classification of Diseases 11th Revision*. Geneva: WHO: 2018. https://icd.who.int/

## 9: Abstinence and Harm Reduction, in Adolescence and Recovery

(fn 10): more moderate drinking by their youths. Phillipe De Witte and Mark C. Mitchell Jr. (Eds.), *Underage Drinking*. Luvain-La-Neuve, France: Presses Universitaires de Louvain, 2017. https://books.openedition.org/pucl/3263?lang=en
(fn 11): Stanton Peele, "The limitations of control-of-supply models for explaining and preventing alcoholism and drug addiction," *Journal of Studies on Alcohol*, 48:61-89, 1987. https://www.ncbi.nlm.nih.gov/m/pubmed/3821120/
Stanton Peele, "Alcohol as evil—Temperance and policy," *Addiction Research and Theory*, 18:374-382, 2010. http://www.peele.net/lib/evil.html
Stanton Peele, "End alcoholism—bomb Spain," *Psychologytoday.com*, April 4, 2008. https://www.psychologytoday.com/us/blog/addiction-in-society/200804/end-alcoholism-bomb-spain

Stanton Peele, "I'm single-handedly preserving the world's wine cultures—Any help out there?" *Huffington Post*, September 13, 2010. https://m.huffpost.com/us/entry/706015

Stanton Peele, "In 2018, the Temperance movement still grips America," *Filtermag.org*, September, 25, 2018. https://filtermag.org/2018/09/25/in-2018-the-temperance-movement-still-grips-america/

comparing drinking by Italians and Finns. Sara Rolando, Franca Beccaria, Christoffer Tigerstedt, and Jukka Törrönen, "First drink: What does it mean? The alcohol socialization process in different drinking cultures." *Drugs: Education, Prevention and Policy* 19(3):201-12, 2012. http://www.academia.edu/11769578/First_drink_What_does_it_mean_The_alcohol_socialization_process_in_different_drinking_cultures

Note on international life expectancy. Rob Picheta, "Spain to lead Japan in global life expectancy, US continues to slide, *CNN.com*, October 18,

2018. https://www-m.cnn.com/2018/10/17/health/life-expectancy-fore-casts-study-intl/index.html

as expressed. Will Godfrey, "How far can Ethan Nadelmann push America's drug laws?" *The Fix*, June 30, 2013. https://www.thefix.com/content/ethan-na-delmann-drug-policy91855

without abstaining entirely. Stanton Peele, "Addiction as disease: Policy, epidemiology, and treatment consequences of a bad idea," in J. Henningfield, W. Bickel, and P. Santora (Eds.), *Addiction Treatment in the 21st Century*. Baltimore: Johns Hopkins, 2007, pp. 153-163.

Gallup surveys. Alyssa Brown, "In U.S., smokers light up less than ever," *Gallup*, September 13, 2012. http://news.gallup.com/poll/157466/smokers-light-less-ever.aspx
Pavel Somov and Marla Somova, *The Smoke-Free, Smoke Break*. Oakland, CA: New Harbinger, 2011.

drug consumption sites. EMCDDA, *Drug consumption rooms*. Geneva: EM-CCDA. Lisbon, Portugal: EMCDDA, 2018. http://www.emcdda.europa.eu/topics/pods/drug-consumption-rooms_en

similarly beneficial outcomes. Transform, "Heroin-assisted treatment in Switzerland," Tdpf.org.UK, January 10, 2017. https://www.tdpf.org.uk/blog/heroin-assisted-treatment-switzerland-successfully-regulating-supply-and-use-high-risk-0

states with dispensaries for medical marijuana have witnessed a decline in opioids deaths. David Powell, Rosalie Liccardo Pacula, and Mireille Jacobson, "Do medical marijuana laws reduce addictions and deaths related to pain killers," *Journal of Health Economics*, 58(March 2018):29-42, 2018. https://www.rand.org/pubs/external_publications/EP67480.html

can be addicted. Stanton Peele, "Marijuana is addictive—so what?" *Stanton Peele Addiction Website*, January 7, 2006. http://www.peele.net/lib/addictive.html

encourage drug use. Rod Rosenstein, "Fight drug abuse, don't subsidize it," *New York Times*, August 27, 2018. https://www.nytimes.com/2018/08/27/opinion/opioids-heroin-injection-sites.html

David Sheff, *Beautiful Boy: A father's journey through his son's addiction*. New York: Mariner, 2009.

Nic Sheff, *Tweak: Growing up on amphetamines*. New York: Atheneum, 2009.

David Sheff, *Clean: Ovecoming addiction and ending America's greatest tragedy*. Boston: Houghton Mifflin Harcourt, 2013.

Nic Sheff, *We All Fall Down: Living with addiction*. New York: Hachette, 2011.

resulting in more drug use. Wei Pan and Haiyan Bai, "A multivariate approach to a meta-analytic review of the effectiveness of the D.A.R.E. program," *International Journal of Environmental Research and Public Health*, 6(1):267-77. http://www.mdpi.com/1660-4601/6/1/267/html

explains how. Barry Lessin, "How harm reduction made me a much better family therapist," *FSDP*, October 12, 2015. http://fsdp.org/2015/10/12/harm-reduction-made-me-a-much-better-family-therapist/

## Chapter 10: The Limits of the 12-Step Approach

Overall impact is harmful. Marc Lewis, "Why the disease definition of addiction does far more harm than good," *Scientific American Blogs*, February 9, 2018. https://blogs.scientificamerican.com/observations/why-the-disease-definition-of-addiction-does-far-more-harm-than-good/

he is labeled. Ruth Fowler, "10 people revolutionizing how we study addiction and recovery," *The Atlantic*, October 6, 2011. https://www.theatlantic.com/health/archive/2011/10/10-people-revolutionizing-how-we-study-addiction-and-recovery/246202/#slide10

After 75 years of Alcoholics Anonymous. Maia Szalavitz, "After 75 years of Alcoholics Anonymous, it's time to admit we have a problem," *Pacific Standard*, February 10, 2014. https://psmag.com/.amp/social-justice/75-years-alcoholics-anonymous-time-admit-problem-74268

an unconstitutional practice. Tom Horvath, "Court-ordered 12-step attendance is illegal," *Practical Recovery*, undated (accessed December 14, 2018). https://www.practicalrecovery.com/court-ordered-12-step-attendance-is-illegal/

hundreds of thousands of people annually. Stanton Peele, "The five ways hundreds of thousands of people are coerced into 12-step programs," *Raw Story*, "two years ago" (accessed December 14, 2018). https://www.rawstory.com/2016/12/the-five-ways-hundreds-of-thousands-of-people-are-coerced-into-12-step-programs/amp/

Panatalon pointed out. Ziba Kashef, "Yale scientist joins U.S. Nobel Conference to address addiction treatment," *Yale News*, October, 2015. https://news.yale.edu/2015/10/05/yale-scientist-joins-us-nobel-conference-address-addiction-treatment

Delray Beach, Florida. Lizette Alvarez, "Haven for recovering addicts now profits from their relapses," *New York Times*, June 20, 2017. https://www.nytimes.com/2017/06/20/us/delray-beach-addiction.html

"I am an addict." Stanton Peele, "Philip Seymour Hoffman was taught to be helpless before drugs," *Reason*, February 4, 2014. https://reason.com/archives/2014/02/04/what-the-philip-seymour-hoffman-story-te

cause of Hoffman's death. Stanton Peele, "Rehab as cause of death," *Psychology Today Blogs*, July 15, 2013. https://www.psychologytoday.com/us/blog/addiction-in-society/201307/rehab-cause-death

offer equivalent benefits. Tracy Chabala, "SMART, LifeRing, and Women for Sobriety are as effective as AA, study shows," *The Fix*, March 20, 2018. https://www.thefix.com/smart-lifering-and-women-sobriety-are-effective-aa-study-shows

after the first month. *Rational Recovery*, "Why people drop out of AA," 1992. https://rational.org/index.php?id=56

## Chapter 11: Recovery in the Real World

CDC issued a report. CDC, "Suicide rising across the U.S.: More than a mental health concern," *Vital Signs*, 2018. https://www.cdc.gov/vitalsigns/suicide/

How Suicide Quietly Morphed Into a Public Health Crisis. Benedict Carey, "How suicide quietly morphed into a public health crisis," *New York Times*, June 8, 2018. https://www.nytimes.com/2018/06/08/health/suicide-spade-bordain-cdc.html

research. T. Moses, "Self-labeling and its effects among adolescents diagnosed with mental disorders," *Social Science and Medicine*, Feb;68(3):570-8, 2009. https://www.ncbi.nlm.nih.gov/pubmed/19084313

Richard Friedman declared. Richard Friedman, "Suicide rates are rising: What should we do about it," *New York Times*, June 11, 2018. https://www.nytimes.com/2018/06/11/opinion/suicide-rates-increase-anthony-bourdain-kate-spade.html mythical narrative. Editorial, "An opioid crisis foretold," *New York Times*, April 21, 2018. https://www.nytimes.com/2018/04/21/opinion/an-opioid-crisis-foretold.html

disproved by research. Jacob Sullum, "America's war on pain pills is killing addicts and leaving patients in agony," *Reason*, April, 2018. http://reason.com/archives/2018/03/08/americas-war-on-pain-pills-is

declined dramatically. Associated Press, "Number of prescriptions for opioid painkillers dropped dramatically in U.S.," *NBC News*, April 20, 2018. https://www.nbcnews.com/news/amp/ncna867791

continue to accelerate. NIDA, "Overdose death rate," *National Institute on Drug Abuse*, August, 2018. https://www.drugabuse.gov/related-topics/trends-statistics/overdose-death-rates

Stanton Peele and Ilse Thompson, *Recover!: An empowering program to help you stop thinking like an addict and reclaim your life*. Berkeley, CA: Da Capo, 2015.

redefined recovery. Stanton Peele, "The meaning of recovery has changed, you just don't know it," *Psychology Today Blogs*, February 1, 2012. https://www.psychologytoday.com/us/blog/addiction-in-society/201202/the-meaning-recovery-has-changed-you-just-dont-know-it
remains incredibly profitable. Lizette Alvarez, "Haven for recovering addicts now profits from their relapses," *New York Times*, June 20, 2017. https://www.nytimes.com/2017/06/20/us/delray-beach-addiction.html

Koren Zailckas, *Smashed: Story of a drunken girlhood*. New York: Viking, 2005.

She now writes novels about people who aren't alcoholics. Koren Zalickas, *The Drama Teacher*. New York: Crown, 2018. https://www.publishersweekly.com/9780553448092

to avoid and to escape this identity. Life Process Program, "Alcoholic denial—can it help you to recover from addiction?", Lifeprocessprogram.com, undated (accessed December 18, 2018). https://lifeprocessprogram.com/alcoholic-denial-can-help-recover-addiction/

## Chapter 12: Raising Our Non-Addicted Next Generation

deciding not to have children. Claire Cain Miller, "Americans are having fewer babies. They told us why." *New York Times*, July 5, 2018. https://www.nytimes.com/2018/07/05/upshot/americans-are-having-fewer-babies-they-told-us-why.html reproduced for decades. Stanton Peele, "The new thalidomide," *Reason*, July, 1990.https://www.peele.net/lib/thalidomide.html

*Harvard Medical School Health Blog.* Howard LeWine, "Drinking a little alcohol early in pregnancy may be okay," *Harvard Medical School Health Blog*, January 8, 2018. https://www.health.harvard.edu/blog/study-no-con-nection-between-drinking-alcohol-early-in-pregnancy-and-birth-prob-lems-201309106667

*less likely.* Lillian Gleiberman, Ernest Harburg, Wayne deFranceisco, and Anthony Schork, "Familial transmission of alcohol use: V. Drink-ing patterns among spouses, Tecumseh, Michigan," *Behavior Genet-ics*, 22(1):63-79, 1992. http://citeseerx.ist.psu.edu/viewdoc/download?-doi=10.1.1.587.751&rep=rep1&type=pdf

Amy Klobuchar, *The Senator Next Door: A memoir from the heartland*. New York: Holt, 2015.

brief intervention. Ziba Kashef, "Yale scientist joins U.S. Nobel Conference to address addiction treatment," *Yale News*, October 5, 2015. https://news.yale.edu/2015/10/05/yale-scientist-joins-us-nobel-conference-address-addic-tion-treatment

research by Vincent Felitti. Vincent Felitti, Robert Anda, Dale Nordenberg, David Williamson, et al., "Relationship of child abuse and household dysfunc-tion to many of the leading causes of death in adults: The Adverse Childhood Effects (ACE) study," *American Journal of Preventive Medicine*, 14(4):245-58, 1998. http://www.ajpmonline.org/article/S0749-3797(98)00017-8/fulltext

Stanton is not on board with the idea of restricting one's life to a recover-ing identity. Stanton Peele, "Count me out of 'Recovery Nation'—Negative self-identity is the cruelest stigma of all," *Life Process Program*, undated (accessed December 19, 2018). https://lifeprocessprogram.com/count-me-out-of-recovery-nation-negative-self-identity-is-the-cruelest-stigma-of-all/

### Chapter 13: Developing Purpose, Efficacy, and Independence

"Why Are More American Teenagers Than Ever Suffering From Severe Anx-iety?" Benoit Denizet-Lewis, "Why are more American teenagers than ever suffering from severe anxiety," *New York Times*, October 11, 2017. https://www.nytimes.com/2017/10/11/magazine/why-are-more-american-teenag-ers-than-ever-suffering-from-severe-anxiety.amp.html

Alissa Quart, *Hothouse Kids: How the pressure to succeed threatens childhood.* New York: Penguin, 2006.

The findings of this 95-year study. Jeff Haden, "This 95-year Stanford study reveals 1 secret to living a longer, more fulfilling life," *Time,* June 11, 2018. https://www.inc.com/jeff-haden/this-95-year-stanford-study-reveals-1-secret-to-living-a-longer-more-fulfilling-life.html

Motivational interviewing. Rhonda Campbell, "Five principles of Motivational Interviewing," *Chron,* March 19, 2018. https://work.chron.com/5-principles-motivational-interviewing-1836.html
A review of every systematic study of alcoholism treatment. William Miller and Reid Hester, *Handbook of Alcoholism Treatment Approaches: Effective Alternatives* (3rd ed.). Boston: Allyn and Bacon, 2002.

Pantalon's research group. Ziba Kashef, "Yale scientist joins U.S. Nobel Conference to address addiction treatment," *Yale News,* October 5, 2015. https://news.yale.edu/2015/10/05/yale-scientist-joins-us-nobel-conference-address-addiction-treatment

self-efficacy. William Miller, *Motivational Enhancement: Therapy with drug abusers.* Albuquerque, NM: Center on Alcoholism, Substance Abuse, and Addictions (CASAA). https://casaa.unm.edu/download/METManual.pdf

Carol Dweck, *Mindset.* New York: Ballantine, 2007.

## Chapter 14: Overcoming Addiction

Life Process Program. https://lifeprocessprogram.com/

Stanton Peele and Archie Brodsky, *Love and Addiction.* New York: Taplinger, 1975; Watertown, MA: Broadrow Publications, 2014.

Martin Seligman, *Learned Optimism.* New York: Vintage, 1990, 2006.

Addiction is a Disease of Free Will. Nora Volkow, "Addiction is a disease of free will," *Huffington Post,* June 12, 2016. https://www.huffpost.com/us/entry/7561200/amp

Frequent features about addiction. Shreeya Sinha, Zach Lieberman, and Leslye Davis. "Heroin addiction explained: How opioids hijack the brain," *New York Times,* December 19, 2018. https://www.nytimes.com/interactive/2018/us/addiction-heroin-opioids.html

Betty Smith, *A Tree Grows in Brooklyn*. New York: Harper, 1943, 2018 (75th Anniversary Edition).

Jeannette Walls, *The Glass Castle*. New York: Scribner, 2005.

Christina Baker Kline, "Trespassing in Christina's world," *New York Times*, February 17, 2017. https://www.nytimes.com/2017/02/17/well/family/trespassing-in-christinas-world.amp.html

### Chapter 15: Conclusion: The American Delusion

Suicide Prevention is More than Talking Somebody Out of Taking Their Life. Jessica Ravitz, "Calls to suicide prevention hotline spiked after celebrity deaths," *ABC17 News*, June 13, 2018. https://www.abc17news.com/health/calls-to-suicide-prevention-hotline-spiked-after-celebrity-deaths/752584639

Johann Hari, *Lost Connections*. London: Bloomsbury, 2018.

# About the Authors

**Stanton Peele, Ph.D., J.D.,** is an addiction expert who has investigated, written about, and treated addiction over five decades. Based on this work, he was recognized in *The Atlantic* as one of "10 people who are revolutionizing how we study addiction and recovery."

In the course of his life's work, Stanton has identified that addiction isn't limited to drugs, leading to the concept of process addictions. He was among the first to describe natural recovery and its anchorings in life through work, marriage, and family. Along with his 12 previous books and 250 academic and popular articles, he has created the Life Process Program, developed for a successful residential rehab center, the online version of which is now used around the world. Zach works with the online LPP and has expanded it into the family realm.

Photo by Eli Zhou

**Zach Rhoads** is a consultant for families and children. In this role, Zach has demonstrated a gift for communicating with kids who are having difficulties—along with families and teachers who are stymied by their failures to reach these children. Zach developed this empathy through his own problems as a child who wasn't successful at school and for whom standard diagnoses and treatment weren't helpful. Moreover, in his twenties he developed a heroin addiction, which—after several years and a near-death experience—he left behind. Zach is a Life Process Program coach and developer.

Stanton has three adult children, all of whom are engaged in meaningful, creative professional passions and strong intimate relationships. He spends creative time with his three grandchildren, including taking them on trips and other adventures.

Zach (who is 40 years younger than Stanton) is married and is part of a highly supportive family network, to which he and his wife have recently added another member, a daughter, as this book was completed.